CW00751429

JUSTICE, PEACE AND DOMINICANS
1216 – 2001

Justice, Peace, and Dominicans

1216 – 2001

Edited by
John Orme Mills OP

DOMINICAN PUBLICATIONS

First published (2001) by
Dominican Publications
42 Parnell Square
Dublin 1

ISBN 1-871552-77-X

British Library Cataloguing in Publications Data.
A catalogue record for this book is available
from the British Library.

Cover design by David Cooke

Printed in Ireland by
Colour Books, Dublin.

Contents

Contributors

Philippe Denis O.P. teaches at the University of Natal, Pieter-maritzburg, and is author of *The Dominican Friars in Southern Africa. A Social History* (1998) and editor of the forthcoming *Histoire des dominicains en Afrique* (Cerf).

Richard Finn O.P. is Vice Regent of Studies at Blackfriars Hall in the University of Oxford, and Chair of Dominican Peace Action (UK).

Valerie Flessati is Vice-President of Pax Christi.

Viktor Hofstetter, O.P., of the Swiss Province, worked over the last ten years as promoter of the Dominican nuns. Prior to that, he was provincial in Switzerland and regional promoter of justice and peace for northern Europe.

Carlos Josaphat O.P. was a professor of the University of Fribourg, lectures in the Dominican School of Theology in São Paulo, and is author of *Las Casas. Todos os direitos para todos* (2000).

François Leprieur, who was closely associated with the worker-priest movement, has taught widely on Church history and is author of *Quand Rome condamne* (1989).

John Orme Mills O.P. is Chairman of the Eckhart Society, Prior of St Dominic's in Newcastle-upon-Tyne, and former Editor of *New Blackfriars*.

Jim Nuttall O.P., who for a long time has worked in Pakistan, was until recently Dominican Promoter of Justice and Peace in the Asia Pacific Region.

Brian Pierce, O.P., is a member of the Dominican Province of St Martin de Porres (USA) and has served for nine years in Central America, principally Honduras, training lay preachers and ministering to people with HIV-AIDS.

Timothy Radcliffe O.P., has been Master of the Order of Preachers 1992-2001.

Roger Ruston taught moral theology for many years, and is now Christendom Research Fellow in Cardiff University Law School.

Nicholas Sagovsky is a Fellow and Tutor of Clare College, Cambridge, and William Leech Professorial Research Fellow in Applied Christian Theology, University of Newcastle upon Tyne.

Hugh Walters, who is a teacher of religious education, is co-author of *Earthen Vessels. The Thomistic Tradition in Education* (2000).

Brian Wicker for long lectured in English Literature at Birmingham University and then was Principal of Fircroft College of Adult Education. In retirement he is Chairman of the Council on Christian Approaches to Defence and Disarmament.

Acknowledgements

Authors Richard Finn, John Orme Mills and Roger Ruston, and also Associate Editor David Sanders O.P. and translator Colin Carr O.P., are all members of the Justice and Peace Commission of the English Dominican Province, which initiated the idea for this book. The Commission is deeply grateful to the Master of the Order, Timothy Radcliffe, for the generous support he has given to the project. We are indebted to the many people round the world, especially but not solely Dominicans, who by the giving of their knowledge and advice have made the project possible. We are indebted in a particular way to Bernard Treacy O.P. of Dominican Publications, with whom the project was discussed in its earliest days and who has seen the book through to publication, and also to Fergus Kerr O.P., the Editor of *New Blackfriars*, in which quite a lot of the text first appeared.

Preface

TIMOTHY RADCLIFFE, O.P.

This fascinating book is more like a family photograph album than a family history. Rather than a continuous story of the evolution of the Order's commitment to justice and peace, and occasional failures, it offers snapshots. We meet individual friars pursuing this commitment in an extraordinary diversity of ways: settling civil disputes in thirteenth century Italy, and reflecting upon usury in the fifteenth century; defending indigenous people in the newly discovered Americas and in Africa; developing theories of international law in sixteenth century Spain; healing the sick with traditional herbal medicines in seventeenth century Peru; fleeing the cities to found a community of artists in early twentieth century England, and leaving the priories to work in factories in mid-twentieth century France; opposing apartheid in South Africa; working for refugees in late twentieth century Japan.

What do they have in common, these friars who were, among other things, philosophers, artists, lawyers, and factory workers? Are there any common threads that run through this book? In the first case, practical action for justice is in nearly every case linked with theological reflection. These actions are part of our preaching. The engagement of the brethren in peace negotiations in thirteenth century Italy was an expression of Aquinas' vision of justice as the right ordering of all our lives, individually and communally, according to God's will. Las Casas' defence of the Indians in Hispaniola was deeply linked with Vitoria's reflections on international law in Salamanca. The foundation of the Ditchling community went with a study of St Thomas' views on property. Chenu explored the doctrinal foundation for the worker-priest movement. The resistance to nuclear weapons was rooted in a renewal of the reflection upon the concept of a just war.

This theological exploration is not just apologetic, a justification for action, or an explanation of why some Dominicans behaved oddly. A true understanding of what it means to be human, live in a community and obey God's will belongs to the construction of a just society. Rigorous thinking, in the light of the gospel, is an essential part of the commitment to justice and peace, because God made us to live in a world that makes sense. Also it shows that justice and peace can never be a private and individual commitment. It is the work of a community which will include thinkers, those who have practical skills or are involved in politics, and those who are immersed in the messy world of human suffering.

Secondly, there is a connection, I believe, between the way in which these friars sought justice and the Dominican way of life. A way of life which is founded upon the search for the common good, through debate and discussion in the Chapter, is likely to give a particular colouring to the Dominican conception of justice as the building of community. Congar argued that our democratic form of government and fraternal life gave us a space in which the brethren could seek the truth, with a certain freedom from the prejudices and pressures of the time. He believed that this was why the worker-priest movement was especially linked to the Order. One could also argue that St Antoninus' work for the poor in the city of Florence and his reflections upon usury were deeply linked to his way of life as a friar. As Richard Finn writes, 'The heart, the purse and the voice are formed in a single apostolic life.' Martin de Porres' compassion for the poor was a profound expression of that mercy which is at the heart of Dominican life, even if he did not always receive it from his brethren! The fact that other brethren who shared this same way of life often took precisely opposite views does not invalidate this hypothesis. It confirms that in the Dominican tradition union is not identified with uniformity and communion gives space for diversity.

Although this book does not offer a history of an evolving tradition, yet one can sense moments of profound transition in our understanding of what it might mean to seek justice and peace. The conquest of the Americas posed immense new challenges to an understanding of justice that was born in the context of the medieval city. It provoked the birth of international law. The Dominican Order must also reflect upon what is demanded of us in today's new situation. Between the end of the Second Vatican Council and the fall of the Berlin Wall, our understanding of a commitment to justice was largely shaped by the context of the conflict between capitalism and communism. Commitment meant taking sides in an ideological conflict that split the Church and many religious orders, including our own. To be for 'justice and peace' often implied belonging to a group within the province. It meant that one was 'left wing'. It seemed to involve endless protests: against the war in Vietnam, apartheid, racialism, and the possession of nuclear weapons. Some friars were often seen on the street demonstrating. Others stayed at home and watched them on television, uncomfortable in being implicated!

We who now live and preach after the fall of the Berlin Wall must discover how to work for justice and peace in a new situation. The virtual collapse of communism has liberated the Church from a neurosis that often deformed our commitment to the gospel. Now the 'preferential option for the poor' and a commitment to human rights are no longer the cry of a minority but part of the ordinary teaching of the Church, even if not always implemented in practice. We can hope that the discourse of 'justice and peace' may cease to represent the concern of a group in the Church, and be seen as an ordinary part of the Christian vocation. Prophets will always make us uncomfortable and suffer persecution, but they are more likely to be heeded if they are not seen as belonging to a 'party'.

On the other hand, the triumph of the global market is profoundly discouraging for those who dreamed of a world made new. Consumerism is virtually unchallenged as the dominant philosophy of our age. God's creation has become a commodity, and his children are transformed into producers and consumers. What utopias are left to keep alive our hope of the coming of the Kingdom? At a recent meeting in Latin America, the brethren shared their conviction that now one can only struggle for justice if one is sustained by a profound spirituality, walking to Jerusalem without yet glimpsing Easter. If we are to be faithful in the struggle, then we must be contemplative.

My hope is that the Order may now be able to make a small contribution to the search for a just world, offering a discourse in which rigorous reflection, spirituality and the commitment to justice are knitted together again. In Aquinas and, according to John Mills, in the fourteenth century Rhineland mystics, we see a tradition that predates the fracturing of theology into specialised compartments. Prayer, reflection on the gospel, and analysis of human society belong together. This wholeness is needed for a preaching that addresses the mind, the heart and the soul, and which gives hope for a better world.

The days of protest are not over. We still face a brutal embargo against Iraq that must be opposed; there are still thousands of nuclear weapons, whose existence remains a threat to humanity's future; and there are campaigns still be continued against the proliferation of mines and small arms, for the elimination of the crucifying burden debt, and for a just price for medicines for poor countries. But there is a shift. Now there is not so much the dream of an imminent and radical transformation of social structures as the focus on small projects that give hope and show that the world can change, such as the experiment in ecological farming by our brother Nzamujo Ugwuegbula at Songhai, Benin, which is being studied and imitated all over Africa. There is an increasing stress on advocacy, joining the debate and trying to win the argument. Next year we will have an international conference on finance and ethics in Madrid. The presence of the Order, in collaboration with the Franciscans, at the Human Rights Commission in Geneva gives us a new voice.

Finally, religious orders such as our own may have a special contribution to make today because the challenges to justice and peace are linked with globalisation and we are among the oldest international organisations in the world. Our brothers and sisters are present in the United States and the European Union, whose economic and political policies have profound consequences on the lives of other countries where we are also present. How can we as an Order respond globally? The delegations of members of the Dominican Family in the United States to the brethren and sisters in Iraq may be suggestive of future developments.

In every photograph album, there will be some members of the family who get left out, or are only glimpsed at the back of the group. I would have loved, for example, to hear more of Louis-Joseph Lebret, whose *Economie et Humanisme* had such an immense influence in the French-speaking world. And of course this is a photo album in which only the friars appear, except in the chapters on Africa and Asia. This is inevitable if the book were not to swell unmanageably. We can hope for companion volumes that will tell the story of how other branches of the Dominican Family have laboured for justice. We will hear of Dominicans such as St Catherine of Siena and her struggle to bring peace to a divided Christendom; St Rosa of Lima and her criticism of racialism in seventeenth century Lima; Blessed Marie Poussepin and her response to the industrial revolution, and Blessed Giorgio Frassati, and his opposition to fascism in Italy before the last world war. We need to hear their stories too, because in this new moment in the history of the Order, the commitment to justice and peace will be a shared task of the whole Dominican Family.

Introduction

Trying to Make the World Better

JOHN ORME MILLS, O.P.

Is the world a better place because Christians have been in it? That, very basically, is what this book is about ... or, more accurately, this is the question that niggles away behind all the other questions raised in this book. Nearly all Christians and even the vast majority of Christian theologians would say the answer to the question was obvious. Academic historians, on the other hand, would be far from sure. They would almost certainly say that humanity's story during these past two thousand years is far too complex for us to be able even to start to make a judgment.

We believe a more useful contribution to the debate than guessing what the whole Christian world has done to bring peace and justice to the earth would be to look at what one definable group of Christians has achieved. So we are offering here a review of what people belonging to one great religious tradition have contributed to the promotion of peace and justice during the length of its lifetime. One of the things that makes it a particularly interesting group to study is, in fact, the sheer length of its history, stretching across eight hundred years, right back to the feudal period.

St Dominic, who was born in Old Castile about 1172 and died in Bologna in 1221, believed that the way to overcome the division and conflict in his world – the medieval world – was not by mass slaughter but by effective preaching and studying and teaching of the Christian gospel, and he created a group of men united by religious vows, to be dedicated to this work. Their official title still is 'the Order of Preachers', but they have long been better known as 'Dominicans', and now there are many more Dominican sisters than Dominican brothers. The Dominicans and Franciscans were the two international families of friars (*fratri*, 'brothers') which had such an enormous effect on Western Christianity in the later middle ages. And the lives of today's Dominican brothers are still governed by a basic constitution not profoundly different in essentials from the constitution created by St Dominic in 1220.

Even so, this seemingly homogeneous group has, of course, altered in all sorts of ways during these eight centuries. Political and social structures have changed out of all recognition; and our culture, our understanding of the world, and the Christian world itself have all changed. So it is dangerous to make loose generalisations about Dominicans of all ages. Yet there are certain important things they have in common.

Concern in the Roman Catholic Church with questions of peace and justice did not begin only with the publishing in 1965 of *Gaudium et Spes*, the document issued by the Second Vatican Council on the Church in the Modern World. Neither did it begin only with the publishing in 1891 of *Rerum Novarum*, the first papal encyclical on questions of social justice. Nor, for that matter, did it begin only in 1269, when the most famous of all Dominicans, St Thomas Aquinas, made his important pronouncement in article 7 of question 66 of section 2a 2ae of his *Summa Theologiae*, stating that people in desperate need had a moral right to take what they needed for their survival. No, the promotion of peace and justice has been part of the teaching of Christianity ever since St Paul's time. It has been interpreted in all sorts of different ways in different times and places, but it is part of the vision at the heart of the Christian message – the vision that has shaped the Christian idea of heaven and the Christian idea of what the world should be like.

One of the ways of talking about a particular group of people – the Dominicans, for example – is to talk about their way of responding to this challenge. However, what confronts us is not a history of consistent advance, any more than the history of mystical theology is a history of consistent advance. In this book Richard Finn quotes the thirteenth century Dominican Humbert of Romans as saying:

There are some preachers who are so averse to taking part in the affairs of the world that they refuse to help their neighbour, even spiritually; they are like the ostrich which does not take care of its young. Their conduct does not conform to the example set by Our Lord.

And in this book Finn also quotes the twentieth century Dominican Vincent McNabb as writing that there can be no appreciation of God's mercy where there is no appreciation of his justice and of our sins against it:

If our mission is the salvation of souls, the aim stated by our fundamental constitution, we must give hope to those who long for God's justice.

What we see here is a history of discovery (or, rather, rediscovery) in successive ages, as needs and circumstances change.

Moreover, a thing that has struck me as editor of this book has been the *ambiguity* of the Dominican tradition. Here, after all, is a venerable Christian tradition which has produced not only a whole number of men and women dedicated to what most of us today would call the causes of peace and justice, but also a lot of people who have seen themselves as authentic followers of St Dominic yet have had a very different outlook – who have, in one way or another, supported what many of us would label control and domination. This, in fact, has been their understanding of what peace and justice is.

It has not been possible to give much space to this alternative vision in this book, but that does not mean that this 'alternative vision' has been unimportant. In Madrid, in the Museo del Prado, there is a painting by the fifteenth century Spanish artist Pedro Berruguete. It shows St Dominic sitting high up on a splendid throne, witnessing the carrying out of a sentence imposed by the court of the inquisition in Albi. Below him, two young Albigensian heretics have been tied to stakes, ready to be burned. The vast majority of our contemporaries would see the picture as a portrayal of cruelty and oppression. But the majority of Berruguete's contemporaries (including undoubtedly the Dominicans who commissioned the picture) would have seen it as a portrayal of the exercise of justice and the establishing of peace.

The tension between these two conflicting visions has been – at least sometimes – a creative tension. In fact, it could even be argued that most Dominicans of any note have, at least in parts of their lifetimes, shared something of both the visions.

How far, though, did the people written about in this book in actual fact manage to challenge their culture, or at least be effective critics of it? And how deeply did they influence their followers? After all, even St Thomas's teaching did not have a powerful immediate influence.

The extent of the influence of these people varied enormously. Generalising about them, we can, however, say that all of them did at least help to create a mood, a feeling, that did extend beyond their lifetimes. But if that is all they did, did they labour in vain? Not really. If one has left that much behind, one has left a lot. Admittedly, unlike peace treaties and legal reforms, moods and feelings are immeasurable, but sometimes they have started things more momentous than treaties and reforms.

And, next time we are asked to say what good Christianity has done to the world, this is something well worth telling our interrogators.

1

Early Voices for Justice

RICHARD FINN, O.P.

Preachers often find it difficult to make themselves heard. Humbert of Romans, fifth Master of the Order, emphasised the need for a measured delivery in a strong voice; but getting a hearing has always been more than a matter of mere audibility.[1] The first Dominican chapels were small, built on the cheap in the expectation that the friars would find a welcome and a pulpit in others' churches. They had not reckoned on the hostility of parochial clergy. It was soon discovered that they would have to build large churches of their own. From its earliest years the Order of Preachers had to adopt new ways of communicating the Gospel, or go unheard. A certain ingenuity and willingness to copy a good idea is traditional for the Order, where we do not decline. In Florence not only the church but also the piazza outside Santa Maria Novella would have to be enlarged after 1245 to accommodate the crowds who attended the open air sermons. And now the Dominican Family has its presence on the Internet.

In this tradition we should place the creation in January 1998 at Geneva of an office, a joint initiative with the Franciscans, at the Human Rights Commission of the United Nations Organisation. And most provinces now have Justice and Peace Commissions. These are faint echoes in a modern key of the petitions that Dominicans like John of Darlington and Walter Winterborne handled in their role as confessors to the Plantagenet kings for almost 150 years. Our voices can be heard, however quietly, in a newsletter or at the conference table. And such actions, however faltering, amateur, or unlikely to succeed, are themselves part of what it takes to preach with authority and credibility.

To what extent, though, can we speak of a perennial Domini-

1. Humbert of Romans, *Treastise on Preaching*, ed. W. Conlon, O.P., Blackfriars Publications 1955, p.41f.

can vocation to preach on issues of social justice and politics, of war and peace? When the friars at the General Chapter of 1977 started to include expressions of 'solidarity' with the poor among their legislative *acta*, and the commitment to 'strive for the establishment of a more just society', when members of the Dominican Family played a prominent role in the peace movement of the 1980s, it seemed to some that we had jumped on a bandwagon, adopted the latest theological fashion. The suspicion lingers that the rhetoric, the structures, with their promoters and conveners, offices and commissions, were something of a pose, talking largely to the converted, littering yet other desks with brown envelopes. Dominic was not known for preaching against injustice, but for preaching God's mercy towards sinners and recalling them to the practice of the Catholic faith. Is it not enough for us to do the same?

The answer has to be No. Not if what is meant is a neglect of justice. Preachers, wrote Vincent McNabb in the opening issue of *Blackfriars*, must give 'others their due of truth ... as in kindred matter ... their due of justice' and that includes the truth about justice, the significance of this cardinal virtue in any human life and in the fully human life of the saints.[2] To preach in the cause of justice has been a perennial Dominican vocation – as we can see from the example of such well-known figures as Eckhart, Antoninus of Florence, Bartolome de Las Casas and Martin de Porres. But there are other, lesser known Dominicans, those who heard the call of *Rerum Novarum* and brought to contemporary debates about economics and social justice their Thomistic training, those who took to the streets in the various peace movements of this century, and those who contributed to the development of liberation theology.

How we remember these figures, their achievements and failings, alters how we see ourselves as their successors and how we approach the present in all its complexity. For, on the one hand, there is a danger that we kid ourselves, recreate the past to suit current priorities or prejudices, and in the process neglect warnings and lessons from that past. And, on the other hand, there is a perennial temptation not to get involved.

2. V. McNabb, 'Our Aim of Truth', *Blackfriars*, Vol. 1, No. 1, April 1920, p.8.

Humbert observed that 'there are some preachers who are so averse to taking part in the affairs of the world that they refuse to help their neighbour, even spiritually; they are like the ostrich which does not take care of its young. Their conduct does not conform to the example set by Our Lord.'[3]

What, then, of Dominic himself and the first friars? Dominic's concern for justice among the brethren was certainly shown by his willingness to punish them. That we know from the testimony of Brother Ventura for the canonization process of 1233.[4] Yet much of the lives of the first brethren and their preaching in the thirteenth century is hidden from us and what we do know we must be careful not to misinterpret to fit our own slant.

It is true that the brethren often numbered the poor among their neighbours. But it was scarcity of land and its high price inside the towns that determined the location of priories on the then edge of town either just within the walls, as at York, or in the suburban ring, an area into which newcomers increasingly crowded, pushing back the market-gardens, like those near the first London priory at Holborn.[5] It was among this shifting population of artisans and merchants that the battle with heresy was to be fought in the cities of Northern Italy and elsewhere.[6] The location was not determined by zeal for the poor who were found in these 'working-class areas of the suburbs.'[7] The friars often moved when and where larger and more central sites became available.

So, too, the voluntary poverty and mendicancy that marked Dominicans and Franciscans alike should not be misread as an act of solidarity with the oppressed poor. For the Franciscans it was first an act of solidarity with the poor Christ, an entry into his sufferings. For the Dominicans it would appear to have been

3. Humbert, *op. cit.*, p.141.

4. S. Tugwell O.P., *Early Dominicans*, p.67.

5. Guillaume Pelhisson, O.P., attributed the modest scale of building at the Toulouse priory in the early 1230s – domos valde pauperes, parvas et humiles' – to *penuriam loci et defectum expensarum, Chronique*, ed. J. Duvernoy, Paris, 1994, p.40.

6. Lambert, *Medieval Heresy*, p. 118.

7. C. Morris, *The Papal Monarchy*, p.460. Hinnebusch argued that the poor had no particular quarter in (English) medieval towns. But a modern study of Siena by Daniel Waley describes the poor concentrated in the suburbs just beyond the walls.

a badge of apostolic authority. How they were seen affected how they were heard.

That explains Dominic's insistence on the relative poverty displayed in their churches, the absence of 'purple or silk vestments' or 'vessels of gold or silver, except chalices.'[8] Hence also the penance meeted out to the Newcastle Dominican who turned up at the London General Chapter of 1250 on horseback.[9] Poverty had a missionary purpose. Guillaume Pelhisson, a Toulouse Dominican in the mid-thirteenth century, spoke of voluntary poverty in food and dress 'for the name of Christ and the implanting of the faith.'[10]

We must also recognise that what we regard as wrong and unjust may have struck medieval men and women as wrong but vicious in some other way and *vice versa*. What we regard as an infringement of human rights might have been repugnant as an act of cruelty. What we see as selfish, they might consider a failure to give others their due. And as the friars sought the conversion and reconciliation of those to whom they preached, we should not expect from their sermons a denunciation of sins committed by others.

If we survey the early Dominicans' concern for peace and justice we see first the brethren's interest in a proper understanding of the issues. William of Moerbeke was the first to provide a complete Latin translation of Aristotle's *Politics* (*ca* 1260). Albert lectured and wrote on Aristotle's *Ethics* and *Politics* at Cologne. Aquinas commented on the *Ethics* and *Politics* (Books I-II and part of III), the former probably in 1271-1272, the latter perhaps a few years earlier.[11] It was, on the one hand, the biblical sense of God's good order in creation, a goodness to which we are attracted and in which we can share through our use of reason, and, on the other hand, Aristotle's understanding of our flourishing in society that set the context for Aquinas's

---

8. Testimony of Br Amizo of Milan during the canonization process of St Dominic, trans. in S. Tugwell O.P., *Early Dominicans*, p. 71.

9. A. Emden, *A Survey of Dominicans in England*, Rome, 1967, p.18.

10. *Chronique, op. cit.*, p.40.

11. There is some doubt as to whose commentary on the *Politics* came first. See the discussion in the Leonine edition of Aquinas, *Opera Omnia*, xlviii, Rome 1971, which also has a valuable appendix on Aquinas and the *Nicomachean Ethics*.

discussion of justice in the *Summa* as a particular virtue disposing us to give others their due as God's creatures and our
neighbours. Justice is served by human laws and partly determined by legislation and consent. But the laws must themselves
conform to the pattern of God's justice. And the just owe
worship and obedience to God.

In the *De regimine principum* Aquinas argued that justice was
best served by one man's rule in defence of the common good,
though the injustices of a democracy were preferable to the
crimes of a tyrant and tyranny was to be avoided by constitu-
tional checks. Later works, like the 1278 *Determinatio compendiosa
de iurisdictione imperii* by Ptolemy of Lucca and the treatises *De
bono pacis* and *De iustitia* of Remigio de' Girolami, attempted to
establish the proper exercise of civil and ecclesiastical authority, to sort out the competing claims of popes and emperors,
and relate the demands of justice to the need for peace.

We also see how frequently the friars were involved in the
practical search for a just peace, the establishment of good
order. Yet that search brought with it major problems. These
might occur when the justice the friars espoused was Roman or
of a novel kind disputed by their neighbours. Or, it might be
that, even following traditional forms of arbitration, they proved
unable to find impartial settlements in political disputes, especially those between regional powers. Peace seemed both to
require justice and yet also to demand its subordination.

For many, the arrival of the Dominicans raised questions of
justice because these newcomers were seen as acting unjustly.
They appropriated revenues belonging to existing clerical and
monastic institutions or to the poor dependent on alms distributed by those institutions. The Cistercians at Scarborough, who
held the advowson of the parish church, long sought to expel
the friars and charged them with breach of royal and ecclesiastical legislation. At Bristol the Benedictines objected. At Oxford
and Dunstable it was the local canons. Appeal to papal privilege
rode roughshod over local rights. It did not always work. In 1250
Innocent IV found in favour of the cathedral chapter at Her-
eford in their efforts to prevent the foundation of a Dominican
house in the city. Alexander IV confirmed the decision in 1254.

The legal battle continued to the end of the century.[12] The secular clergy at Cologne found apt words for what many thought of these new arrivals: 'they have put their sickle into another man's harvest.'[13]

Questions of justice were raised by the Dominicans' early association with the newly created papal inquisition into heresy. Gregory IX established in 1233 what one historian describes as 'both a new procedure, a rational inquiry by a judge, and a new institution, a papal agency designed to utilize this new procedure for uncovering and trying alleged heretics.'[14] Gregory appointed individual friars in a given region to carry out the preaching which preceded an investigation and to undertake the judicial investigation itself.

Medieval attitudes towards heresy defy simple generalisations. Death, long considered the just penalty for persistent heresy, had been imposed by secular rulers. Suspected heretics, like witches, faced in most places mob hatred and lynching, so that the inquisitors had to distinguish between true and false charges, protect against unjust accusation and punishment. In other towns, particularly those in the Languedoc and in Northern Italy caught up in the conflicts between pope and emperor, heretics might enjoy toleration and be unpunished by local diocesan courts. In these places the friars had to search out heretics. But the procedures adopted by the inquisition and the new punishment of burning inflicted by the secular authorities on the guilty who relapsed into heresy after their first conviction, brought a legal justice at odds with customary rights and loyalties.[15]

The friars faced much hostility. At Toulouse they were ejected forcibly from the town in November 1235 and kept out for some months. The priory at Orvieto was sacked in 1239. The

12. W. Hinnebusch O.P., *The Early English Friars Preachers*, Rome 1951, p. 98 and pp. 109-113.

13. C.H. Lawrence, *The Friars*, 1994, p. 107.

14. A. C. Shannon, O.S.A., *The Medieval Inquisition*, p. 67.

15. Heresy became punishable by burning in imperial territories by a decree of 1224. Imperial laws on heresy were adopted by Italian cities over the next decade. The papal decree Ad extirpanda of 1252 provided for the legal torture of certain suspects, a measure already legal in certain Italian towns, but there is no clear evidence for the regular use of torture by the inquisition in this period.

Dominican inquisitor Peter Martyr was assassinated near Milan in 1252. The house at Parma was broken into in 1279. At Bologna there were ugly scenes in 1299. What the brethren saw as 'the working out of God's just judgement' on the wicked, others saw as cruelty.[16] Arnaud Sans, the blacksmith, shouted to his fellow townsfolk, as he was led to the stake, 'See, all of you, what wrong they do me and this town ... '[17]

As outsiders who could be expected to be impartial in local matters to which they were strangers, and then as clerics educated in the Scriptures and canon law, the friars were frequently asked to arbitrate in disputes. They could be called upon by secular or religious leaders to take part in sensitive negotiations. In 1226 Guala of Bergamo, O.P., was appointed a papal negotiator at peace talks between the emperor Frederick II and the Lombard League.[18] In 1229 he negotiated a truce between Bologna and Modena.[19] The English Provincial William of Southampton served on the royal commission in 1277 that negotiated the peace with the Welsh Prince Llewelyn. The next year he was a mediator between Anthony Bek and Roger de Seiton over a church at Briggenhem.[20] Peter Martyr arranged treaties between hostile towns in the Romagna. Ambrose Sansedoni was sought out by the Sienese in 1273 both as a renowned preacher of peace and as an ambassador to reconcile the city with Pope Gregory X, who had placed Siena under an interdict. In 1276 Ambrose negotiated a peace between Florence and Pisa. The friars were seen to enjoy a spiritual authority to make peace. They could reconcile opponents in calling the parties to a common repentence mindful of God's judgement and so to a common acceptance of God's peace. Theobald of Albinga, whom Dominic clothed in the habit in 1220, was held to have a 'special grace of healing enmities.'[21]

16. The phrase '*iusto Dei iudicio operante*' describes the imprisonment and burning of Cathar heretics by Fr. Ferrarius, O.P., in certain manuscripts of Pelhisson's *Chronique*, p.46.

17. '*Videte, omnes quam iniuriam faciunt mihi et ville* ... ' ibid, p. 60.

18. C. Maier, *Preaching the Crusades*, pp.29-30.

19. A. Thompson O.P., *Revival Preachers and Politics*, Oxford, 1992, p. 51,

20. Hin-nebusch, *op. cit.*, p. 479.

21. *Lives of the Brethren*, trans. P. Conway, London, 1955, p. 194.

Arbitration might prove time-consuming, however, and decisions unpopular, turning people against the preachers. The *acta* of thirteenth century chapters testify to the difficulty of reconciling potentially conflicting demands: warnings and prohibitions are balanced by exceptions in cases of grave necessity.[22] Humbert warned that the 'preacher ought to shun jobs which incur men's dislike, such as arbitrating settlements, official investigations, visitations and other such judicial work, in the course of which it is frequently impossible to avoid offending many people.'[23] If it is true today that 'the credibility of the churches depends upon their attitudes towards institutionalised injustice, and this affects the credibility of those who claim to proclaim the good news,'[24] the medieval friars found that a reputation for giving justice was a mixed blessing. It could both enhance and compromise their status as God's preachers. It could rob them of a hearing: 'For when one who is dressed in a holy habit permits himself to become immersed in worldly affairs, it is as if he were to lose caste in the eyes of men, and the respect which they had for him were to vanish.'[25]

Such difficulties can be studied in the history of the renewal movement known as the Great Devotion or Alleluia that swept through the towns of Lombardy in 1233. Preachers like the Franciscan Gerard of Modena and Dominicans, Jacopino of Reggio, John of Vicenza, and Bartholomew of Breganza, came to exercise for a few short months great political power in towns disturbed by internal factions, unstable government, rivalry with other towns, and the pursuit of vengeance in the name of honour. Crowds poured in from the countryside to take part in the colourful and noisy processions and to hear the sermons with their call for reconciliation. The friars settled all kinds of disputes, over property and inheritance, over civil and ecclesiastical jurisdiction, between individuals, families and factions. A witness at Dominic's canonization process stated that 'almost all the cities of Lombardy and Marche handed over to the friars

22. Hinnebusch, *op. cit.*, pp. 423-424.
23. S. Tugwell, *Early Dominicans*, p. 310.
24. *Acta* of the Quezon City General Chapter, cited in the 1978 Acta of the English Province.
25. Humbert, in S. Tugwell, *Early Dominicans*, p. 143.

their acts and statutes for adjustment and amendment according to their will, to erase, add, subtract and change as seemed appropriate to them. And this they did to end the warfare and make and establish peace among them, and to restore usury and wrongful acquisitions ... '[26]

This is no exaggeration. The friars legislated in Parma, Modena, Bologna, Vercelli, Monza and many other cities. At Bologna the oaths which bound the members of each faction to vengeance were suppressed and political prisoners released from gaol. John of Vicenza preached before hostile armies drawn up on the battlefield and dispersed them. At Verona he was appointed *dux et rector* of the city with a mandate to reconcile old enemies.[27]

The high ideals that motivated the renewal proved difficult to embody in practice, especially where the disputes were political in nature. At Piacenza the peace brokered in July by the Franciscan Leo de' Valvassori of Perego broke down one month later in rioting and expulsions. Even a short-lived peace could be costly. John ordered the burning of sixty heretics in Verona, who would not swear to his settlement. The peace John proclaimed before the crowds at Paquara on the feast of Saint Augustine proved unacceptable to the Paduans and led to renewed conflict.

The call to reconciliation was heard because of the spiritual authority of the preacher. It often foundered in the politics of the peace determined on, when that determination, partial and imperfect, robbed the preacher of his authority. To a political theorist, Remigio de' Girolami, at the turn of the century it seemed that an answer to all these disputes required a rigorous subordination of many just claims to the overriding good of peace, of the individual to the common good, although he was careful not to ignore the claims of the poor. But those with a genuine grievance find it hard to surrender their claims, and tyranny can wreak havoc in the name of security and public order. It would be a mistake, however, to write off the Great Devotion as misguided or as a total failure. Many of the agree-

---

26. C. Morris, *The Papal Monarchy*, p.459.
27. A. Thompson, *op. cit.*, pp. 57-58, p. 60, and p. 71.

ments were being reaffirmed thirty years later.[28]

Throughout Western Europe the friars were often appointed to the specific mission of preaching the crusades, receiving the vows of would-be crusaders and collecting alms for the liberation of the Holy Land. In 1291, for example, Pope Nicholas IV requested the English Dominican provincial to preach the Crusade and appoint fifty others to the same mission.[29] This might not strike modern readers as evidence for a perennial vocation to preach justice and peace, but in their age the crusades to the Holy Land were understood as just wars for Christ's patrimony, an inheritance unjustly taken from his people, and for the liberation of Christians from oppression. Humbert of Romans in his treatise on preaching the crusades expected the preacher to know the history of infidel aggression. The crusades were also presented as a form of penance, as something owed to God. The Dominican William Peyraut in a sermon for the Fourth Sunday of Lent described the crusader as doing an exemplary penance.

Yet, here, too, the brethren found themselves required to advocate wars the justice of which might be disputed, especially when not every crusade was to the Holy Land. In the 1240s crusades had to be preached against the German emperor Frederick II and the General Chapters of 1246–1248 instructed the brethren to co-operate. For one Swabian Dominican it was too much. He wrote a tract in which he accused the pope of being the Anti-Christ.[30]

Dominicans have also long had a professional interest in other people's money. We know, thanks to a Parisian manuscript at Canterbury, that Jordan of Saxony preached on the text that 'it is easier for a camel to pass through the eye of a needle'.[31] Dominicans, like other mendicants, often preached against usury as a form of injustice and not simply of greed.[32]

---

28. *ibid*, pp.200-201.

29. Hinnebusch, *op. cit.*, p.330.

30. C. Maier, *op. cit.*, p.115, p.113 and p.72.

31. Fr Morenzoni, 'Les sermons de Jourdain de Saxe', in *Archivum Fratrum Praedicatorum* LXVI (1996), p. 217.

32. '*accipere usuram pro pecunia mutuata est secundum se iniustum ...* ' *Summa Theologiae*, 2a 2ae, q. 78, a. 1.

The *exempla* or stories for use in sermons compiled by a thirteenth-century Cambridge Dominican include graphic images
of toads with coins in their mouths found in the putrid corpses
of dead usurers.[33] Ambrose Sansedoni died as a result of
bursting a blood vessel while condemning usury. Wealth was a
danger to those who misused or hoarded their riches.

The almsgiving that we might see as generous and merciful,
Aquinas with other, and earlier, medieval theologians saw as
something owed to the poor: 'whatever surplus some people
possess, belongs by natural law to the relief of the poor.'[34] For
justice in this view involves recognition of no absolute right to
the continued use or disposal of private property:

> in this respect ... a person should not hold things in the world
> as his own, but as communal, so that he is ready to share them
> with others in their need.[35]

We must not, however, ignore those who criticised the
Dominicans. There were soon those who charged the new
arrivals with a failure to preach against the sins of the powerful.
Grosseteste reputedly made this complaint on his death-bed.
The friars' reliance on wealthy donors could silence them. The
Franciscan chronicler, Thomas of Eccleston, tells on the authority of one Friar John, visitor of the English Dominican
Province in the thirteenth century, how the king had criticised
another Dominican, William of Abingdon: 'Brother William,
there was a time when thou couldst speak of spiritual things;
now all thou canst say is, Give, give, give.' These are serious
charges, for it was the duty of those in power to secure peace and
justice. A distinction in the margins of what is probably a
Dominican collection of sermons and preaching aids from
Oxford in the late thirteenth century summed up the king's
duties as to 'protect their subjects, defend against all-comers, re-
establish peace, punish disturbers of the peace, give each their
due, to attack and destroy enemies.'[36]

33. Miri Rubin, *Charity and Community in Medieval Cambridge*, p. 89.
34. *Summa Theologiae*, 2a 2ae q.66. a.7. For the views of earlier writers see
Rubin, *op. cit.*
35. *Summa Theologiae*, 2a 2ae q.66. a.2.
36. M. O'Carroll, *A Thirteenth-Century Preacher's Handbook*, p.182.

But the English friars certainly spoke out on occasion against the powerful, or the excesses of their soldiery. Matthew Paris related that Dominicans and Franciscans in October 1233 rebuked the English king for ravaging the estates of noblemen who had not been tried and convicted by their peers. The Dominican Archbishop of Canterbury, Robert Kilwardby, wrote in 1277 to the Earl of Warwick and other field commanders of the troops then fighting in Wales to complain about the army's conduct.[37] The friars collected *exempla* with which to warn the powerful of the eternal punishments brought on them by their own savagery, like the story recorded by the Cambridge Dominican of the clerk who witnessed in a vision the torments of his former princely patron.[38]

The early Dominicans reveal both how much and how little can be achieved. These friars remind us of how difficult it is for the preacher to determine a disputed justice and how easily our own comforts may silence us. They remain an inspiration in their ability to integrate preaching, practical action, and personal virtue in the search for a just peace. Sansedoni was reported to have told an angry opponent of his mediation: 'since God is a peace-loving king, his servants must love and wish for peace, but to find peace, one must first grant it to others …' He admitted with candour that he too was a sinner, apologised for any fault, volunteered to pray that God would not count his opponent's angry words against him, showed himself undaunted by the threat of violence. His gentle resolution so unnerved and disarmed his attacker that the man found himself on his knees begging pardon and God's peace.[39]

37. Hinnebusch, *op. cit.*, p. 64., p.467 and p. 476.

38. S. L. Forte, 'A Cambridge Dominican collector of Exempla', *Archivum Fratrum Praedicatorum* XXVIII (1958), pp. 145-6.

39. *Vie des Saints et Bienheureux de l'ordre des Frères Prêcheurs*, Lyon, 1887, Vol.

2

Thomas Aquinas on Justice

NICHOLAS SAGOVSKY

INTRODUCTION

For Thomas, there is nothing abstract about justice: it is the dedicated, personal practice of a cardinal virtue. Those who practise justice are those who are determined to do the will of God which has been made plain in the law of God. In a fallen world, the practice of justice will doubtless involve both self-denial and suffering. The practice of justice is, however, the way which fulfils God's purpose for humanity not just individually but corporately. Thomas's teaching about justice became, as it continues to be today, integral to the way of life espoused by his own Dominican Order. It has for seven hundred and fifty years inspired not only Dominicans, but many other Catholics and many other Christians, to follow the way of justice which leads to peace.

Thomas[1] views creation as an ordered whole, the order of which reflects the ordering creativity of its Creator. His visionary understanding of God and creation is most fully set out in his *Summa Theologiae*, which is a carefully structured exposition of Christian doctrine (*sacra doctrina*), the 'holy teaching' of the Christian Church. 'In Christian doctrine', says Thomas, 'all things are considered in relation to God (*sub ratione Dei*), either because they are God himself, or because they have their place (*ordinem*) relative to God as their origin and their end.'[2]

1. In this essay, I shall broadly follow Thomas's treatment of justice in the *Summa Theologiae*, using the Blackfriars edition, 60 volumes (London: Eyre and Spottiswoode and New York: McGraw-Hill, 1964-1981). Helpful guides to overall structure have been the Marietti (Leonine) edition (4 vols, Rome, 1952-6) and T. McDermott ed., *Summa Theologiae, a Concise Translation* (London: Eyre and Spottiswoode, 1989). For background details I have used J.A. Weishepl, *Friar Thomas d'Aquino* (Oxford: Basil Blackwell, 1975). Translations are my own. I have retained Thomas's gendered pronouns since they reflect his gendered construal of natural order.

2. *ST*, 1a, q. 1, a. 7: '*Omnia autem pertractantur in sacra doctrina sub ratione Dei vel quia sunt ipse Deus; vel quia habent ordinem ad Deum, ut ad principium et finem.*'

Two terms here are almost untranslatable, but are central to everything that follows. First, the *ratio Dei* ('God's reason' or 'rationality'), and second, *ordo* ('order' or 'place' in that order). Thomas's account of creation is shot through with wonder at its immanent order, which is the product of God's transcendent ordering rationality.[3]

To understand what anything is – whether it be an object, an animal, a virtue, or a human being – we have to understand its place and purpose in the ascending tiers of God's cosmic order. We have to look at it *sub ratione Dei*. We have to understand where everything created by God comes from and what, in the purposes of God, it is for – so that we can use it aright. Similarly, we have to understand God's own nature and purposes, since the very heart of the Christian faith is an invitation to right relation with God. Justice must be understood at both levels. It is a virtue to be cultivated by the right use of this world's goods, but a full understanding of justice must begin from and culminate in the knowledge of God himself.

JUSTICE IN GOD AND IN HUMAN BEINGS

Thomas's sustained treatment of justice is part of the lengthy discussion of moral theology in the *Secunda Secundae* of the *Summa*. Following his discussion of the three theological virtues (faith, hope and charity), Thomas turns to the four cardinal virtues (prudence, justice, courage and temperance). His treatment of justice is far longer than that of any of the other virtues: sixty five questions are given over to an extremely wide-ranging discussion. However, before he comes to this discussion of justice among the virtues, he touches on justice in a number of other contexts.

Thomas first discusses the theme of justice in his consideration of the action of God.[5] In this way he establishes the divine 'origin and end' of justice before he concentrates on the worldly justice

3. Thomas speaks of 'the beauty of order' (*pulchritudo ordinis*), *ST*, 1a, q. 96, a. 3.

4. Thomas's sources include Aristotle's *Nicomachean Ethics* and Cicero's *De Officiis*. His commentary on Aristotle's *Ethics*, probably written towards the end of his life (1268-73), is an important additional source for his views on justice.

5. *ST*, 1a, q. 21, aa. 1-4.

that is to be enacted by humans. When expounding 'the justice and mercy of God', Thomas introduces an idea to which he repeatedly returns: 'The just act is that which renders what is due (*Actus iustitiae est reddere debitum*).'[6] This is the key to all Thomas has to say about justice, both human and divine. God renders to each their due, even making provision that the worship and obedience which is his own due shall be rendered to himself. The pattern of this 'distributive justice' was established from the beginning in the very way God ordered creation. God 'exercises justice when he gives to each one what ought to be given to that one (*quod ei debetur*) according to (the ratio of) its nature and condition'.[7] This giving 'what ought to be given', is what God wills for himself and for all his creatures. To do this, whether as a rational creature or as God, is to act in accordance with God's justice. 'When ... [God] acts according to his will he acts justly (*juste*), just as when we act according to the law we act justly (*juste*).'[8]

The human exemplar of such justice is the unfallen Adam. Thomas believes that Adam was created with all the virtues, since the virtues are 'perfections by which the reason is directed (*ordinatur*) towards God and the lower powers are exercised in accord with the rule of reason'.[9] Adam was endowed with 'original justice' (*justitia originalis*) in that his reason was, by grace, supernaturally subjected to God.[10] In the same way that God governs the universe by his reason, so, before the Fall, Adam governed his passions by reason. However, this justice was not incorruptible: though 'just', Adam was able to fall, because his state was not that of the blessed (*beati*) who enjoy the open vision of God from which they cannot fall away.[11]

6. *ST*, 1a, q. 21, a. 1.
7. *ST*, 1a, q. 21, a. 1.
8. *ST*, 1a, q. 21, a. 1. See *ST*, 1a 2ae, q. 93, a. 1: '*Ratio divinae sapientiae moventis omnia ad debitum finem obtinet rationem legis* (The rationality of the divine wisdom moving all things to their right end finds expression in the rationality of law).'
9. *ST*, 1a, q. 95, a. 3.
10. Thomas's view of the unfallen Adam is well illustrated by lines from Gerard Manley Hopkins' 'As Kingfishers Catch Fire, Dragonflies Draw Flame':
> 'I say more: the just man justices;
> Keeps grace: that keeps all his goings graces;
> Acts in God's eye what in God's eye he is ... '
11. *ST*, 1a, q. 100, a. 1-2.

The Fall entailed the loss of 'original justice': following the disruption of 'right order' in the cosmos (there are fallen angels) and the Fall of Adam, disorder became endemic in the natural world, in human society and in individual human beings.[12] The 'justification' of human beings, through the forgiveness of sins, represents the restoration to the sons and daughters of Adam of what we might call 'justice lost'. Justice, which 'in its rationality implies a certain rightness of order (*de sui ratione importet quamdam rectitudinem ordinis*)', can be taken in two senses.

First, there is the right ordering of a person's actions, whether with respect to another individual or in terms of obedience to the law, which orders human actions in the service of the common good. Then, there is the ordering of a person's interior disposition, 'namely when what is highest in man is subject to God and the lower powers of his soul are subject to what is supreme, which is the reason'. This is the state in which Adam was created, and this is the state to which the sinner is restored by the working of grace and the forgiveness of sins. Thomas sums up: 'Justice in its widest sense implies complete rightness of order (*totam rectitudinem ordinis*).'[13]

In his discussion of law, Thomas explains that God's order, the reflection of God's *ratio*, can readily be known in the world.[14] He sees God's law not as inert patterning of the world, but as the mode of God's providential governance of the world.[15] God governs all things according to law, which is the expression of

---

12. Thomas's moral cosmology is similar to that of Shakespeare's Ulysses:
   'The heavens themselves, the planets, and this centre,
   Observe degree, priority, and place,
   Insisture, course, proportion, season, form,
   Office and custom, in all line of order ...
   Take but degree away, untune that string,
   And, hark, what discord follows! ...
   Force should be right; or rather, right and wrong, –
   Between whose endless jar justice resides
   Should lose their names, and so should justice too.'
                              Troilus and Cressida, Act 1, Scene 3.
13. *ST*, 1a 2ae, q. 113, a. 1.
14. *ST*, 1a 2ae, qq. 90-97.
15. *ST*, 1a 2ae, q. 93, a. 5: 'Eternal Law is the rationale of divine providence (*Lex aeterna est ratio divinae providentiae*).' See 1a 2ae, q. 93, a. 1.

his own rationality ('Law is something that belongs to reason').[16] Law exists to guide humans in the way of God's justice: 'It is the function of law to direct human actions according to the order of justice (*secundum ordinem justitiae*)'[17] – guidance to which fallen human beings cannot respond without the aid of grace.

Beyond time, God promulgates his Eternal Law through his Eternal Word.[18] Within time, God ordains the 'natural law' which reflects the Eternal Law and regulates creation according to his will. Human beings, who by their rationality participate in the law's rationale, have, as it were to make explicit what they already know implicitly (a task requiring practical reason, or prudence), and then to enact their obedience to the natural law (a task requiring justice).[19] Human rulers have to implement specific laws, which, since they are fallen and fallible, will need at times to be corrected and amended in the light of new understandings of natural law. The standard of good government is the law we have in us by nature, and law framed by human beings is law only to the extent it derives from that law.[20] Humanly enacted laws can be just or unjust. To be just they must serve the common good, must not exceed the lawmaker's authority, and must fairly apportion the burdens of serving the common good amongst all members of the community.[21] Just laws oblige us in conscience because they derive ultimately from the Eternal Law. Laws can, however, be unjust when they serve not the common good but some lawmaker's greed or vanity, or when they exceed the lawmaker's authority, or when they

16. *ST*, 1a 2ae, q. 90, a. 1: '*Lex [est] aliquid pertinens ad rationem.*' For Thomas, the law is not only in the *ratio* of the governor, but also in the *ratio* of the governed. He also says, quoting Paul's 'lex membrorum' (see Rom 7:23), that a human inclination may derivatively be called a 'law' (see. Rom 2:15). His account of law, like his later account of justice, is thoroughly participatory.

17. *ST*, 1a 2ae, q. 91, a. 5.

18. Thomas makes it clear that, following Augustine, he sees Christ as the personification of the Eternal Law ('*ipse est lex aeterna per quamdam appropriationem*', *ST*, 1a 2ae, q. 93, a. 4). In accord with this, he suggests that Christ may be seen as 'justice personified' (*ST*, 3a, q. 59, a. 2), a point he would doubtless have elaborated had he completed his treatment of the Last Judgment.

19. *ST*, 1a 2ae, q. 91, a. 5: Thomas says, 'It pertains to the law to direct human deeds according to the *ordo* of justice.'

20. *ST*, 1a 2ae, q. 95, a. 2.

21. *ST*, 1a 2ae, q. 96, a. 4.

unfairly apportion the burdens of serving the common good. Such laws are not really laws at all, but forms of violence which do not oblige us in conscience.

The natural law is in accord with the divine law to which Scripture bears witness. Scripture tells us of the Old Law, which is to be found in the commandments of the Old Testament, and of the New Law, which, while evident in the commandments of the New Testament, is primarily to be understood as the Law implanted by grace within the hearts of believers. Thomas writes that the New Law is 'above all the very grace of the Holy Spirit, which is given to those who believe in Christ'.[22] Thus, the New Law not only shows human beings what they should do but, unlike the Old Law, gives them power to do it. The truly just person will enact a 'fourfold' obedience to the law: they will at one and the same time obey the natural law, written on the human heart, the 'positive law' of the land, inasmuch as it reflects the natural law, the divine law as it is written in the Scriptures, and the Eternal Law which is the eternal will of God for the good of his creation. Thomas quotes Augustine with approval: 'I reckon the just to act according to the eternal law.'[23] The just ruler will seek to render to each person what is due to them in accordance with the law, and so to uphold the divine order which is an expression of the *ratio Dei*. In a fallen world none of this will be easy. Justice, which enacts such rational obedience, is a costly virtue to be cultivated by the ruler and the ruled alike with the help of God's grace.

THE ANATOMY OF JUSTICE IN A FALLEN WORLD

There is a brief preview of Thomas's treatment of justice among the virtues in the *Prima Secundae*, where Thomas discusses the virtues in general. He argues, in line with the tradition that stretches back to Aristotle, that there are four cardinal virtues: prudence, justice, courage and temperance (or moderation).[24]

23. '*Justos sub aeterna lege agere existimo*' (*De lib. arbit.* 1.15, quoted *ST*, 1a 2ae, q. 93, a. 6. Augustine actually has *beatos* rather than *justos*, PL 32, 1238).

24. For a discussion of the Four Cardinal Virtues, see *ST* 1ae2ae 61.2. Compare Wisdom of Solomon 8:7: 'And if anyone loves righteousness, her labours are virtues; for she teaches self-control and prudence, justice and courage (*sobrietatem et prudentiam docet, justitiam et virtutem*); nothing in life is more profitable for

Prudence has a special place because it is a virtue of the intellect, of practical reason. The other virtues are dependent on the exercise of ordering rationality (*ordo rationis*): in the case of justice with respect to deeds and in the case of courage and temperance with respect to the passions. Amongst these three moral virtues, says Thomas, justice is preeminent.

Thomas's substantive treatment of justice comes in the *Secunda Secundae*.[26] Here prudence is seen as a virtuous articulation of the reason, justice of the will, temperance and courage of the emotions. The practice of these virtues is the hallmark of the virtuous person. They do not spring up overnight. A disposition to act in accord with these virtues must be carefully and energetically cultivated so that the strength to adhere to virtuous action is present in time of trial, when such adherence, though it serves the common good, appears to be of no benefit to the individual.

Thomas begins from a discussion of prudence, which he says is 'knowing what to want and what not to want'. It does not mean simply 'carefulness', but appropriate and skilled exercise of judgment. He quotes the Scriptural injunction (Mt 10:16) in the form, 'Be prudent [we are more used to "be wise"] as serpents'. The exercise of prudence is the exercise of practical reason. Prudence does not actually set the goals of virtue, but determines by reason the means to those goals in particular circumstances, and justice then acts upon what it has determined. Prudence is a practical virtue, which may be exercised in various spheres such as the personal or the domestic, but its highest form is political prudence exercised in statesmanship or lawmaking for the common good.

---

mortals than these.' Augustine talks of 'four virtues of the soul whereby it lives spiritually in this life, namely prudence, temperance, fortitude, and justice', adding that 'the fourth which is diffused through all the others is love of God and neighbour' (*De Div. Quaest.* LXXXIII 61, PL 40.51). Gregory the Great says that 'the entire structure of morality' is built on four virtues, namely prudence, temperance, fortitude and justice (*Moralium Libri in Job* II.49, PL 75, 592). Thomas wrote a number of articles on 'The Virtues in General' and 'The Cardinal Virtues', probably in 1269-72. See the Marietti Edition of *Quaestiones Disputatae*, vol. 2 (Rome, 1965), especially pp. 707-51, 813-28.

25. *ST*, 1a 2ae, q. 66, a. 2.

26. *ST*, 2a 2ae, qq. 57-122.

Thomas then turns to extended discussion of his second cardinal virtue: justice. First he deals with it is in general; then he considers many forms of injustice; then he considers just behaviour towards God; finally he considers just behaviour in the human community, concluding with a discussion of equity (*epieikeia*).

Thomas approaches his subject indirectly by considering the relationship between the right (*ius*) and justice (*iustitia*).[27] He argues that the use of the term 'justice' implies a certain balance (*aequalitas*) in things, because the very word 'justice' suggests that when they are out of balance they should be 'adjusted' (he uses the Latin *justari*) to be brought back into balance. Justice is not a virtue that pertains to the individual alone; it pertains to how the individual relates to others and this should not be 'out of kilter'. Thus, for example, there is a 'just' (or 'commensurate') payment for a service rendered. We can speak of 'the just thing' (for example 'the just outcome' or 'the just wage') which has about it an element of objectivity. Thomas equates *ius* and *iustum*, 'the right' and 'the just thing'. What 'the right' or 'the just thing' is depends upon who you are dealing with. A son may be said to 'belong' to a father, and a slave to a master, so there is only a modified and limited version of the 'just thing' to be established between them. Between a husband and wife there is also a specific form of the 'just thing': *'justum oeconomicum'*.[28] However, when two members of a society, neither of whom is subordinate to the other, meet as equals, the just thing (*justum*) can be established between them in the fullest sense, because it is a matter of equality.

When Thomas turns to discuss justice directly, he first considers how it should be defined, settling with the Roman lawyers for justice as the 'habit [a habit is a settled disposition] whereby a person with a lasting and constant will renders to each his due'.[29] The allusion is clear: *iustitia* is the will to give to

27. *ST*, 2a 2ae, q. 57. For a discussion of the relation between law, right and *ius*, see A.P. d'Entreves, *Natural Law* (second edition, London: Hutchinson, 1971, p. 61).

28. *Iustum oeconomicum* is derived from the Greek word *oikos*, here meaning 'household' or 'domestic'.

29. *ST*, 2a 2ae, q. 58, a. 1: *'Iustitia est habitus secundum quem aliquis constanti et perpetua voluntate jus suum unicuique tribuit.'*

each their *ius*. Justice is a virtue that is always exercised towards another. It requires a diversity of persons and is only properly used of one person towards another. However, by analogy, we may speak of 'diverse principles of action', such as the reason and the desires, within one individual. Justice would obtain within an individual whose reason controlled his desires, so that each part of his personality played its proper role. Thomas follows Aristotle, who saw this as a metaphorical use of the term 'justice'. The proper use of the term 'justice' is for action towards another.

Justice is a virtue because it regulates human action according to a standard of right reason, and so renders it good. It is seated in the will, which is 'the rational appetite'. Reason grasps the proportional relation of things to each other and the will enables us to enact that perception justly: justice is seated in the human faculty from which action flows, that is the will. Thomas says explicitly 'we are not said to be just because we know something correctly'. We are called just 'in that we do something rightly'. 'The just thing (*justum*)' or 'the right' must be enacted.

Thomas speaks both of 'general' or 'legal' justice, which is concerned with the good of all (the 'common good') and 'particular justice' which is concerned for the good of one other person. The act proper to justice is to render to each person what is rightly theirs, according to 'a certain proportional equality' (Thomas is no believer in absolute equality). General justice, with its concern for the common good, outshines the other virtues because the common good surpasses the specific good of one other person. Aquinas quotes Aristotle to the effect that 'justice is the most splendid of the virtues, and neither Morning nor Evening Star is so wonderful'.[30] Particular justice also shines brightly among the moral virtues because it is seated in the nobler parts of the soul, the will rather than the passions, and because it is concerned for the other rather than the individual.

When he turns to particular justice, Thomas follows Aristotle in making a key distinction between 'commutative' and 'distributive' justice. Dealings which relate one person to one other

---

30. *Ethics* V.1 (1129b); *ST*, 2a 2ae, 58, a. 12.

are in the field of commutative justice: that is, justice in exchanges. But the whole must also relate to its part, the community to its members. Such dealings are the field of distributive justice, according to which a person in authority apportions from the common resources that which is right for the individual. Distributive justice dictates that such common goods are to be shared out according to the status in the community of the recipient – though the priority remains meeting the needs of all. A person's status is thus directly relevant to the exercise of distributive justice; it will also affect commutative justice in so far as it affects the balance of indebtedness between two individuals. Commutative justice governs such dealings between two people. Some inter-personal dealings are involuntary: examples would be theft, bodily harm, false witness and public accusation, adultery or enticement of servants. Other dealings are voluntary: buying and selling, loans and hiring, deposits and pledges. All inter-personal dealing falls within the realm of commutative justice. There must be equitable recompense in all such transactions. Thomas says it is as a measure of equitable recompense in commercial trans-actions that money was invented (here he follows Aristotle closely). The proper act of restitution is characteristic of commu-tative justice. Where, after a wrong, there cannot be physical restitution, money may be used for an appropriate and equalising repayment. There may well be a judicially imposed penalty; a 'judicious' penalty.

While Thomas's analytical discussion of justice is obviously indebted to Aristotle's *Ethics*, his detailed description of the virtues and vices which constitute the practice of justice is much more like a manual for confessors. For instance, the vice opposed to distributive justice is failure to take into consideration that which makes for a person's dignity or worth: a form of partiality. The vices opposed to commutative justice, which are many, begin with homicide and proceed through bodily harm, theft, legal malpractice, slander, fraud and usury. Thomas famously allows that people in desperate need, who cannot meet their need in any other way, may provide for themselves from another's property.[31] Though the details of some of his

31. *ST*, 2a 2ae, q. 66, a. 7.

teaching (for example on suicide, punitive mutilation, and corporal punishment) make uncomfortable reading today, the principles which govern his theological jurisprudence remain starkly challenging to possessive, individualistic thinking: just as an individual limb is a member of the whole human body and exists 'for the sake of the whole', so each person is 'purposefully ordered to the whole community of which he is a part.'[32] It is the good of the community, and, within that, the good of individual persons, which governs Thomas's thinking about justice and about private property.

Embedded within Thomas's account of the vices and virtues associated with justice is his account of 'true religion': the proper worship due to God, against which he measures forms of superstition or irreverence. Religion is a moral virtue because it offers to God the worship that is rightfully his[33] but since humans can never fully render to God the worship that is rightfully his, religion must remain subordinate to justice. Thomas moves through a series of virtues which he sees as 'a part of justice', all of which go some way to offering what is due to God and one's neighbour: piety, gratitude, truth, friendship, and generosity.

Thomas turns, finally, to a discussion of *epieikeia*, which is usually translated 'equity'. He argues that since laws can only apply to general cases 'legislators take into account what is ordinarily the case and formulate a law accordingly', but there are cases where the slavish following of the letter of the law would amount to an evil. As an overriding principle, 'it is good to follow what the meaning of justice and the public good demand, setting the letter of the law aside.'[34] The key point here is Thomas's conviction that it is possible to transcend legalism and grasp the *justitiae ratio*. He gives the well-worked example of the madman who loans a sword and then demands it back when 'in the grip of his madness'. In a case of such manifest danger, *epieikeia* would overrule the normal demand of justice that a person's property should be returned on demand. *Epieikeia*

32. *ST*, 2a 2ae, q. 65, a. 1.
33. *ST*, 2a 2ae, q. 81, a. 5.
34. *ST*, 2a 2ae, q. 120, a. 1: '*Bonum autem est, praetermissis verbis legis, sequi id quod poscit justitiae ratio et communis utilitas.*'

does not subvert what is just absolutely, but, in exceptional and clear-cut cases (*in manifestis*), it moderates the inappropriate application of human law.

Thomas thus argues that it is possible to enter into the spirit of the law, or what the legislator intended, and to act justly in a way that transcends legalism. He quotes Aristotle to the effect that '*Epieikeia* is itself a form of that which is just' (*quoddam justum*), but it is also 'a kind of higher rule for human actions'.[35] It cannot be included within 'legal justice' if 'legal justice' is a matter of observing the laws without adverting to the intention of the legislator, but if the intention of the legislator is taken into account, then *epieikeia* is the 'principal form' of legal justice. In this way it acts as a moderating influence on legalistic approaches to justice.

The implications of what Thomas says are enormous. His remarks on *epieikeia* suggest it is possible so to enter into the 'spirit' of justice that one can discern clearly where the normal rules of 'justice' do not apply. In this discussion Thomas makes no explicit theological link with the Holy Spirit, nor with the Pauline contrast between the Spirit and the Law, but in the wider context of the *Summa* [36] it is clear that the transcendent *ratio Dei* and the *ratio justitiae* were for Thomas accessible through the *ratio* which the believer exercises and the grace in which the believer participates. In the end, the exercise of justice is a participation in the *ratio Dei*, in the mind of God. The discernment of the intention of the legislator is a discernment of God's intention in the promulgation of 'natural law' and of the fallibility of human legislation which must be general in its provision and so cannot illuminate the demands of justice in each specific situation. In each specific situation the exercise of justice depends upon prudential discernment, whether it be the discernment that this is a situation appropriately covered by the general law, or the discernment that in this situation 'equity' must overrule. In the end, it is not the keeping of law, but the outworking of the spirit of the law in responsible action which is the key to Thomas's understanding of justice.

35. *ST*, 2a 2ae, q. 120, a. 2.
36. Compare (as above, note 22) *ST* 1a 2ae, q. 106, a. 1.

Thomas correlates his discussion of the seven theological and cardinal virtues with the tradition of discussion about the seven gifts of the Spirit in Isaiah 11:2. The gift he correlates with justice is piety, because it 'does not only offer honour and duty to God, but also to all people inasmuch as they are related to God'.[37] He also correlates with each of the virtues specific injunctions by which they are enjoined. In the case of justice, he specifically commends the Ten Commandments, reading them as 'precepts of justice'. He concludes:

> After three command-ments pertaining to religion by which that which is due is rendered to God; and after a fourth commandment, enjoining the piety which renders to parents that which is their due, in which is included all that is due for any other special reason (of affiliation); it was then necessary to include all the other commandments pertaining to justice in its proper sense, which impartially renders to each what is their due.[38]

For Thomas, the Ten Commandments sum up perfectly God's guidance for the practice of justice.

THE JUSTICE OF CHRIST AND THE JUSTICE OF THE FATHER

For modern readers, it is striking that the *Summa Theologiae* postpones Christology until the *Tertia Pars*, which begins with the discussion of the Incarnate Word. The *Tertia Pars* is written predominantly in the mode of fulfilment, and so brings in the perspective of eschatology. Christ, like the unfallen Adam, had 'all the virtues'.[39] Though Christ naturally shrank from suffering, he still yielded himself obediently to the suffering that was his Father's will for him. What Christ wanted above all was that the will of his Father should be fulfilled.[40] In every way, Thomas argues, Christ demonstrated his justice by keeping the precepts of the Law.[41] Christ was justice incarnate,[42] voluntarily offering

37. *ST*, 2a 2ae, q. 121, a. 2.
38. *ST*, 2a 2ae, q. 122, a. 6.
39. *ST*, 3a, q. 7, a. 2.
40. *ST*, 3a, q. 18, a. 5.
41. *ST*, 3a, q. 40, a. 4.
42. *ST*, 3a, q. 46, a. 2: '*Cum ipse sit iustitia*'

himself to suffering in fulfilment of the will of God. His justice was instrumental in obtaining the liberation of humanity.[43]

When Thomas has considered at length the crucifixion, resurrection and ascension of Christ, he turns to the power of Christ as judge (*judiciaria potestas*), though he postpones a full discussion of the Last Judgment until his never completed consideration of what will happen at the end of the world.[44] The premise for this discussion has been stated much earlier: 'Judgment is an act of justice, inasmuch as the judge restores those things which are able to produce a situation of inequality to the equality that is justice.'[45] The authority to judge human beings rests first with the Father but the power of judging is delegated from the Father to the Son: 'According to the justice of God, he who fought and overcame on behalf of God's justice, and was (himself) unjustly judged, is the judge.'[46] However, so long as the present age continues, there can be no perfect and open judgment. 'There must, then, be a final judgment on the last day, on which there will be adjudged perfectly and openly that which is right for every person.'[47] In other words, God in his justice and mercy will in Christ bring to completion his 'lasting and constant will to render to each his due'.

There is a thought-provoking coda to Thomas's reflection on justice in the *Summa Theologiae*. The last section he was able to write, which was on penance, includes a section on repentance as a virtue specifically related to justice. Thomas describes repentance as 'a kind of human justice with respect to God (*justitia quaedam hominis ad deum*)'.[48] Repentance is a virtue because it is a matter of the will and it is impossible without

43. *ST*, 3a, q. 46, a. 1.

44. The *Supplementum* to the *Summa Theologiae* (Marietti Edition, vol. 3, Rome, 1956), compiled largely from Book 4 of the *Scriptum Super Libros Sententiarum* (1252-6), covers this ground. See especially qq 88-90. There is also relevant material in the *Summa Contra Gentiles* (1259-64). I have borne this in mind when assembling clues from the *Summa Theologiae*.

45. *ST*, 2a 2ae, q. 63.4: '*Judicium est actus judiciae, prout judex ad aequalitatem justitiae reducit ea quae inaequalitatem oppositam facere possunt*'; see *ST*, 2a 2ae, q. 60, a. 1.

46. *ST*, 3a, q. 59, a. 4.

47. *ST*, 3a, q. 59, a. 5.

48. *ST*, 3a, q. 85, a. 3.

grace. Repentance is unique because it opens the door to all the other virtues. Repentance and justice go together because repentance opens the way for the human sinner to render to God, in whom are his origin and end, the worship and thanksgiving due to God alone.

CONCLUSION

We have seen how Thomas's cosmology is structured by his thought about Eternal Law, natural law, divine law, and positive law and how his belief that these exist in mutually supportive correlation is rooted in his notion of the *ratio Dei*. Thomas's ordered universe, and its ordering law, is a magnificent, but to many modern thinkers, impossible vision. In our own time, confidence in any pre-ordained, hierarchical *ordo*, in rationality freed from ideology and the struggle for power, in justice as manifestly 'fair' recompense, has largely gone. In its place, there is a sharp awareness of justice as a contested concept and the struggle for justice as one that involves a succession of challenges to the received social order, be that order monarchy, liberal democracy, state socialism, or global capitalism. Modern thinkers are likely to ask, whose *ordo*? what rationality? how much will the market, or popular opinion, stand? For Thomas, however, the practice of justice involved a kind of 'tuning in'. It was like finding the wavelength, helped by both reason and Scripture, to receive a broadcast emanating from a not-so-distant homeland. Now that in Western societies there is no supportive public consensus for belief in a divinely grounded natural law, the notion that there is a universal moral rationality by which construals of justice may be broadly determined begins to look not only counter-intuitive but, more than that: prophetic.

We may find it hard to weave together the many strands of Thomas's thinking as he does, but the strands that can be woven together provide a remarkably sound base for the critique of injustice. Thomas's notion of justice requires of individuals a passionate commitment to the common good, so that they seek consistently to discern and to follow what is good not merely for themselves but for all. Central to his notion of commutative justice is his conviction that there is good or 'dignity' in all things and that there is a proper use of money which is conditioned by the recognition of this dignity (and not the other way round). There is a 'just price' for goods, which is determined by the amount of labour that goes into their manufacture, not simply the price that the market will stand. There is a 'just price' for labour which ensures that people have what is their due: only by providing what is sufficient to meet their needs do we recognise their dignity as human beings. Thomas's view of society, money, labour, property and human need provides the ground for a radical critique of global capitalism and the unjust systems which perpetuate poverty, hunger and social exclusion. Thomas's participatory and integrated view of what we call politics and economics provides the grounds for a critique of any system which perpetuates exclusion and marginalisation. The roots of this lie in his theologically based humanism, in his prophetic affirmation of the dignity of every human being and 'the right' which demands that their needs must be met.

It is, then, no surprise that Roman Catholic lawyers, indebted to Thomas, played a major part in the drafting of the Universal Declaration of Human Rights (UDHR), which begins with an affirmation that 'recognition of the inherent dignity and of the equal and inalienable rights of all members of the human family is the foundation of freedom, justice and peace in the world'.[49] The UDHR is distinguished from many later statements of human rights by the way in which it holds together civil and political with economic and social rights. In this, as in its emphasis on social participation, its proclamation of correlative duties as well as rights, and its fundamental conviction of the dignity of every human being, it is clearly indebted to Thomas's view of justice. The UDHR is an attempt at a statement for the modern, pluralist era of what it means to have a 'lasting and constant will to render to each person their due'. Just as with the *Summa Theologiae*, which is a statement of fundamental Christian

49. Preamble to the Universal Declaration of Human Rights (1948), quoted P. Sieghart, *The Lawful Rights of Mankind* (Oxford: Oxford University Press, 1985), p. 172.

doctrine, the UDHR, which is a statement of fundamental human rights, now provides a radical basis for the confrontation of injustice in the hope of lasting peace. Where Thomas would take issue with it is, of course, in its lack of a theological grounding. For Thomas, there cannot be one without the other.

3

The Medieval Rhineland

Eckhart and Popular
Theological Preaching

JOHN ORME MILLS, O.P.

1. WHY ECKHART?

Thirty years ago the very idea of including the Rhineland mystics in a series of essays on the role of the Dominicans in the promotion of peace and social justice would have been seen as intolerably bizarre. At that time it was still widely taken for granted that mysticism and dedication to the promotion of social justice were irreconcilable: that they belonged to profoundly different ways of understanding the world and understanding the teaching of Jesus Christ. There were, of course, some remarkable people who seemed to be able to keep a foot in both the camps, but lesser mortals who attempted this were in danger of not being taken seriously by the occupants of either.

In spite of the massive changes which have taken place since then in politics, the culture and the Church, even today the presence of the Dominican Rhineland mystics in this series demands some explanation. By 'the Dominican Rhineland mystics' we mean, first and foremost, three friars of the Dominican Province of Teutonia: the brilliant but controversial Meister Eckhart (*ca* 1260-c.1328) and two of his disciples, Johannes Tauler (*ca*1300-1361) and Henry Suso (1295-1366). At first sight the only things which these men seem to share in common with, for instance, the French Dominican worker-priests of the 1950s or the Brazilian Dominican liberation theologians of the 1970s are membership of the same religious order and considerable strength of character.

After all, Frank Tobin has said that Eckhart's sermons 'center so exclusively on what is within and are so utterly devoid of any comments that might be used as references to time and place that they might just as well have been delivered on the moon as in turbulent fourteenth-century Strasburg or Cologne.'[1]

And Eckhart himself says in his Latin work *The Book of the Parables of Genesis:*

> It is order that makes something good, so that it is impossible for there to be good outside order and conversely for there to be evil where order exists. A natural order is one in which the highest point of what is inferior touches the lowest point of its superior ... In the contact, meeting and union of what is essentially superior with the highest point of its inferior both sides kiss each other and embrace in a natural and essential love that is inward and very delightful.[2]

So inequality is an essential constituent of perfection; it is our duty to remain where God has put us. Not, of course, that there is anything particularly original about what Eckhart is saying here. He was a medieval man. He accepted uncritically the general neo-Platonic notion of a divinely-willed hierarchical order of the cosmos, and, like many other learned men of his age, he saw the feudal system as exemplifying it. As Richard Woods has said: 'His harshest detractors never accused him of fomenting insurrection or even mouthing social criticism.'[3]

It is, of course, well to bear in mind the argument of the Russian historian Aron Gurevich that it is 'much more productive to interpret medieval culture as "another" culture, admitting that it is not our culture and that the criteria for evaluating it must be sought within itself.'[4] Also, for that matter, Richard

1. *Introduction to Henry Suso: The Exemplar, with Two German Sermons,* Paulist Press, New York 1989, p.15.
2. nn. 139, 146. Augustine discussed the relation of the good to order in *The Nature of the Good* 3qq., and Thomas in e.g. *Summa Theologiae* II-IIae.q. 81,a. 2. Eckhart's direct source for the notion of the concatenation of all reality into the great chain of being appears to be the Pseudo-Augustinian The Spirit and the Soul.
3. *Eckhart's Way,* Darton Longman & Todd, London 1987, p.216. Cf also Bernard McGinn, 'Meister Eckhart: An Introduction', Paul E. Szarmach ed. An *Introduction to the Medieval Mystics of Europe,* Albany: State University of New York Press 1984, p.238.
4. *Medieval Popular Culture: Problems of Belief and Perception,* Cambridge 1988, p.216.

Finn's remark in the first essay in this series – namely, that we must recognise

> that what we regard as wrong and unjust may have struck medieval men and women as wrong but vicious in some other way and vice versa. What we regard as an infringement of human rights might have been repugnant as an act of cruelty. What we see as selfish, they might consider a failure to give others their due.[5]

However, even assuming we do take on board what Aron Gurevich and Richard Finn are saying to us, this does not lead us suddenly to see that Eckhart was a campaigner for social justice after all. It is just possible to put up an argument that Tauler had a social conscience (much depends on how one reads some of his sermons),[6] but not Eckhart and not Suso.

Why, then, are Eckhart and his followers here? To answer that, we must first put these men in their context.

2. ECKHART'S WORLD

Ever since the publication in 1979 of *A Distant Mirror: The Calamitous Fourteenth Century*, Barbara Tuchman's study of the similarities between the disasters of the fourteenth and twentieth centuries, popular interest in the world of the Rhineland mystics has grown.

Eckhart and his followers lived in an age of turmoil, uncertainty, scandals and fiascos. While the towns were still steadily increasing in power and importance, Central Europe's overall population and productivity had already begun to decline even before the Great Famine of 1315-17. The collapse of the Hohenstaufen dynasty and the Interregnum of 1254-73 had severely weakened the Holy Roman Empire as a political force. In 1307, in the face of political upheaval in Italy, the papacy withdrew to

---

5. See p. 22, *supra.*
6. See, for example, the loving respect he shows in sermon H47 for cobblers and ploughmen, his statement in sermon H40 that 'an uncouth peasant' will be a thousand times more welcome at the heavenly banquet than 'vain worldlings', and his criticisms in sermons H23 and H27 of 'great lovers of themselves' who 'will rob one another of their rights by injustice, fraud and violence'and 'dominate' their neighbour.

Avignon, and it had lost much of its moral leadership. The feudal system respected by Eckhart was beginning to break up, and chivalry declined as the knightly class became economically weaker – many knights were having to take up trades in the towns or become outlaws. The Black Death of 1347-9 wiped out approximately one-third of the population.

Confronted as they were by so much insecurity and so little promise, it is not surprising that the interior life became of immense importance to a relatively large number of people, both clerical and lay. However, it would be unwise to make a simple connection between the crises just listed and the growth of mysticism. The tendency to 'turn inward' was part of a bigger social development which the crises promoted. In the opinion of some modern historians,[7] it was during the two centuries in which the lives of Eckhart and his followers fall, the thirteenth and fourteenth centuries, that – at least partly as a result of the growth of urban life and of the arrival of the mendicant orders – Western Christianity changed from being predominantly 'a religion of the churchmen', of a minority of the population, to being a 'religion of the masses' ... by which is meant one more extensively adapted to the spiritual needs and aspirations of ordinary lay people.

A remarkably large number of outstanding mystical writers were alive in the fourteenth century, scattered right across Western Europe (in England were Richard Rolle, Julian of Norwich and the author of *The Cloud of Unknowing*). However, quite exceptional was the popular wave of religious fervour of this kind which spread through the regions adjacent to the Rhine – along its upper reaches (Suso spent much of his life at Konstanz), in the neighbourhood of Strasburg and Cologne (cities where both Eckhart and Tauler lived), and in the Low Countries.

Those three Dominicans directly or, more often, indirectly influenced the lives of thousands, for at least three categories of people were being drawn to that fervent and profoundly inward spirituality. The first of these were members of the mendicant

7. See, for example, Georges Duby, *The Age of the Cathedrals*, Chicago 1981, p. 268.

orders, and particularly Dominican nuns. The next, Beguines and Beghards – in other words the large number of women and smaller number of men who could not enter an ecclesiastically-approved religious house with a formally constituted rule but lived a vigorous spiritual life in communities loosely affiliated to one or other of the mendicant orders. Lastly, many laypeople, most of them living in towns. The potential audience was not an elite clique.

The basic contention of this article is that, although they did not offer a programme of social reform, Eckhart and to a lesser extent his followers were concerned with transforming the quality of people's lives, with changing them – not only the lives of clerics but also of women religious and of laypeople (including laypeople who were not wealthy).

3. THE PREACHING

'Medieval popular preaching' is a loose term covering all preaching other than the preaching done in Latin by theologians in a clerical milieu. We find among the surviving collections of sermons of parish priests and missionaries of the earlier middle ages some impressive attempts to transform Christian doctrine into the world-view of the mass of the people. This was achieved by avoiding any kind of abstract reflection, using simple language and keeping to subjects within the mental horizon of the audience.[8]

Long before Eckhart's time the medieval preacher had been equipped with guides to effective popular preaching, and firmly in this tradition is the compendium called *Memorable Histories*[9] written in Eckhart's own time by Rudolph of Schlettstadt, a Dominican of Eckhart's own province. It was written to help priests teach the faith to the uneducated, largely with the aid of entertaining examples from ordinary life and stories about saints and visits to the Other World. It presupposes both

8. See G.R. Owst, *Literature and Pulpit in Medieval England*, Oxford 1961, *Preaching in Medieval England*, Oxford 1965; M. Richter, 'Kommunikationsprobleme im lateinischen Mittelalter', *Historische Zeitschrift* 1976, 222:43–80.

9. E. Kleinschmidt ed., Rudolf von Schlettstadt: *Historiae Memorabiles. Zur Dominikanerliteratur und Kulturgeschichte des 13. Jahrhunderts*, Cologne-Vienna 1974.

readers and listeners who are totally unfamiliar with theological literature.

In the thirteenth century the sermon in the German vernacular was, then, flourishing. Yet were the preachers reaching everybody's needs? In 1266 appeared the first systematic listing of different kinds of audiences: *De Eruditione Praedicatorum* by Humbert of Romans.[10] His writing of it is an indication of the new social reality and awareness which the Dominican preacher was facing in later medieval times.

In the province of Teutonia shortly after 1300 there were seventy convents of Dominican nuns, seven of them in Strasburg alone. Each convent contained about fifty women, and in a few cases nearly eighty, some of them very intelligent and with a knowledge of Latin. The dramatic growth in the number of these convents had stirred up a lot of unease at the highest level in the Church. The outbreak of antinomianisn among the so-called Brethren of the Free Spirit was soon to reveal the problems that could arise when the serious pursuit of the interior life became popular among people with no formal education in theology. Also the nuns themselves had stressed their need for spiritual instruction. Primarily to instil order and control among the nuns, Pope Clement IV in 1267 officially commanded the Dominican Order to provide preachers and confessors for the spiritual welfare of these women. Later their responsibility was extended to women of other religious orders also.

Nobody at the time would have guessed that almost certainly this was the decisive event which led to the flowering of mysticism in the Rhineland. To quote Frank Tobin: 'This combination of enlightened spiritual advisers and recipients who were both eager and qualified provided the basis for much of the intense spiritual activity of the times.'[11]

In 1313 Meister Eckhart, then about fifty years old, was assigned to Strasburg as Vicar-General with oversight of the many women's convents in south-west Germany. He had already twice

10. Simon Tugwell, *Early Dominicans: Selected Writings*, Paulist Press, New York 1982, pp.201–3.

11. *op. cit.* p.16.

held a chair in theology at the University of Paris (the only other person to achieve that honour was St Thomas Aquinas) and been a very successful first Provincial of the new Dominican province of Saxonia. He was appointed to Strasburg almost certainly because the Council of Vienne (1311-12) had accused Beguines in that area of heresy. He was now more closely involved than he had ever been with the problems of this multitude of religious women, but, far from ruling them with a rod of iron, he displayed a very real sympathy for them ... and thirteen years later was to be accused of heresy himself.

Inevitably, because the movement was a popular one, most of the writing and preaching on 'the God within' had to be done in the vernacular, and erudite thinkers and deeply sensitive spirits – of whom by far the most prominent was Eckhart – had to struggle to put into their native language ideas which hitherto they had assumed could only be satisfactorily expressed in Latin. In the words of Bernard McGinn: 'It was in the creative turn to the vernacular that the German mysticism found its distinctive voice.'[12] We may call the German sermons of Eckhart 'popular theological preaching' or 'mystic sermons', but this certainly does not mean they avoided the serious questions. Loris Sturlese has said they 'may be regarded as an attempt to convey in German to a German audience a sophisticated philosophy which had as its goal a redefinition of the relationship between God and humanity'.[13]

The effect which Eckhart had on the lives of those women and, for that matter, their influence on him, is difficult to gauge. We are dependent for our information largely on what we find in the one hundred or so authentic German sermons of Eckhart, nearly all of them taken down by the nuns themselves. In 1329, one year after his death, the highly controversial papal bull *In Agro Dominico* was published, condemning twenty-eight propositions based on his teaching. It had a disastrous effect on his reputation, which has only very recently fully recovered from it. Tauler and Suso kept his memory alive for a while and copies of

12. *ibid.* p.3.
13. 'Mysticism and Theology in Meister Eckhart's Theory of the Image', *Eckhart Review* 2 (1993), p.30.

a few sermons went on circulating, usually anonymously, but whereas Tauler's sermons were widely read and studied right down through the centuries and, of all devotional books, Suso's *Horologium Sapientiae* was surpassed in international popularity in the late middle ages only by the *Imitation of Christ*, Eckhart was a half-forgotten figure until the mid-nineteenth century. Fragments of his teaching continued to be remembered, but out of their context. Recovering his thought in its integrity has been a big scholarly exercise, and there is still work to be done.

4. THE TEACHING

Eckhart opens sermon 53 (22 in the Walshe translation):[14]

When I preach, I am accustomed to speak about detachment, and that a man should be free of himself and of all things: second, that a man should be formed again into that simple good which is God; third, that he should reflect on the great nobility with which God has endowed his soul, so that in this way he may come to wonder at God; fourth, about the purity of the divine nature, for the brightness of the divine nature is beyond words.

What we have here is in fact not merely an outline of how Eckhart presented his ideas in his preaching, but a very brief summary of his spiritual doctrine.

In it he says that he usually begins by urging his listeners to free themselves of themselves and of everything. One of the things which is striking about Eckhart's spirituality is how liberating it is, compared with most late medieval spirituality. This is the characteristic of it on which this essay is focussing, and we will consider it under three headings.

First of all, note how Eckhart helps us to be aware of our limitations. As Bernard McGinn has pointed out,[15] for Eckhart

14. The first number is of the sermon in the Quint edition of the German works, *Meister Eckhart: die deutschen und lateinischen Werke*, Kohlhammer Verlag, Stuttgart and Berlin 1936–; the second number is of the translation in M. O'C. Walshe, *Meister Eckhart: German Sermons and Treatises*, Element Books, Shaftesbury 1979–87.

15. Edmund College and Bernard McGinn, *Meister Eckhart: The Essential Sermons, Commentaries, Treatises and Defense*, Paulist Press, New York 1981, p.31.

theology's task was not so much to reveal a set of truths about God as to frame the paradoxes that would highlight the inherent limitations of our minds and mark off the boundaries of the unknown territory where God dwells. 'Only when we have come to realize what it is that we cannot realize can we begin to live out of the unknowable divine ground of our being.'

Secondly, he makes bold claims about our accessibility to God. For example, in sermon 26 (W58), on the relationship between God's goodness and human goodness, he says:

> There is no-one here so coarse-grained, so ignorant or unprepared but if, by the grace of God, he can atone his will purely and totally with the will of God, then he need only say with desire: 'Lord, show me your dearest will and strengthen me to do it!' and God will do so as truly as he lives, and God will give to him in as bounteous fullness and in every way as perfectly as He ever gave to that woman [by the well in John 4]. So you see, the most benighted of you, the most insignificant of you all might have got all this from God before he leaves this church today, in fact before I have finished preaching, in very truth as surely as God is God and I am a man

Ultimately any way can be the way to God and every way is also a nonway, because we can break through simply by detaching ourselves and being completely open to God.

Thirdly, it is for this reason important for us to understand what precisely Eckhart means by *abegescheidenheit*, usually translated from Eckhart's Middle High German as 'detachment'. It is one of his most central teachings, and also one of the most difficult. He does not mean by this word a cold withdrawal, a negative world-rejection, but a stripping of the self, a freeing of the self. For him, all moral and ascetical advance is rooted in a sovereign and grace-filled intervention of God in the depths of our being. In the treatise *On Detachment* he says:

> You should know that true detachment is nothing else than for the spirit to stand as immovable against whatever may chance to it of joy and sorrow, honour, shame and disgrace, as a mountain of lead stands before a little breath of wind.

This immovable detachment brings a man into the greatest
equality with God, because God has it from his immovable
detachment that he is God, and it is from his detachment that
he has his purity and simplicity and his unchangeability.

In sermon 52 (W87) he argues that 'A poor [i.e. detached]
man wants nothing, and knows nothing, and has nothing.'

'People should not worry so much about what they should
do; rather about what they should be,' he insists elsewhere.[16] At
the level of ordinary living, the process of detachment begins
with the giving up of our own will, the giving up of the sense of
being in possession of things. And, surprisingly, one of the
things that being 'detached' in the Eckhartian sense does to us
is to make us care more for other people, not less. We will care
for them more like God does. 'You must,' he tells us in sermon
5a (W13a), 'make no distinctions in the way you relate to
people, being no closer to yourself than you are to anyone else.'
Richard Woods has even gone so far as to claim: 'Eckhart calls
us freshly to transformation, to a rebirth into God-centred
contemplation of the world's weals and woes, to a greater, freer
commitment to social justice, inclusive love, and effective action.'[17]

Important consequences followed from the teachings re-
viewed above. Firstly, to quote Richard Kieckhefer: 'Eckhart did
not view ecstasy or abstractive union with God as integral to the
life of the soul, or even as a goal to be sought or particularly
treasured'.[18] He encouraged his listeners to cultivate a habitual
awareness of God continuous and compatible with ordinary
experience in the world. In fact, he glorified the everyday life of
active service, infused with consciousness of God's presence, as
the highest ideal, and applied to this life the mystical terminol-
ogy hitherto reserved for distinctive forms of experience.[19] He
was not particularly interested in discussing ecstatic states.

16. *Meister Eckhart: die deutschen Werke* vol V p.192.
17. *op. cit.* p.219.
18. 'Meister Eckhart's Conception of Union with God', *Harvard Theological Review*, 71 (1978), p.224.
19. Richard Kieckhefer: *Unquiet Souls – Fourteenth-Century Saints and their Religious Milieu*, Chicago U.P., 1984, pp.150–1.

Secondly, Eckhart recommends the dropping of particular devotional practices, if these are felt to obstruct our union with God. 'Our blessedness does not lie in our active doing, rather in our passive reception of God,' he says in sermon 24 of Oliver Davies's Penguin Classics translation (W2). As he rather tartly remarks in sermon 5a (W13a): 'We are the cause of all our obstacles.' When he was Prior of Erfurt and still in his thirties, in talk 2 of his *Talks of Instruction* he tells his young Dominican brothers:

A free mind can achieve all things. But what is a free mind? A free mind is one which is untroubled and unfettered by anything, which has not bound its best part to any particular manner of being or devotion.

More bluntly, in an often-quoted extract from sermon 5b (W13b) we hear him saying to his audience:

If a man thinks he will get more of God by meditation, by devotion, by ecstasies or by special infusion of grace than by the fireside or in the stable – that is nothing but taking God, wrapping a cloak around his head and shoving him under a bench. For whoever seeks God in a special way gets the way but misses God, who lies hidden in it. But whoever seeks God without any special way gets him as he is in himself, and that man lives with the Son, and he is life itself.

He is equally blunt talking about external observances in the much less well-known sermon 30 in the Davies translation:

I will not say that those who hold external observances to be the best shall be damned, but only that they shall not come to God without great purification in Purgatory. For these people do not follow God if they do not abandon themselves; rather they follow the self-esteem in which they hold themselves.

Neither has Eckhart much room for intercessory prayer as that term is ordinarily understood, insisting in sermon 65 (W5):

When I pray for aught, my prayer goes for naught; when I

pray for naught, I pray as I ought. When I am united with That wherein all things are existent whether past, present or future, they are all equally near and equally one; they are all in God and all in me. Then there is no need to think of Henry or Conrad [in other words, Tom, Dick or Harry].

What, though, did Eckhart's audiences think of the things he was telling them?

5. THE AUDIENCE

Eckhart believed that what he was offering people was 'freedom' – that they should be 'free of themselves and of all things'. His popular theological preaching was consistent with this aim, and he clearly had a respect for the intelligence of the people whom he preached to, and especially the women religious. He did not equate lack of education with lack of intelligence, and in reply to the criticism that he should not preach on such elevated topics to unlearned audiences he replied:

If we are not to teach people who have not been taught, no one will ever be taught, and no one will ever be able to teach or write. For that is why we teach the untaught, so that they may be changed from uninstructed into instructed.[20]

Nevertheless, some of the most basic ideas in Eckhart's preaching seem to be attacking the religious practices of his hearers.

The increasing literacy in late medieval Europe, and the spread of lay piety which was partly a result of that, brought about what Kieckhefer has called 'a democratisation of mysticism', with broader audiences not only reading about the mystics but also emulating them.[21] Yet this was at the same time a period when women, particularly religious women, were finding themselves increasingly constricted – when there was a tightening-up of clerical control over them. The spiritual life of the fourteenth-century devout person, and particularly of the devout woman, was a world made up of scores of observances:

20. Colledge and McGinn, *op. cit.* p.239.
21. *Unquiet Souls*, p.150.

of devotions and ascetic practices and affective prayer. Furthermore, among devout women in particular a lot of importance was placed on mystical visions – not only on hearing and reading about them, but on actually being granted them. Mystical and paramystical experiences were attributed to women much more often than to men. In the words of Grace Jantzen:

> if women were to have or exercise spiritual authority, it would have to be grounded somehow; and the grounding which was available to religious men – good Latin education, ecclesiastical validation – was largely and increasingly not open to religious women. At least from the time of Hildegard of Bingen [1098–1179], women were consciously grounding their religious authority on their visionary experience.[22]

There is no doubt, though, that Eckhart felt that what he saw as excessive emphasis on particular devotions or particular ascetical practices could positively hamper an individual's union with God, and so could reliance on mystical visions. In sermon 16b (W14b) he says:

> Some people want to see God with their own eyes, just as they see a cow; and they want to love God just as they love a cow. You love a cow because of the milk and cheese and because of your own advantage. This is how all these people act who love God because of external riches or because of internal consolation. They do not love God rightly; rather they love their own advantage.

What kind of impact would this have had on the nuns and beguines whom he was preaching to, for whom quasi-sensory religious experience was so important? It is Grace Jantzen's conclusion that Eckhart's writings 'do not offer the resources for a liberating spirituality',[23] by which she means a spirituality which confirmed women as being in no sense inferior beings to men. However, other scholars would say that what Eckhart was criticising was not *all* the devotions or ascetical practice or quasi-sensory religious experience of the women he was counselling

22. 'Eckhart and Women', *Eckhart Review* 3 (Spring 1994), p.41.
23. op. cit. p.46.

but their *excessive* reliance on these.[24]

None of the feedback from Eckhart's audiences has survived. On the other hand, it was members of his audiences, and above all religious women, who took down those sermons (including ones criticising some of their religious practices) and preserved them in their houses. In fact, Saskia Murk Jansen has only very recently shown that good copies of Eckhart's works continued to circulate in women's religious houses in the Low Countries despite the condemnation of him.[25]

Furthermore, recent scholarship has revealed just how much respect Eckhart and his followers had for outstanding religious women and for the women in their charge, in spite of the negative attitude to women of so many senior ecclesiastics of their time, Inquisitors particularly. These Dominicans were open to learning from them, and did so. As John Coakley has put it, in the women they found the charismatic gifts they themselves lacked.[26] There are grounds for thinking Eckhart read some of the writings of Hildegard of Bingen, Mechthild of Magdeburg and Margaret Porete.[27] Tauler visited a number of times the mystic Margareta Ebner, a Dominican nun. Elsbeth Stagel, another Dominican nun, contributed to the composition of Suso's masterpiece, *The Life of the Servant.*

There is no doubt at all that the Dominican mystics of the Rhineland profoundly influenced some aspects of the spirituality of the late middle ages, but this is not our concern here. We have argued here that themes in Eckhartian theology led these Dominicans to attempt through their teaching to make at least some of the people living in that stifling and insecure world freer in spirit. It could be said that Eckhart's teaching on 'inwardness' was an early contribution towards the making of the

24. See e.g. Frank Tobin, *Meister Eckhart: Thought and Language,* Philadelphia 1986, pp.116f; Oliver Davies, *Meister Eckhart: Mystical Theologian,* London 1991, pp.76–8.

25. 'Apocryphal Followers of Meister Eckhart?', *Eckhart Review* 7 (Spring 1998) pp.3–13.

26. 'Friars as Confidants of Holy Women in Medieval Dominican Hagiography', Renate Blumenfeld-Kosinski and Timea Szell, ed.: *Images of Sainthood in Medieval Europe,* Cornell U.P. 1991, p.225.

27. See Oliver Davies: *Meister Eckhart: Mystical Theologian,* SPCK London 1991, chapter 3: 'Meister Eckhart and the Religious Women of the Age.'

modern identity. It did not endure: it was swallowed up in the maelstrom of high ecclesiastical politics, and for long was almost forgotten. If, however, we only wrote about Dominicans whose contributions to the cause of social justice succeeded, this collection of essays would be brief indeed, surely?[28]

---

28. Translations from Eckhart's Middle High German and Latin are taken from M. O'C. Walshe: *Meister Eckhart: Sermons & Treatises I–III*, Element Books, Shaftesbury 1979–1987; Edmund College and Bernard McGinn: *Meister Eckhart: The Essential Sermons, Commentaries, Treatises and Defense*, Paulist Press, New York 1981; Bernard McGinn: *Meister Eckhart: Teacher and Preacher*, Paulist Press, New York 1986; Oliver Davies: *Meister Eckhart: Selected Writings*, Penguin Classics, London and New York 1994.

4

Recovering the Apostolic Life

Antoninus of Florence

RICHARD FINN, O.P.

The Acts of the Apostles relates how in the Jerusalem church 'the whole group of those who believed were of one heart and soul, and no one claimed private ownership of any possessions, but everything they owned was held in common. With great power the apostles gave their testimony to the resurrection of the Lord Jesus, and great grace was upon them all.'[1] The author of Acts is not simply reporting three separate facts about the apostles, how they felt, how they lived, and how they preached. Their preaching gains its power from their common faith and life. Their rejection of private property and redistribution of wealth, cutting at the roots of avarice, form an eloquent expression of their faith in the God who hears the cry of the poor, whose day of justice is at hand. The heart, the purse, and the voice are formed in a single apostolic life.

This picture of the apostolic life was at the heart of St Augustine's vision of religious life and dear to the early Dominicans who adopted his *Rule*. The fifth Master of the Order, Humbert of Romans, in his *Commentary on the Rule* was adamant that the brother who even said 'that's my book!' and meant it committed mortal sin. All things had been shared before the Fall and would be in the Kingdom. Private property was a frequent cause of envy and strife. It tied down the heart.[2]

Humbert set out the different reasons why voluntary poverty was integral to the office of preaching. Preachers have to go everywhere and not everywhere could afford to support the retinue, the horses and servants, of a rich prelate. Preaching bore fruit in confession and spiritual direction, but the poor in

---

1. Acts 4:32–33.
2. *Expositio regulae B. Augustini*, in *Opera de Vita Regulari*, ed. J.F. Berthier, Turin 1956, Vol. 1, pp. 79–80.

the congregation would not have the nerve to approach some-one whose fine clothes set them apart. Above all, the friar had to preach 'the poor Christ and evangelical poverty'. Who could doubt, Humbert asked, 'that such preaching was more effective in the mouth of a poor than a rich man?'[3]

In the second half of the fourteenth century, however, after the Black Death had more than decimated the friars and killed a generation schooled in the traditional observance, the breth-ren led an increasingly privatised and more comfortable life. Instead of pooling all available income, friars began to keep some of the alms they received from preaching in their districts and with these or other private means built and decorated apartments for themselves within the houses. Rather than come together for meals in the refectory, they either had better food brought in or dined out, eating meat normally forbidden by the Constitutions. Individuals bought better clothes and excused themselves from the tiring business of joining the community for the Night Offices in church.

Attempts to stop the rot fell on deaf ears. The 1353 General Chapter at Besançon required the provincials to stop friars from dining out more than two or three times a week. In 1370 the Valencia chapter only tried to get them into the refectory at least once a week.[4] In 1390 Raymund of Capua dispatched one William de Bartelen as prior to Newcastle to assemble there '*fratres devotos de observantia.*'[5] It was not a signal success. Not surprisingly, how the friars lived shaped how they were seen. Their reputation fell. The Dominicans, together with the Franciscans and others who had made similar compromises, were dismissed as hypocrites.

Something of all this can be caught in *The Vision of Piers Plowman.* On the one hand 'Ancres and heremytes, and monkes and frères Peeren to Apostles through hire parfit lyvynge.'[6] On the other hand friars, who should 'lyve by litel and in lowe

3. *ibid,* pp. 51–53.
4. Mortier, *Histoire des Maîtres Généraux de l'Ordre des Frères Prêcheurs,* vol. III, pp. 289–305.
5. Mortier, *op. cit.,* p. 570.
6. Langland, *The Vision of Piers Plowman,* ed. AV.C. Schmidt, London 1978, xv, ll. 415–416.

houses'[7] reliant on alms, have become greedy flatterers, and hypocrisy has laid siege to the Church. In such circumstances the preachers are still teaching that 'alle thynges in hevene oughte to ben in comune,'[8] but that message is not heard as a call to give justice. It is heard as an incitement of the poor to envy and social strife.

It is against this background that St Antoninus of Florence (1389–1459) stands out as an apostolic preacher against avarice in a city of both great wealth and destitution, but whose work also betrays the difficulties faced by Christians in working out where avarice begins and ends. The boy who at the age of fifteen in 1405 committed himself to the austere common life of the Dominican reform movement, or Observance (when the priory at Fiesole was still a building site) became the friar who brought the Observance and its preaching into the civic heart of Florence with the foundation of San Marco in 1436, who founded in 1442 an exemplary confraternity dedicated to almsgiving, the *Buonomini di San Martino*, and who as archbishop from 1446 was often pragmatic and outspoken in seeking the distribution of wealth proper to a Christian society. Yet he was also the teacher who rigidly adhered to a traditional scholastic interpretation of usury which most Catholics later rejected. His life shows the profound virtue of sticking to your principles and the difficulty in finding the right principles at which to stick.

The link between lifestyle and preaching was already evident in the career of the friar who had done much to inspire the young Antonino's vocation, Giovanni Domenici, chosen by Raymund of Capua – Master of the Order – to lead the reform first in Venice and then elsewhere in Italy at Chioggia, Lucca, Fabriano and Cortona. Domenici is the inspiration behind Antoninus's account of preaching in his *Summa Moralis*, where he explains the preacher's mendicancy: 'the Lord established that those who were to preach the Gospel should live by the Gospel … '[9] Domenici taught Antoninus that, in practising asceticism, the friars inherited the mantle of the prophets. He

7. *ibid*, xv, 1.421.
8. *ibid*, xx, 276.
9. *Summa Moralis*, 3a pars, tit. xviii, cap. 1, ii.

wrote in one of his letters how 'religious men and women were to be beacons and a mirror for the fallen world, not only enjoying peace but in that peace supporting all the afflicted and strengthening them in their patience.'[10] Antoninus himself witnesses to Domenici's power as a preacher capable of converting even obdurate sinners. He was repeatedly asked at Florence to preach in Advent and Lent.

The voluntary poverty sought by the Reform stemmed in part from a view of private property as encouraging a selfish anxiety or worry. Common ownership also has its worries in looking after things, as any bursar will tell you, but in the *Summa* Antoninus notes that worrying over common property may be part of our love for others, is not self-seeking.[11] Private property could not be abolished in society at large 'for the world would be turned into a desert.'[12] But within the ordered life of brethren vowed to obedience its abolition was an exemplary model of right relations where each received what each needed.

The Observance did not demand the extreme renunciation of all but the barest essentials for each day associated with the early Franciscans. Nor, on the other hand, would it settle for the common ownership of much land and not a little wealth practised by the monks. The *Summa Moralis* sees the mendicant poverty envisaged by the Dominican constitutions as lying between these two extremes: 'owning something in common, though only a moderate amount, enough to suffice for food and clothing for a certain period of time if not too long.'[13]

This was not seen as a compromise. It was justified in terms of the Order's purpose. It gave adequate freedom from daily anxiety about where the next meal was coming from, a freedom that served contemplation, and provided sufficient resources

10. 'Debbono i religiosi e religiose essere luce e specchio del mondo caduco e non solo avere pace in se ma a pace confortare tutti i tribulati e in pazienza confermare.' *Letters*, p.94.

11. *Summa Moralis*, 3a pars, tit. xvi cap. 1, iii 'sollicitudo, quae adhibetur circa res communes, pertinet ad amorem caritatis, quae non quaerit quae sua sunt, sed communibus intendit.'

12. *Summa Moralis*, 3a, iii, 2, i, citing the Franciscan John de Ripa, trans B Jarrett, *Medieval Socialism*, London, p.50.

13. *ibid*, cap. 1, iii; 'habere aliquid in communi, moderate tamen, quod sufficere possit ad victum et vestitum pro aliquo tempore non prolixo.'

for the preaching mission.[14] Domenici taught that in normal circumstances the mendicants should not accept property which brought in rents or other annual incomes, but he recognised that in exceptional circumstances, by papal decree, a house could receive such a fixed income for the sake of its mission.[15] This is not a history of the Observance,[16] but it is important to see how it formed Antoninus, who was not, for example, sent to the international study houses at Paris, Bologna or Oxford, and how his promotion of the Reform was integral to an apostolic preaching on property.

In this context belongs the foundation of San Marco, authorised by a papal bull of January 1436, on the site of a dilapidated Silvestrine monastery. It was unusual to establish a reformed house in a town that already contained a Dominican priory. The highly visible presence of Eugenius IV and the papal court at Santa Maria Novella, the great unreformed house, perhaps gave added reason for the move – as well as added impetus, since Eugenius was a known supporter of the Observance. Antoninus, by now vicar-general of all the reformed houses in the Roman province, would have taken a leading role in discussing plans for the new house, in gaining the extensive patronage of Cosimo de Medici necessary in order to finance the re-building, and in deciding which friars were to move into the new community (juridically still a part of the Fiesole priory).

In this way Antoninus set up before his fellow citizens an attractive model of the common life largely dependent on their generosity. He accepted Cosimo's patronage which extended far beyond the initial building costs to presenting novices with their first tunic and paying for bread, salt and medicines, as well as the extra food (wine, fish and eggs) on the feasts of the Epiphany, of St Mark, and of Sts Cosmas and Damian. In so doing he accepted money made by a banker whose trading practices were tainted with suspicion of usury (though a mani-

14. *ibid*, cap. 1, ii: 'In religione autem illa, quae est ordinata ad tradendum aliis contemplata per doctrinam et praedicationem, congruit permaxime illa paupertas, quae mobilia pro tempore reservat in communi...'

15. *Summa Moralis*, 3a, xvi, 1, xii.

16. See R. Creytens, O.P., and A. D'Amato, O.P., 'Les actes capitulaires de la Congregation dominicaine de Lombardie', *Archivum Fratrum Praedicatorum* (1961).

fest usurer would be excommunicate) and an oligarch who rigged the city taxes in ways that impoverished his opponents but left intact his own fortune. He allowed him the prestige associated with charitable giving and the display of family symbols in the decoration of the priory.[17] Cosimo retained a cell there with a fresco of the Adoration by Gozzoli. The theme was closely associated with the Medici and San Marco. It also spoke of giving away wealth in love of Christ.

The foundation of San Marco in this way presented Florentines with two separate images of virtue: the perfection of mendicants holding in common the few things necessary for life through partial withdrawal from the world, dependent on the second, the generosity to be found within this world in giving alms. Both images and practices involved the redistribution of wealth as expressing love for fellow members of the Body of Christ.

It is a measure of how important Antoninus thought the project, but also of how difficult it was to maintain, that he later had to seek the papal dispensations necessary for the Observant house to draw on a more secure income: in 1443 Eugenius entrusted to San Marco the care of the local parish with its associated income; and in 1455 Calixtus III permitted the friars to own property which would bring in further revenues. Mendicancy was valued, but unlike the common life, was not a principle on which to stick.

Through his preaching and in other ways Antoninus fostered the right use of wealth in the wider city. Fifteenth century Florence was more prosperous than it had been a century before when the starving had been heard to cry out in the streets 'Mercy! Have compassion on us so that we do not die of hunger in this Easter Week! Console us and help us for the love of Jesus Christ.'[18] Yet it has been calculated that in the 1420s only 100 families, 1% of the total number of urban households, owned a quarter of the city's wealth and six families (the Strozzi, Bardi,

17. M. Hollingsworth sees Cosimo as breaching all rules that restrained the self-aggrandizement of patrons in their commissions – *Patronage in Renaissance Italy*, 1994, p. 55.

18. Domenico Lenzi, *Specchio umano*, 1329, cited J. Henderson, *Piety and Charity in Late Medieval Florence*, Chicago 1994, p.276.

Medici, Alberti, Albizzi and Peruzzi) owned 10% of all taxable wealth.[19] It is true that the practice of almsgiving was a well known part of Christian charity and civic duty. The state itself gave annual funds to a number of hospitals, which not only tended the sick but served as soup kitchens, and in times of emergency the state regularly doled out grain. In 1411 the sum of 64,000 florins was spent on grain.[20] But endemic poverty, 'maximam paupertem', remained.[21] When the population were taxed in 1427, one third had no surplus to tax beyond the bare essentials with which they scratched their living, no reserves to fall back on if their wages dropped below the bread line.[22] Malnutrition weakened resistance to the plague which even in a good year accounted for two in every five deaths.[23] And the three confraternities which had previously given much poor relief – the *Orsanmichele*, the *Misericordia* and the *Bigallo* – now gave much of their moneys to other causes.

Against this background may be set, first, the actions of Antoninus to establish in February 1442 the *Provveditori de' poveri vergognosi*, known popularly as the *Dodici Buonomini di San Martino*. This was a charitable confraternity which would buy bread with money received from its benefactors for distribution to a number of impoverished artisans. It was something new in giving this targeted relief in kind to vulnerable workers and their families over a long period of time.[24] Here, too, Antoninus collaborated with Cosimo de' Medici, for Cosimo was to be by far the chief benefactor.[25] The founding statutes set out the confraternity's aims:

> Considering the present famine and the multitude of poor in the city and surrounding district of Florence, especially of

19. D. Herlihy and C. Klapisch-Zuber, *Tuscans and their Families: a Study of the Florentine Catasta of 1427*, Yale 1985, p.100.

20. J. Henderson, *op. cit.*, p.361.

21. Report by the captains of the Orsanmichele in 1413, cited I. Henderson, *op. cit.*, p. 382.

22. Herlihy an Klapisch-Zuber, *op. cit.*, p. 100.

23. *ibid*, p.279.

24. J Henderson, *op. cit.*, pp. 388–397.

25. D. Kent, 'The Buonomini di San Martino' in *Cosimo il Vecchio ...* ed. F. Ames-Lewis, Oxford 1992, p.50. Cosimo was behind half of all the money given in the first three years.

those who are not accustomed to beg ... 'inspired by God' ...
the twelve citizens inscribed below decided to become procu-
rators for the shamed poor ... by seeking all together or
separately according to their discretion, aid or alms from any
lord, either spiritual or temporal, and from citizens or other
persons, to be distributed from time to time to those shamed
poor.[26]

In seeking to distinguish the recipients from regular beggars
and in making repeated though modest grants it might be said
to have been welfare for work that avoided dependency. It was
a modest achievement, with small costs, reaching perhaps only
some four hundred people in any one year. Yet it was known and
remembered by many as exemplary, spoke to others of their
duties.

When Antoninus became a reluctant Archbishop of Florence in 1446 much more was to be expected of him. He met and
exceeded those expectations in often surprising ways. He took
on a role in which it was traditional to be a protector and
benefactor of the poor, but also to cut a great figure and to
display the spiritual importance of episcopal office in orches-
trated magnificence and it was all too usual for bishops thereby
to neglect the poor and succumb to worldly ambitions. How
Antoninus viewed these matters is evident in the *Summa Moralis*
where he cites and then comments on a passage of Jerome:

Whatever the clergy possess belongs to the poor and their
houses should be the common property of all. They should
feed not dogs and birds, not horses, but men, not lords and
soldiers in order to buy their friendship, not relatives, in
order to enrich them, not performers and concubines, but
their subjects, those in need, and they should feed them
much rather with the spiritual nourishment of the sacraments and preaching.[27]

26. *ibid*, p.52.
27. 'Quidquid habent clerici, pauperum est, et domus eorum omnibus
debent esse communes. Non canes et aves, non equos, sed eos, scilicet homines,
debent pascere, non dominos et milites, ut sibi eos amicos faciant, non histriones
aut concubinas, sed eos, scilicet subditos, indigentes, et multo magis pascere
debent cibo spirituali sacramentorum et praedicationum.' 3a, xix, 11, i.

The new archbishop set a startling example of simplicity from the first days of his solemn entry into Florence and installation. It was customary for the new bishop to arrive on horseback in fine clothes surrounded by his entourage. Antoninus kept his religious habit and refused the horse. The same simplicity would be kept in his travels round the diocese, when, still in his simple habit, he would go either on foot or on a donkey lent by Santa Maria Nuova.[28] An inventory of the furnishings and properties of the episcopal palace undertaken after Antoninus's death reveals a like austerity. His bedroom was sparsely furnished with a bed, a wooden chair, a desk: his study was unadorned. Throughout the house the notary who drew up the inventory found only 'sad and wretched furniture.'[29] There were no works of art.

The archbishop kept where possible the poverty he had practised as a friar. In part this was because he considered himself still bound to those obligations of the *Rule* which did not conflict with his new status.[30] But he was also motivated by a lively sense of not wasting what could be better spent elsewhere. On being presented at table with a pheasant his complaint was that the money could have fed a poor man's entire family for a day.[31] The household itself was minimal: a secretary, a lay brother who was attached to the bishop as valet, a chaplain, a vicar general, chamberlain and seven others.[32] They led a communal and quasi monastic life with silence and readings at mealtimes. According to the secretary, Castiglione, there were no security guards. The doors were always open.

Antoninus gave away whatever he considered himself free to give away – he would not, for example, give away the money

28. Vespasiano da Bisticci, *Vita*, ed. A. Greco, Florence 1970, vol. 1, p. 228.

29. R. Morcay, *Saint Antonin*, Tours, p. 133.

30. In the *Summa* Antoninus distinguishes between the poverty and chastity to which a religious is still bound after the consecration as a bishop and the withdrawal from public life, silences and fasts from which he is dispensed by reason of his public duties (3a, xx, vii). Bisticci's description of the palace furnishings repeats the phrase *come i frati*.

31. *Vita S. Antonii, Summa Moralis*, Verona. 1740, cap. 2. 10. n 4.

32. *ibid*, where the *Vita* describes it as 'modestissimam.' Da Bisticci's *Vita* puts a figure of 500 florins on his household expenses from an income of 1,500 scudi. *op. cit.*, p. 228.

required for the repair and upkeep of the city churches. Anything he thought a luxury, however, rarely stayed long in his hands. The theology was traditional. It was the practice which astounded. One of the richer citizens presented him with a sumptuous satin counterpane, only to find it on a merchant's stall soon afterwards, having been sold and the proceeds given to the poor. The donor bought the counterpane a second time, presented it to the archbishop, only to find it back on the same stall a few days later. He bought it back again, again presented it, again found that it was sold to provide alms for the poor![33] When he had no money of his own to help the starving he successfully petitioned the pope for further funds.[34] When he had no money at all to dispense he was known to give away articles of clothing or let people grow food on his land. The archbishop, typical in this respect of many fifteenth century Florentines, showed particular generosity not only to individuals but to charitable institutions, such as the big hospital of Santa Maria Nuova immediately outside the old city walls, which could house some two to three hundred patients at any one time and was at the centre of the commune's response to poor relief and aid for the victims of plague.[35]

Plague was a recurrent bane. In 1448–9 it struck with renewed ferocity. Many who could afford to do so fled. Antoninus remained. According to one of those who testified during the canonisation process Antoninus would take a donkey laden with food and medicines and go into the poorest hovels and the prisons to comfort the sick. His example was followed by the friars at San Marco, Fiesole and Santa Maria Novella, with the result that many died. The archbishop was given 3000 florins by the city authorities to give out on their behalf.[36] In a move thought to be inspired by Antoninus, the Signoria 'appointed additional priests to hear confessions and administer the sacraments, four physicians and four barber-surgeons, forty women and twenty men to attend the sick, particularly the indigent, and

33. Morcay. *op. cit.*, p. 176.

34. Vespasiano da Bisticci, *op. cit.*, p. 230.

35. K. Park, 'Healing the Poor' in J. Barry and C. Jones, *Medicine and Charity before the Welfare State*, London 1991, p. 32.

36. Morcay, *op. cit.*, p 178.

they considered the necessity of a special hospital for plague patients.'[37] Not for the first time, Antoninus' personal example gave an authority which led to concerted action and institutional reform.[38]

In what has so far been described Antoninus co-operated with the tight-knit oligarchy comprised of the city's leading merchant bankers. He re-directed something of their wealth and relied on their support. This did not prevent the archbishop from challenging the oligarchy where he saw fit, or as prudence determined, in particular when they failed to give justice to the Church, to the commune, or to the poor.

Antoninus did not object to properly authorised taxation of the Church, which was normally exempt. He even oversaw the necessary collection at his own suggestion to ensure its fair administration, but he opposed any laws or taxes 'against the liberty ... of ecclesiastical persons and charitable institutions' and threatened the authorities with excommunication after a proposal in 1451 to levy a gabelle of twenty five percent on sales of property passing from taxpayers to non-taxpayers, a move which he denounced as 'contrary to your salvation and the salvation of those who enacted it, those who support and enforce it, and those who do not work for its repeal.'[39] Yet he acquiesced in another levy that same year which had received papal approval.

It was the same concern for legality or procedural justice that brought him into further public conflict with the governing elite a year before his death. For many years Cosimo de' Medici and his fellow oligarchs had ensured that their political opponents were kept out of office by suppressing the traditional practice of drawing lots and introducing ten *accoppiatori*, popularly known as the Ten Tyrants, whose task was to choose the new officials or priors every two months from among the names

37. A. Carmichael, *Plague and the Poor in Renaissance Florence*, CUP, 1986, pp. 101–102.

38. Gilbert Márkus has also linked Antoninus with the establishment of the *montes pietatis* (*The Radical Tradition*, p. 80), but most historians date their foundation to the work of the Observant Franciscans at Perugia in 1462. It was they who set up a *monte pietatis* in Florence after Antoninus' death in 1488.

39. P. Gavitt, *Charity and Children in Renaissance Florence*, Ann Arbor 1990, pp. 96-97.

in the *burse*. In 1455, however, the secret ballots had been restored. When the oligarchs attempted to reverse the decision in July 1458 Antoninus vigorously opposed them. He fixed an uncompromising declaration to the cathedral doors and a number of other churches setting out the impropriety of the changes. Failure to return to the legal method which the officials had sworn to uphold would be met with excommunication. It is said that the archbishop was threatened with the loss of his see. He stood firm. The oligarchy, led by Luca Pitti, the *gonfaloniere*, summoned a 'parliament' or popular assembly under the eyes of its soldiers to approve the measures. Antoninus did not win, but in the series of banishments which followed (of the Barbadori, Brancacci, Bardi, Peruzzi, and Strozzi) Antoninus was left untouched and named among the orators sent to congratulate the new pope Pius II. The fifteenth century life by Vespasiano da Bisticci rightly said of Antoninus that he was able to '*stare fermo nella giustitia et da quella non si muovere.*'[40]

How did Antoninus view the business practices which underlay the prosperity of the governing elite? Florence's wealth came from a combination of industry – in particular the weaving and dyeing of cloth – commerce and banking. These were international operations and the first was unworkable without the drafts and bills of exchange provided by the third. All three had their risks. Wealthy bankers had gone bust in the mid-fourteenth century when the King of England defaulted on his loans. Yet the merchant bankers also made huge profits from such money-lending at high rates of interest.

It was here that Antoninus was a vocal, if largely unoriginal, preacher against the sin of usury. Antoninus' teaching against usury in the pages of the *Summa Moralis* is marked, on the one hand, by sticking to the principle that all secure lending at interest for the sake of coming out richer is usurious and avaricious (rather than defining usury as lending at excessive rates which impoverish the borrower) and, on the other, by the detailed analysis of financial instruments and practices, as well as the discussion of arguments by other moralists. Like Aquinas, Antoninus allowed lending at interest in limited circumstances

40. Da Bisticci, *op. cit.*, p.235.

as damages for late repayment. Following Peter of Ancarano, he also allowed interest to be paid on the grounds of *lucrum cessans* where the loan deprived the merchant or investor of capital previously earmarked for legitimate business (though this exception did not apply to loans made in the express hope of making money from them, only charitable loans to the indigent).[41] He accepted the Florentine practice of paying interest on compulsory shares in the public debt or *monte*, though not the speculative trade in those shares. He did not condemn the bankers for dealing in bills of exchange and charging a rate of commission for various transactions, but like other moral theologians condemned any attempt to disguise profit-making loans as foreign currency exchanges (*cambia sicca*).[42] He also ruled out as usurious the so-called 'gifts' of interest made by bankers to their depositors.

For several hundred years the Church would continue to rehearse the same principle, though finding its teaching less and less acceptable or workable. One question must be whether Antoninus did not in this respect do us a disservice, did not put the weight of his authority behind a traditional but wrong view of money and money-lending which meant that, when one view of usury was gradually abandoned, there was little teaching on ethics in finance to put in its place.

Antoninus' teaching on industry and commerce, however, if similarly detailed, was grounded in a wider understanding of justice. He argued that citizens could invest money in a business providing that the risks as well as profits were shared.[43] Importers and exporters could sell at a higher price than they bought to cover costs and make a living, but no one was to hold on to goods in order to sell them later at an unfair price.

Two further practices came in for his particular condemnation. The first was the truck system in the textile industry, where if business was bad wages were paid in kind when the contract called for cash, leaving workers with goods they could not sell at a decent price. The second was the debasement of the silver

41. De Roover, *San Bernardino of Siena and Sant' Antonino of Florence*, Boston 1967, p. 31.
42. *Summa Moralis*, 3a, tit. 8, col. 299a.
43. *ibid*, 3a, 8, col. 312a,

coinage in which wages were paid, without debasing the gold florins which made up the merchants' wealth or altering the nominal wages.[44]

The impact of Antoninus' teaching is impossible to assess. His *Summa*, written between 1440 and 1454, proved highly popular. Parts circulated in manuscript before its final completion. By the end of the century it had run through nine editions and many parts had once again been published separately.[45] His diocesan secretary Castiglione commented:

> He not only wrote about universal things, but he also adapted doctrine, coming down to the particulars, to our very way of living, to the basic practice of the specifics of human life.[46]

In this and in synthesising other writers' works to make their teaching more accessible to busy clerics you could say that Antoninus showed the same attitude to intellectual property that he did to other goods. What mattered was getting the goods to where they were needed. If one quotation from his writings were to sum up his unchanging theory and practice it would be the assertion that 'only our sins properly belong to us: all goods must be the common property of all, even the spiritual goods'.[47]

44. De Roover, *op. cit.*, pp. 26-27.
45. P. F. Howard, *Beyond the Written Word: Preaching and Theology in the Florence of Archbishop Antoninus 1427–1459*, Rome, 1995, p. 25.
46. *ibid*, p. 52, n. 40.
47. R. Morcay, *op. cit.*, p. 184.

5

Francisco Vitoria

The Rights of Enemies and Strangers

ROGER RUSTON

Under the heading 'Vitoria, Founder of International Law' *Blackfriars* of October 1946 devoted a whole issue to the Spanish Dominican who had died four hundred years earlier. The timing could not have been more appropriate: what one might call the 'legal audit' of the Second World War was in full swing. Uppermost in the minds of the contributors were the Nuremberg Trials (verdicts delivered that month). Article 6 of the Tribunal Charter defined crimes against 'humanity' (the contemporary, secularized version of natural law) in terms that would have been recognizable to Vitoria, and indeed – via four hundred years of development – owed much to his original concept of the law of nations.[1] Then there were the atomic bombs used the previous year. The end of the world war had left a legacy of guilt about the practice of destroying whole cities by strategic bombing, culminating at Hiroshima and Nagasaki. This put the principle of non-combatant immunity – fully integrated with just war theory for the first time by Vitoria – at the centre of the arguments for and against the new weapons. Further, the revival of international law in the first half of the twentieth

---

1. 'Crimes against Humanity: namely murder, extermination, enslavement, deportation, and other inhumane acts committed against any civilian population, before or during the war, or persecutions on political, racial or religious grounds in execution of or in connection with any crime within the jurisdiction of the Tribunal, whether or not in violation of the domestic law of the country where perpetrated. Leaders, organizers, instigators, and accomplices participating in the formulation or execution of a common plan or conspiracy to commit any of the foregoing crimes are responsible for all acts performed by any persons in execution of such plan.' See Adam Roberts and Richard Guelff, *Documents on the Laws of War* (Oxford: Oxford University Press, 1982), p. 155.

The point is that in the natural law tradition, to which both Vitoria and the Nuremberg Tribunal belong (despite the 400 years and a change of vocabulary), it is individuals – not only States – whose rights are to be protected in law, and individuals who must be held responsible when these are violated.

century had issued the previous October in the United Nations Charter and would lead in 1948 to the signing of the Declaration of Human Rights and the Genocide Convention; and in 1949 there was to be the first of the Geneva Conventions on the limitation of warfare.

In the studies of the origins of international law that had preceded all this postwar legislative activity – largely the work of secular American and Jewish scholars – it was Vitoria the Spanish Catholic theologian who had been identified as the 'founding father', the one who had first established basic principles for the coexistence of independent sovereign states in the global community of the modern world.[2] Perhaps rather too much was claimed by way of Vitoria's modernity – he was after all a scholastic, lecturing on medieval texts; he had some medieval attitudes, notably towards Saracens and heretics, and Christendom was still a reality for him. But his timely birth and the momentous events taking place during the period of his mature work – together with his special genius for bringing universal principles into relation with the big political events of the day in a clear and intelligible manner, and his undoubted respect for the human dignity of non-Europeans – made all the difference to his future relevance.

One article every fifty years on a Dominican theologian of such contemporary importance is not a lot, and it suggests the need for a little biographical detail.[3]

* * *

Francisco de Vitoria was born in 1483, probably in Burgos to a family from the Basque town of Gasteiz/Vitoria. He was nine years old when Columbus, back from his first voyage, was

2. International law has several such 'founding fathers' who took it new directions, most notably the Spanish Jesuit, Francisco Suarez (1548–1617), and the Dutch Calvinist, Hugo Grotius (1583–1645), both of whom acknowledged a debt to Vitoria.

3. A lot more attention has been paid to Vitoria and other great figures of the Salamanca school in other European countries, Spain in particular, and of course in Latin America, with critical editions of his works, institutes of human rights named after him, international congresses on his thought, etc. It is a pity that, apart from the excellent translations of Pagden and Lawrence (see below), not much of this activity is finding its way into English.

received by Ferdinand and Isabella in Burgos, then the Spanish capital. The revolution in European consciousness that began with that discovery was the background of Vitoria's early years and it is clear that he followed reports of that astonishing conflict with great attention. At the same time the Protestant Reformation was tearing Christendom into irreconcilable fragments and a new era of 'holy wars' was about to begin.

In Spain it was also a time when religious orders – including the Dominicans – were experiencing regeneration through a return to their sources. The young Francisco soon followed his elder brother Diego into the priory of Burgos and was professed in 1506. The following year he was sent to Paris where he became a master and teacher of theology, returning to Spain in 1523 to teach at Valladolid. There he lectured on grace, sin, human society and the two areas of law, ecclesiastical and civil.

Then in 1526, when he was forty-three, by popular choice of the students of the University of Salamanca he was elected to the leading theological post in Spain – that of Prima Professor. The title referred not to his rank but to the time of his lecture: 6 a.m., immediately after the Office of Prime, and presumably before breakfast (and about a hundred years before coffee). This was the *lectio* or 'reading' – though unlike some other teachers, Vitoria did not just read the text.

Moreover, he broke with the age-old custom of lecturing on the *Sentences* of Peter Lombard, and took the *Summa Theologiae* of Aquinas as the standard text and thus the foundation of theological teaching – a change already initiated in Paris by his teacher, Peter Crockaert. It represented a resourcing of scholasticism after generations of baroque decline and subsequent retreat in the face of the new humanism. It was to become the basis of the so-called 'Renaissance Scholasticism' of sixteenth-century Salamanca, led first by Vitoria and then by the Jesuit, Francisco Suarez. But they were less concerned with looking back to the past than with the problems of their own epoch, notably the laws of war, colonialism, slavery, and resistance to unjust governments.

Eye-witnesses tell us that Vitoria's lectures were meticulously prepared – giving him little time to do anything else in his career – delivered with great clarity and wit, and always relevant to contemporary events. He usually answered questions, even during the lecture, which, given that he could be speaking to up to nine hundred students, tells us something about the attention he commanded. None of the lectures survive except in the form of students' notes. He never gave the same lecture twice, rewriting his course for every one of his twenty-six years at Salamanca, and would tell his students it was no use their using last year's notes since he was constantly rethinking his theology.

More important for posterity is the special annual lecture, called *relectio*, or rereading, in which Vitoria would formally discuss some important topic of the day in the light of the theological principles they had been studying through the year. Since the *relectio* was governed by a time limit of two hours, the material was presented with sharp focus on the main point. The university published these and we have a fair number of them. There is an immense amount of learning behind them, worn very lightly. The most important and influential for European thought are undoubtedly the two he wrote on the treatment of the inhabitants of the New World, *De Indis Noviter Inventis* (On the Indians Lately Discovered) and *De Jure Belli* (On the Law of War made by the Spaniards on the Barbarians). It is their brevity and clarity which makes these texts so accessible – something that has done a lot for their continued influence.

A modern reader finds it difficult to decide whether Vitoria is a theologian, a political moralist or a lawyer. But none of these over-defined categories can contain his writings.[4] He was employed as a theologian, choosing as his text the *Summa* of Aquinas, behind which, of course, lay the Scriptures. But the theology he inherited from this source covered everything governed by divine or natural law. It was jurisprudence in the most comprehensive sense. He deliberately narrowed the scope of his public utterances, however, and was so much the more

4. Vitoria himself was well aware of the difficulties: 'The office and calling of a theologian is so wide, that no argument or controversy on any subject can be considered foreign to his profession ... perhaps this is the reason why there are now, to put it no more strongly, so few really good and solid theologians.' (*On the Civil Power*, Prologue, in Anthony Pagden and Jeremy Lawrance, *Francisco Vitoria Political Writings* (Cambridge: Cambridge University Press, 1991), p. 3.)

effective for that.[5] He specialized in what we would call 'political
theology'. The topics he chose to engage with were the most
contested ones of his day: the powers of the pope; the nature of
civil power; the wars between Christian powers (France and
Spain); the marriage and divorce of monarchs (Henry VIII and
Catherine of Aragon, daughter of Ferdinand and Isabella); the
rights of newly discovered peoples to possess their land and
govern themselves; the right and wrong methods of spreading
the Christian faith to pagans; how to deal with people whose
religion requires human sacrifice; whether they can be forcibly
baptized. Vitoria never sidesteps conclusions which might be
politically unwelcome to the powers – notably the King of Spain
and the Papacy. At a time when political theology really mattered,
as never before, or perhaps since, Vitoria's was the voice which
carried most weight, but it was an independent voice, never that
of a 'court theologian'.

For the first time ever in theology, Vitoria addressed the
problem of Christian states confronting organized, peaceful
non-Christian communities with their own political authority,
with their own laws. Previously there had been barbarian raiders
– and Saracens. But unlike these 'enemies of Christendom', the
newly discovered peoples were assumed not to be hostile to
Christianity. They may have been 'barbarians', but it was the
Christians who were the raiders.

His two treatises amount to a code of ethics for first contact:
what can be assumed on behalf of the humanity – and, to use a
modern term, the human rights – of these non-Christians when
confronted by the claims of their European 'discoverers'. The
basic concept was the Roman Law category of *jus gentium*, which
until then had been understood to be the 'common law' of the
Roman/Christian world, governing contact between different
jurisdictions and subject nations, but under the same notional
authority. The discovery of quite new areas of the globe which
owed nothing to Roman order or to Christianity but which
consisted rather of independent, autonomous peoples, each

5. 'In this broad and mighty field of universal theology, whose acres are
infinite, I have chosen for myself a single little corner ... My subject is the
commonwealth (*res publica*)' (*Ibid.*).

with their own governments, required a rethinking of this concept. By a deployment of the Thomist category of natural law, Vitoria was able to think through to something like a *jus inter gentes*, an order of law binding peoples together in virtue of their common human need for government, freedom of ownership, and pursuit of their lives in communities unhindered by attacks from outside. Such needs were there by 'nature', irrespective of any agreement or contract between rulers, or religious allegiance:

> The law (*jus*) of nations does not have the force merely of pacts or agreements between men, but has the validity of a positive enactment (*lex*). The whole world, which is in a sense a commonwealth (*res publica*), has the power to enact laws which are just and convenient to all men; and these make up the law of nations. From this it follows that those who break the law of nations, whether in peace or in war, are committing mortal crimes ... No kingdom may choose to ignore this law of nations, because it has the sanction of the whole world.[6]

In an era which has seen the appearance of a retired Latin American dictator in the dock of a British court on charges of murder and torture in his own country, this passage has a particular resonance. In the *relectio On Civil Power* just quoted, Vitoria may have been speaking primarily of Christian nations, but the ground is well prepared for a real intellectual revolution: the globalization of the common good realized in the two *relectiones* on the war against the Indians.

As a young Dominican Vitoria may have read the reports of Las Casas on the treatment of the Indians of the new World, and his stance in maturity was essentially the same as that of Las Casas, even though he never went to the Indies to find out for himself. On hearing of the destruction of the Inca Atahuallpa by Pizarro and his men in July 1533, he wrote to his Dominican superiors in the following year that 'After a lifetime of studies and long experience, no business shocks me or embarrasses me more than the corrupt profits and affairs of the Indies. Their very mention makes my blood run cold.' The returning conquis-

6. *On Civil Power* 3.4, Pagden and Lawrance, *op. cit.*, p. 40.

tadors were attempting to legalize their robberies by 'compounding' – paying the royal treasury a lump sum – and some of them were doing the rounds, trying to elicit the agreement of the theologians that this was a legitimate practice. Vitoria would have nothing to do with them: 'Sooner my tongue and hand wither than say or write a thing so inhuman, so alien to all Christian feeling! On their heads be it, and let them leave us in peace. There will be no lack of men, even within the Dominican order, to salve their consciences, and even to praise their deeds and butchery and pillage.' As for the war itself: ' ... the justice of this war passes my understanding'; 'there was no other cause for this war than sheer robbery ... Even if the emperor has just titles to conquer them, the Indians do not and cannot know this. They are most certainly innocents in this war.'[7]

Although he stood at the threshold of European colonialism and had no idea what was to come in the centuries ahead, in these two brief treatises the entire course of that colonialism – not just of Spaniards, but of Portuguese, French, British for the following four centuries – has the moral ground pulled from under it once for all. European assumptions of right to rule (though not of cultural or religious superiority) were questioned at their root. Thus he openly proclaimed the limits of the powers of the Pope and the European monarchs over other, non-Christian peoples. This involved confronting the claim often made by the conquistadors and kings that the Pope had the power to grant them the lands of the heathen. Vitoria denied this at length in two relectios.[8] No surprise then that in 1539 Charles I of Spain and V of the Holy Roman Empire tried to get him silenced by his religious superiors. Unfortunately for the Emperor, the prior in Salamanca was Dominic de Soto, the Vespera Professor, who agreed with everything Vitoria said, and did nothing. So Charles had to put up with it, and later on even consulted Vitoria on the revision of the Laws of the Indies (1542), which became the most elaborate and humane (even if unenforceable) body of European colonial law. But Vitoria's

7. Letter to Miguel de Arcos, O.P., Salamanca, 8 Nov. 1534, in Pagden and Lawrance, *op. cit.*, pp. 331–2.
8. I and II *On the Power of the Church* (1532 and 1533), texts in Pagden and Lawrance, *op. cit.*

writings – stating, as they did the limits of papal authority – deeply offended Pope Sixtus V and just escaped being put on the index of forbidden books by the Pope's death.

ON THE AMERICAN INDIANS

The basic issue behind this *relectio* and the one on just war which followed it is the circumstances of the conversion of the inhabitants of the Indies. From the outset, Isabella had declared the sole justification of the Spanish presence there to be that of bringing the Gospel to the heathen. So, by starting his investigation with the great commission at the close of Matthew's Gospel, Vitoria establishes the evangelical framework for everything that follows. The question is: What right have the Spaniards to conquer the Indians, take their land and goods, depose their rulers, and make subjects of them? Is it a necessary consequence of making Christians of them, or something quite alien to this?

Vitoria takes some time establishing the theologian's (and therefore the Church's) right to decide a matter which might seem to be the business of secular rulers and lawyers only. Behind the text one can detect some hostility between the theologians and the secular jurists, acting for people with other objectives, for whom converting the Indians was a means to an end rather than the end itself. He asserts the primacy of a *theological* framework for the judgement of the legality of the wars against the Indians:

> Since these barbarians we speak of are not subjects [of the Spanish Crown] by human law, as I shall show in a moment, their affairs cannot be judged by human statutes, but only by divine ones, in which jurists are not sufficiently versed to form an opinion of their own.

It is a deliberate challenge. Then, with some irony, he establishes that there is sufficient doubt about the legality of what has happened for a fresh judgement:

> At first sight, it is true, we may readily suppose that, since the affair is in the hands of men both learned and good, everything

has been conducted with rectitude and justice. But when we hear subsequently of bloody massacres and of innocent individuals pillaged of their possessions and dominions, there are grounds for doubting the justice of what has been done ... [9]

If all this appropriation and killing is going on in the name of the Christian King, perhaps it is because – as Vitoria's opponents asserted – the Indians, being already natural slaves in the Aristotelian sense, are not true legal owners of their goods and their land, and the Spaniards are simply exercising their rights over them. There was no shortage of theologians to provide the desired arguments on behalf of the conquest – some of them Dominicans. These are some of the arguments designed to show that relieving the Indians of their goods was perfectly right and proper:

1. They are all in mortal sin, so they can have no dominion over anything.
2. They are unbelievers and heretics and so have forfeited any title they might have in law.
3. They are irrational creatures, like children, and no one without the use of reason can have a capacity for ownership.
4. They are all mad. (One senses the incomprehension of the Spanish soldier confronted by the strange and terrified Incas.)

These could all be legal grounds for arguing against ownership in domestic law ,and Vitoria has no great trouble in disposing of them in a few pages of perfectly clear and irrefutable arguments. Then he says:

The conclusions of all that has been said is that the barbarians undoubtedly possessed as true dominion, both public and private, as any Christians. That is to say, they could not be robbed of their property, either as private citizens or as princes, on the grounds that they were not true masters. It would be harsh to deny to them, who have never done us any wrong, the rights we concede to Saracens and Jews, who have

9. *On the American Indians*, Introduction, Pagden and Lawrance, *op. cit.*, pp. 237–8.

been continual enemies of the Christian religion. Yet we do not deny the right of ownership of the latter, unless it be in the case of Christian lands which they have conquered.

It will be repeatedly argued by Vitoria throughout both treatises that what Christians are not permitted to do to Jews and Muslims (i.e., forcibly baptize them, arbitrarily confiscate their property, war against them without just cause) they are not permitted to do to 'barbarians' either – and that what a Christian ruler is not permitted to do to his own subjects he is not permitted to do to foreigners. In any case, writes Vitoria in a bit of creative exegesis, when Aristotle made his fateful remark about natural slaves, he did not mean that anyone had the right to 'seize the goods and lands, and enslave and sell the person, of those who are by nature less intelligent' – even if that were the case.[10] It was intended as an assertion of the best political outcome, not of the rights of the strong over the weak.

Very well, an opponent would reply, perhaps the Indians are true owners of their goods and land, but the Spaniards have legally come into possession of them. These are the arguments put forward to prove this:

1. The Holy Roman Emperor Charles V is lord of the whole world and whom therefore of these barbarians too. He owns everything and can give to whom he chooses. Claims had been made in the past that a Christian emperor obtains his power as a temporal 'vicar of Christ', being endowed with the Lord's plenitude of power over creation spoken of in the New Testament epistles.

2. The Pope has full jurisdiction in temporal matters and consequently he can make the Kings of Spain sovereign over the Indians, and so he has. Several weighty medieval authorities had made such a claim about the Pope's authority before the discovery of the Americas, including the great Dominican bishop of Florence, St Antoninus.

3. The lands belong to the Spaniards by right of discovery. The law of nations allows that deserted lands become the property of the first occupant.

10. *Ibid.*, 1.6, p. 251.

4. Since the natives refuse to accept Christianity, when it was
   clearly set before them and they were warned that it is a
   matter of their eternal salvation, it is right to make war
   against them because they are sinners and the Christian
   King exercises the authority from God that Paul speaks of
   in Romans.

Again, Vitoria demolishes these arguments one by one. The
Emperor is not the lord of the whole earth. The power of Christ
is not the summit of a feudal pyramid, but, in accordance with
John 18:37, is 'not of this world'. And there is no mention in
Scripture of any handing over of such power. In any case,
political power is not a natural given, but a construction of law
and there is no such law in existence, nor could there be. Even
granted that the Emperor were the lord of the world, still that
would not entitle him to seize the provinces of the Indians and
erect new lords there and put down the former ones or take
taxes. He still does not have the right to convert provinces to his
own use or give land away at his own pleasure. He too is subject
to the laws. This, then, shows that the Spaniards cannot justify
on this ground their seizure of the provinces in question.

As for the Pope, he 'has no temporal power over the Indians
or over other unbelievers'. It was the Lord himself who said,
'you know that the princes of the Gentiles exercise lordship
over them ... But it shall not be so among you.' Christ had no
temporal power, and so neither can his representative on earth.
'It is utterly absurd' ... 'utterly sophistical . . .' 'What has been
said demonstrates that at the time of the Spaniards' first voyages
to America they took with them no right to occupy the lands of
the indigenous population'.

As for right of discovery, this is the weakest of all – the Indians
were already in possession. It is nonsense to talk about
uninhabited lands. It provides no support for possession of
these lands, 'any more than it would if they had discovered us':
a neat way of forcing the opposition to look at the implications
of their own arguments. And the fourth claim – that the Indians
wilfully refused to accept the salvation offered to them in Christ
– has many arguments against it. The most powerful appears to
have some sarcasm and anger behind it:

It is not sufficiently clear to me that the Christian faith has up to now been announced and set before the barbarians in such a way as to oblige them to believe it under pain of fresh sin. By this I mean that they are not bound to believe unless the faith has been set before them with persuasive probability. But I have not heard of any miracles or signs, nor of any exemplary saintliness of life sufficient to convert them. On the contrary, I hear only of provocations, savage crimes, and multitudes of unholy acts. From this, it does not appear that the Christian religion has been preached to them in a sufficiently pious way to oblige their acquiescence; even though it is clear that a number of friars and other churchmen have striven industriously by their preaching, and this would have been enough, had they not been thwarted by those with different things on their mind.[11]

And this is the crux of the matter: is the Spanish presence in the New World to be governed by the truth of the gospel, or is it to be managed solely for the purposes of illicit plunder? Who decides what is right? Is it to be the adventurer with his so-called right of conquest or is it to be the theologian, with his right deriving from natural law? Even though the Christian faith may have been announced to the Indians with adequate demonstration and they have refused to receive it, yet this is not a reason which justifies making war on them and depriving them of their property. St Thomas had shown that you cannot compel unbelievers, such as the Jews, to receive the faith. Belief is an assent of the will and the will cannot act properly out of fear – conversion would be a sacrilege unless done freely. And this is the point where Vitoria comes up with one of his most memorable statements: 'War is no argument for the truth of the Christian faith.' This undermined all notions of holy war, then undergoing a revival.

It remains to be considered what rights the Spaniards do have in the New World. Contact has been made and hostilities commenced, after all. It is here, in his answer to this third question, that one sees what a different kind of presence the

11. *Ibid.*, 2.4, p. 271.

Europeans might have made.

There are, first of all, purely natural rights of travel and trade, which anyone should enjoy in a foreign country. The Spaniards have a right not to be molested while doing this, so long as they do no harm to the natives and observe the laws of the land. The laws of hospitality demand this. The Indians can no more keep off the Spaniards from trade than Christians can keep off other Christians. 'Nature has established a bond of relationship between all human beings . . .' (There is a global community, as the far-sighted such as Vitoria were beginning to perceive. The extension of natural law to cover the interactions within this community would be the basis for the subsequent development of international law.) Consequently, if the Indians, misunderstanding the Europeans' purposes (did they?) and being so fearful of the Spaniards, attack them, then the Spaniards have a right to defend themselves

> within the bounds of blameless self-defence; but once victory has been won and safety secured, they may not exercise the other rights of war against the barbarians such as putting them to death or looting and occupying their communities, since in this case what we may suppose were understandable fears made them innocent. So the Spaniards must take care of their own safety, but do so with as little harm to the barbarians as possible since this is a merely defensive war.[12]

Secondly, Christians have a right to preach and announce the Gospel in the lands of the barbarians. Moreover, if the barbarians permit the Spaniards to preach the Gospel freely and without hindrance, then 'whether or not they accept the faith, it will not be lawful to attempt to impose anything on them by war, or otherwise conquer their land'. The basic principle is that 'no war can be just when not preceded by some wrong, as St Thomas says (*Summa Theologiae* II-IIae, q. 40 a. 1)'.

However, such a wrong would be done in the event of the Indians' obstructing the preaching of the Gospel and attacking the preachers and their converts. This looks fair enough, but it is well to remember that Vitoria – in common with everyone of

12. *Ibid.*, 3.1, p. 282.

his time – assumed the cultural superiority of Christian society over any pagan society it was likely to encounter, though he may not have been quite clear about the critical superiority of the Europeans' weaponry. With the hindsight of 400 years of colonialism, one may see just how attacks on missionaries by people wielding spears and arrows might provide the pretext for their pacification and even Christianization at gun-point.

ON THE LAW OF WAR

The conclusion of the first relectio then, is that if the Spanish forces are to occupy the lands of the Indians, this can only be justified, if at all, by the laws of war. Hence the second *relectio, De Jure Belli*, delivered a few months later, in June 1539, and designed to be read along with the first. Often nowadays read on its own, without reference to its context, the treatise on just war is in no way an abstract thesis, but a continuation of the argument about the legality of the conquest ('the case of the Indians, which is now before us').

However, it is Vitoria's foundation of just war on natural law, applying to all human beings, Christian or otherwise, which makes it more than a political tract for the times. What he has to say about the causes of just war (*jus ad bellum*) and about the just conduct of war (*jus in bello*) made this *relectio* highly influential among the jurists of the following century (most notably Grotius) and has continued to make it a reference point for contemporary discussions of just war.[13]

After a traditional preamble establishing the legitimacy of Christians going to war at all, and the need for legitimate authority, it proceeds to a denial of certain commonly held grounds for just war, the first of which is perhaps the most important, both for him and for us:

My first proposition is: Difference of religion cannot be the cause of just war. This proposition was amply proved in the previous *relectio*, where I refuted the fourth title offered to jus-

13. See, for example, James Turner Johnson, *Ideology, Reason and the Limitation of War*, and *Just War Tradition and the Restraint of War* (Princeton, NJ: Princeton University Press, 1975 and 1981).

tify the enslavement of the barbarians, namely, 'that they refuse to receive the Christian faith'. This is the opinion of St Thomas (*Summa Theologiae*, II-IIae, q. 66, a. 8, ad 2.) and of all the other doctors: I know of no one who thinks the contrary.

It requires considerable ingenuity to get the teaching from the cited passage of St Thomas, which allows Christian princes to despoil unbelievers of their goods when they have done something 'illegal'. Vitoria is relying on a creative interpretation of this by the great Dominican Thomist commentator, Cajetan (see *De Indis* 2.2). However, what St Thomas says about the illegitimacy of forcing baptism on Jews and anyone who has never accepted Christianity may be sufficient. What seems clear is that Vitoria was the first theologian – and in flat contradiction of many others of his period – to state unambiguously that 'holy' war is not just war.

Illustrating the contradiction, the American just-war theorist, James Turner Johnson[14] quotes some of the holy-war enthusiasts, among them Cardinal Allen, the enemy of Queen Elizabeth I: 'There is no war so just and honourable ... as that which is waged for religion, we say for the true ancient, Catholic, Roman religion.' It was a common opinion of the time, among both Catholics and Protestants, that the best possible warrant for going to war was a command of God, which could only come through an interpretation of certain Old Testament passages in one's favour. Against such a shallow and self-serving theology, Vitoria understood that a firm grasp of law and justice was itself, at root, deeply theological. Real theology is done, not by a proof (force of arms) of one's privileged position in the eyes of the Creator over against everyone else, but by a regard for the unity of the human race under the one divine law governing the treatment of anyone, whether belonging to one's own religion or not. It is for this reason that Vitoria, when doing his theology, often appears to us to be doing something else – morals, jurisprudence or whatever. It was perhaps only his elevated and totally confident understanding of what theology is that enabled

14. *Just War Tradition*, p. 96.

him to do this with authority and without a hint of the embarrass-ment that would afflict us, after centuries of demoting theology to the category of 'special interest'. If theology had taken the direction indicated by him and his successors at Salamanca, instead of suffering self-destruction at the hands of the holy-warmongers during the era of European wars of religion, it might now be more able to do its rightful job.

Vitoria's conclusion is that 'there is a single and only just cause for commencing a war, namely, a wrong received'. It is a matter of right, rather than righteousness. A ruler has no more authority over foreigners than he does over his own subjects. They too have share in human dignity and if they have done no wrong he is forbidden to attack them.[15] However, Vitoria is quick to add that 'Not every or any injury gives sufficient grounds for waging war'.

There are many, strict precautions to be taken against assuming that any given war will have a just cause. Among them,

> if a subject is convinced of the injustice of a war, he ought not to serve in it, even on the command of his prince. This is clear, for no one can authorize the killing of an innocent person. But in the case before us the enemy are innocent.. Therefore they may not be killed.

As for councillors of state:

> If such men can by examining the cause of hostility with their advice and authority advert a war which is perhaps unjust, then they are obliged to do so … if a man can prevent some-thing which he ought to prevent, and fails to do so, the blame rests with him.

Affinity with the Nuremberg principles is clear.

Vitoria is also noted for being the first to recognize that in some sense it may be possible to fight justly on both sides. Although it cannot in fact be true that the same war is just on both sides, ignorance of the facts or of the law can result in ordinary soldiers on both sides being justified in fighting. This tends to strengthen the affinity between the combatants and

15. *On the Law of War* 1.3.4, Pagden and Lawrance, *op. cit.*, p. 303.

focus the moral question for the soldier not so much on the justice of the war as such, as on the methods by which it is being fought – the *jus in bello*. They are up against men who may also be fighting in good faith. They may not treat them as if they were not fellow human beings.

Vitoria is most remembered, however, for his principled yet realistic approach to non-combatant immunity, which he systematized from medieval antecedents such as the code of chivalry and the writings of the canonists. In spite of the biblical record of Joshua's campaigns against the Canaanites [16] – much invoked by the contemporary enthusiasts for holy war – Vitoria flatly states that 'it is never lawful in itself intentionally to kill innocent persons'.[16] His examples of who may not be killed – women and children of the Saracens (even), *bona fide* travellers caught up in the fighting, clergy and monks (so long as they are not caught fighting), and 'harmless agricultural folk' – make it appear that he is working with a notion of innocence familiar to us. But this is not entirely so. Although there is a strong moral element in it – to be fighting an unjust war is, after all, morally wrong and anything but innocent – it is not entirely a moral category in our sense. The functional element is also strong, and would become stronger as just war theory developed. It is the function of the soldier that is crucial to his status rather than his moral position. He may be morally quite innocent, but nevertheless engaged in some violent harm to the common good, which needs to be prevented. Conversely, the noncombatant may be guilty of hatred, but nevertheless not actively engaged in doing harm, and therefore may not be directly attacked. Sharpening the distinction between moral and functional definitions of innocence – something undertaken by Vitoria's successors – enabled a clearer distinction to be made between those guilty of war crimes and those merely

16. He does not have the space for a proper examination of biblical texts, but simply opposes the Joshua texts with one from Exodus 23.7: 'the innocent and righteous slay thou not'. This may look like a piece of prooftexting, but in its context it simply demonstrates that the case for holy war is thrown into doubt by its own single resource, the Old Testament, whereas the more theological argument of Vitoria, which opposes holy war, does not need to put all its eggs in one basket.

guilty of fighting on the wrong side. It also made easier a denial of the malignant doctrine of collective guilt, already weakened by Vitoria's refusal of religion as a just cause.

But in a passage that causes some trouble to modern commentators, Vitoria allows that one may kill the innocent while attacking 'military' targets,

> for example, during the justified storming of a fortress or city, where one knows there are many innocent people, but where it is impossible to fire artillery and other projectiles or set fire to buildings without crushing or burning the innocent along with the combatants. This is proven, since it would otherwise be impossible to wage war against the guilty, thereby preventing the just side from fighting. Nevertheless, we must remember … that care must be taken to ensure that the evil effects of the war do not outweigh the possible benefits sought by waging it.[17]

He was speaking about fairly primitive cannons, but the fantastically increased power of modern weapons to cause indiscriminate damage has made this a dangerous admission. Vitoria's allowance for what is nowadays called 'collateral damage' needs to be seen realistically in the context of modern methods of war. But what he certainly would not allow is any attempt to win a war by deliberately targeting non-combatants as the most effective method of breaking down resistance.

Although the material conditions of modern war are utterly different from the Conquistadors' campaigns against the American Indians, the moral reality is not so very different, and Vitoria's strict rules of engagement, based on the common human dignity of people on both sides, and their rights to their own lives, property and social order, still have a great deal to say to us. To take a contemporary example: with the stated aim of dislodging the ruler of a sovereign state, the Western nations, since 1992, have aimed severe economic sanctions and sometimes bombs at a large and populous Middle Eastern country. This has resulted in immense hardship, child mortality, hunger and disease, the impoverishment and collapse of ordinary life

17. *On the Law of War* 3.1, Pagden and Lawrance, *op. cit.*, p. 314.

and sometimes sudden death for wholly innocent people. As usual, it is the 'soft target' of the general population that is hit rather than the rulers. We need to ask Vitoria's questions: whether the innocent are being intentionally targeted (if not by the bombs, then by the sanctions) and whether the evil effects of the war – the damage to the human community itself – do not outweigh the possible benefits sought by waging it.

POSTSCRIPT

Often quoted is a passage from Boswell's *Life of Johnson:*

> 'I love the University of Salamanca; for when the Spaniards were in doubt as to the lawfulness of their conquering America, the University of Salamanca gave it as their opinion that it was not lawful.' He spoke this with great emotion …

This was a simplification of history no doubt, and it is always a temptation for the British to point the finger at the Spanish for what they did to the people of the New World. But one is entitled to ask where is the Vitoria of British, French, or Dutch colonialism? Where were the royal consultations, the regard for a law transcending the power of the State, the moral debates, the university opposition, the treatises in political theology demonstrating the illegality of the division of Africa, or the genocide of the North American Indians and Australian aborigines? I am unaware of anything approaching the care that was taken over such matters in sixteenth-century Spain.

6

Las Casas

Prophet of Full Rights for All

CARLOS JOSAPHAT, O.P.

The commemorations of the five hundredth anniversary of the discovery of the Americas in 1492 threw a new light on the figure of Fray Bartolomé de Las Casas (1484-1566). Greater familiarity with the whole corpus of his writings and researches into the whole of his life and into aspects, even today not totally clear, of his activities and attitudes towards the colonisers, the Indians and the Africans, have elevated the Dominican friar to the status of model and champion of social justice, the prophet of all rights for all in America. [1]

COLONISATION: PROBLEMS AND CHALLENGES

When the young Bartolomé de Las Casas landed in Central America in 1502 and settled there as a colonist in 1503, he was joining deliberately and even enthusiastically in the great movement of colonisation. The discoverers were turning into conquistadors. In official texts, the 'Catholic monarchs' of Spain began to adopt with enthusiasm the title 'tamers of peoples'.

The occupation of the new lands, beginning with the Caribbean islands, was carried out energetically and speedily. In ten years, after the installation of some military fortifications and the first residential settlements, the model of colonisation was already clearly drawn. It began by meeting the economic needs of Spain, a country burdened with a huge population without property or income, but also gifted with an active class of merchants, shipbuilders, seafarers and business people, ready to travel and venture.

---

1. As argued by the present writer in: *Las Casas. Todos os direitos para todos.* São Paulo: Loyola, 2000.

America came as the great hope for the whole Spanish nation in process of unification, with its widespread poverty alongside the courage and even idealism of the elites, especially political and economic leaders. Colonisation resulted from a decision by these leaders, but was taken up with a degree of enthusiasm by pioneers and adventurers, but above all by small farmers hoping for favourable conditions in which to improve and even enrich themselves.

These longed for social and economic conditions seemed to be waiting for the lucky colonisers. The soil of the new continent, and its hidden depths, was the first rich promise. Did these tropical regions not present the most luxuriant, beautiful and fertile lands, a paradise never seen before? And were they not also rich, gleaming with gold and silver mines and deposits of precious stones? And these hopes and dreams of avarice were confirmed and encouraged by two other certainties, affirmed by the authorities and the leaders of the colonial enterprise. First, these 'discovered' lands could be occupied, and if necessary invaded by main force; they were considered 'no one's' (*res nullius*) and became the property of the incoming Europeans, possessed of all the skills required to realise their value.

This task required hard and difficult work, in a climate sometimes harsher than that of the Iberian peninsula. But all that initially seemed to presage an obstacle was immediately transformed by the discovery of another miraculous asset. The native population of the country, labelled 'the Indians', was there and totally available. They were savages, without ruler or law, codes or culture. And, above all, they were infidels. They were therefore cheap, even free, labour, requiring no more than maintenance and guidance to learn how to work rationally and profitably for the benefit of the faithful Catholic Spaniards.

At the precise moment when the young Las Casas, descendant of merchants from Seville, came with his relatives and settled as a colonist on the island of Hispaniola (today divided between the Dominican Republic and Haiti), in the vigour of his twenties, the Spanish metropolis began to draft the first legal and political measures to ensure the conquest and colonisation of the 'West Indies'.

Among these measures some were particularly significant and directly relevant to the style of colonisation that was being implanted. In 1502, in Seville, there was founded the House of Trade (*Casa de Contratación*), to encourage and control trade in the colonies. In 1503 approval was given to the *encomienda*, a form of appropriation and cultivation of the land that consisted in assigning to the colonist a piece of ground and a part of the indigenous population living on it, to work free for the fortunate title-holder or *encomendero*. This system, baptised as *repartamiento* or division, revived in a new context an ancient model of slave labour that had already been disappearing at the end of the Middle Ages, that of the glebe serfs. These agriculturalists were tied to the ownership of the land, sold or passed on as a legacy with the rest of the landowner's goods.

It is evident that this model of colonisation was a conjunction of economic, political, cultural and ideological features now backed by the first regulations of colonial law. This system assumed the approval or consecration of religion, appealing to the Alexandrine bulls (issued by the Spanish Pope, Alexander VI). The Spanish monarchs officially received from the Head of the Church the power and the mission to 'bring into submission', to colonise and evangelise the infidel peoples of the newly discovered lands.

This type of colonisation, based on the conquest and division of the land into *encomiendas*, implanted an economy that from the start enriched the coloniser with the twofold gift of real estate and free labour. Seen from the perspective of the metropolis and its emissaries, this system seemed to contain all the ingredients of success. It could rely on the presence and support of Church dignitaries and clergy, whose duty was to assist the colonisers and evangelise the infidels, whose subjugation and enslavement were held up as the ideal preconditions for their efficient evangelisation. In both economic and religious aspects, the colonisation seemed amply to fulfil its promise. After the first twenty years of colonisation, the *encomiendas* were numbered in thousands, parishes and religious houses multiplied, and several dioceses had been created (from as early as 1510).

THE DOMINICANS TAKE ON THE SYSTEM

But this hitherto untroubled colonial system, linked to the mission of evangelisation, was to face its first challenge and encounter its first rough passage with the coming of the Dominican friars, and above all with the conversion of the future Fray Bartolomé de Las Casas.

It all began with the General Chapter that elected Friar Tomás de Vio, Cajetan, Master of the Order at Pentecost 1508. In his eagerness to renew study and the regular life, but above all the missionary zeal of the Dominican order, Cajetan enthusiastically accepted the proposal that Spanish Dominicans should be sent to America. He wanted them to be an evangelising force, a sizable group from the start, fifteen friars from among those committed to the reform of the Order, led by someone with a provincial's authority. A significant detail: the Master of the Order instructed that provision be made for the appointment of four or five deputies for this provincial, should he come to grief or be prevented from exercising his office in these hazardous mission lands.

In the year 1510 the friars arrived, and there was established on the island of Hispaniola that first Dominican priory of fourteen religious, whose prior was Pedro de Córdoba, a great leader and spiritual master only twenty-eight years of age. This community opened a new chapter in the history of America. For a year the friars observed what went on in all spheres of the colonial venture. Then, in an attitude enlightened by their own apostolic experience, prayer and study, they took the decision to offer their diagnosis. It was to be no less than a prophetic oracle, condemning the gross deviations of the colonisers and calling for a new model of colonisation, guided by social justice and inspired by the gospel.

The pronouncement was the famous sermon preached by Antonio de Montesinos on the Fourth Sunday of Advent, 21 December 1511. The text was prepared and even drafted

collectively. Montesinos, chosen for his oratorical gifts, received from the prior at the priory chapter the formal commission to preach to the colonisers, in the name of the
community, this fiery message: 'You are all in mortal sin.' The
explanation was the crimes they were committing against the
Indians: 'By what right' were they conquering this country
and enslaving and oppressing its inhabitants? 'Are they not
human beings' with rights to be respected, and a right to be
loved by you, Christians?

These words momentarily shook the colonisers and authorities, beginning with the Governor, since the whole population had been invited to listen to the friars' preaching. They
were the start of a new effort to humanise the colonisation
process, even prompting the promulgation of 'new laws' (as
early as 1512). But they did not have a general impact, even
among the Dominicans of the metropolis. What finally prevailed was the spirit of accommodation, leading to acceptance
of the colonial model based on plunder, oppression and even
slavery.

But the central transforming effect of the presence and
attitude of the Dominicans was to have its main embodiment
in the conversion of Las Casas.

FROM COLONISER TO LIBERATOR

Bartolomé de Las Casas was already a priest when he came
into contact with the Dominicans in 1510. He respected the
lives and teaching of the friars, but kept a distance from their
views on social justice. This is the first point to be noted about
Las Casas' life. From the start, he was totally dedicated to the
colonial enterprise. The discovery of America had interested
him from childhood. His family were intimates of Columbus'
and the Admiral's family in Seville. At the age of nine or ten
Bartolomé watched in rapture the Discoverer's triumphal
parade through the city. His father took part in Columbus'
second voyage, and gave him a present of an Indian boy he
had brought from America. Bartolomé's childhood and ado-
lescence were marked by this family passion for the New
World.

Las Casas is the perfect example of a Spaniard whose vision of America included some idealism but vast ambition. He crossed the Atlantic, in search of wealth, but also wanting to help with catechesis, for which purpose he received minor orders. He progressed in both his religious and his financial careers, becoming the first priest ordained in America – a fact of which he remained for ever proud. But he became a land-owner priest. More than that, he became an *encomendero,* a recipient under the *repartimiento* system of a generous portion of land and a batch of Indians. He proved a good administrator, got rich, and was held up as a model for the other colonists.

But Fr Las Casas showed some sympathy for the local population. He was a regular visitor to the Dominicans, and even a collaborator with them. His arguments with them were equable. He retained an attitude of realistic attachment to the colonial enterprise, in much the same way as the rest of his compatriots. It was in 1514, at the age of thirty, that he was converted to the cause of the Indians and to social justice. When he told the story of this complete turnabout in his life, he showed that a total upheaval took place in his outlook, as he prepared to celebrate Mass of Pentecost in Cuba, where he had gone with the occupation forces, more or less as military chaplain.

He says that he was converted as he read the text of Sirach (Ecclesiasticus) condemning unjust sacrifices: 'Like one who kills a son before his father's eyes is the person who offers a sacrifice from the property of the poor' (Sir 34:24; see 34:21-7). He clearly sees his conversion as the fruit of the grace of the Spirit and the power of God's word, but doesn't mention any special phenomenon. In fact, he insists, using the term several times, that he 'considered' the lessons he received from the teaching and example of the Dominicans, 'considered' the injustices inflicted on the Indians, the iniquity involved in enslaving them and invading their land. His conversion comes across as the maturing of a free process of reasoning, under the luminous influence of grace acting on a man adult in his actions and ideas.

So, before his conversion, he gave himself with all his intelligence to the task of being a good coloniser. After his conversion, quite calmly, he made use of his experience and put all his knowledge and practical ability at the service of the defence and promotion of Indian rights.

Thus devoting himself to the quest for social justice, his life was a constant advance, as he lived out and proclaimed what became a sort of motto, the need to bring together life and law (*juntar el hecho y el derecho*), to observe what is done, analyse social affairs and strive for 'the right' – what is demanded of all and due to all – and apply the conclusions judiciously and constantly.

This tireless quest for what is right in all circumstances of life and all historical situations gives a profound consistency to Las Casas' struggle, as he matured and evolved in his endeavour to respond to the different challenges and to the adversaries, whether intransigent or hesitant, that this pioneer of justice encountered. The fifty years he was to dedicate to the defence and promotion of justice fall into stages reflecting the problems raised by the advance of colonisation and representing a constant advance in both doctrinal formulation and practical problem-solving.

By way of illustration, I shall highlight some of the main stages of this evolution of Las Casas in his quest for social justice. The first comprises the seven or eight years following his conversion. When informed of Fr Las Casas' intention to relinquish his *encomienda*, free the slaves and devote himself to their liberation, the Governor reacted with the utilitarian and pragmatic theology typical of the good coloniser: 'God desires you working and prosperous. Don't go imitating the silly friars.'

But this was exactly what Las Casas did, following the Dominicans in the pursuit of justice, drawing inspiration from their doctrine but with more of a practical bent, with more realism, drawing on his experience as a rural businessman. In order to advance the rights of the Indians, but without abandoning his work for the welfare of his fellow-Spaniards, Fr Las Casas set himself to invent a good model of colonisation, inspired and energised by the principles of justice and solidarity. For their part, the Dominican friars gave him firm support, especially 'Venerable' (as Las Casas always called him) Fray Pedro de Córdoba.

His aim was to combine European skill and the capacity for work of the American population, and unite them in something like production communities or cooperatives. He did everything with great care. He set up carefully planned projects. He did his best to select and train the partners in the enterprise. But is impossible to sew a new patch on old cloth. How could small fraternal units be launched and made to succeed in a system dominated by ambition and despotism? His generous experiments ended in a blood-bath. The Spanish colonists provoked the Indians, who attacked the team put together by Las Casas and killed some of his main assistants. This terrible failure took place in 1521.

Las Casas blamed no one. He accepted complete responsibility. He regretted having relied on untrustworthy colleagues. He decided to repeat the experiment with more love and even more care. It was at this moment that the words and examples of the Dominicans had their main influence on him. He recognised that the struggle for justice called for work on minds at a deep level, a wide-ranging and permanent preaching activity to influence habits, guide leaders and change the system itself. Study and prayer were the essential preparation. Consequently he decided to enter the Dominican Order, with the more or less conscious intention of going further than they had hitherto in the defence and promotion of full rights for all.

He spent some years in silence, prayer and study to deepen his vocation as a Preacher. He was remarkable for his original and creative way of confronting his own plan of life and action with the venerable tradition of the Order of St Dominic. He devoted especial attention to the teaching of St Thomas, then arousing great interest in the universities, but on many points going much further than the great medieval master, especially in a more modern understanding of justice and even the situation of unbelievers. Las Casas thus inaugurated a new style in his own life and at the same time a new model of Dominican life. In his personal life, he achieved something similar to the mystical and political vocation of St Catherine of Siena or the compassionate zeal to be at the service of the poor that was offered as an example a few decades later by St Martin de Porres and St Rose of Lima.

The Dominican stages of Fray Bartolomé de Las Casas' life were to shine out as typical ways of living *Veritas,* the liberating truth of the Gospel. He was to be a contemplative aware of the demands of justice, committed to discerning courses of action, in a intellectual activity that did not sever links with experience, kept in touch with reality and maintained a constant dialogue with his allies in the fight. This tireless quest of truth, linked always with the struggle for justice, was characterised by study, by an intellectual life constantly renewed and open to the problems thrown up by life. It is a strange and touching image, the missionary Fray Las Casas travelling the roads of America surrounded by Indians eagerly carrying his books, those enormous tomes that were his travelling library, because the Indians knew that all this strange material was used for their service and to defend their rights.

Many of the episodes, the long journeys, Las Casas' meetings with the monarchs, ministers and counsellors, were inspired by his apostolic commitment. He was certain that it was necessary to go to the sources, detect those responsible and try to educate them in an attempt to remove the injustices and establish permanent measures, even create institutions at the service of justice. It could be said that he practised a spirituality of dialogue or even of argument. In the service of this difficult task, this friar preacher travelled by land and sea, spoke and wrote, combining study, discourse and the struggle for justice with the other vital functions of his Dominican existence.

The beginnings of his Dominican life testify to an exuberant, overflowing love, which revealed itself in admiration for the peoples inhabiting America and delight in the land, its beauty and the happiness, actual or potential, it offered. For him, mission had no sense of external obligation. It grew from the urgings of a heart enchanted by the discovery of the other, of human beings that were different, but lovable and precious in their difference. He did not treat the term 'savage' as pejorative. This was a new, vigorous humanity, endowed with different forms of civilisation and culture. As he devoted himself to evangelisation, defending, often forcefully, the rights of the Indians, he constantly marvelled at the customs of the pre-Columbian peoples. He observed, noted, and compared the new features he found with what he had learned in his studies about the cultures, religions and peoples of antiquity. And, especially in his monumental 'Brief Apologetic History' (*Historia Sumaria*), he wrote treatises on cultural ethnology, clearly with the intention of celebrating the Indians and their culture despite the contempt of the colonisers. But, above all, his developing body of writing bears witness to the fruitfulness of his mission, inspired and shot through with love for justice and truth.

He accepted appointment as Bishop of Chiapas, and was consecrated in 1544. His aims and pastoral plans were now directed to introducing to the Church (in the middle of the Council of Trent) a new model of bishop, dedicated to social justice and the defence of the poorest and most defenceless. The symbol of this new model of Church and ecclesiastical authority is his attempt to make the confessional an instrument for the liberation of slaves and for realistic solidarity between human beings. He did not give absolution, and ordered that it should not be given, to slave-owners if they had not first made a legal grant of freedom. This Gospel-based, liberating vision of episcopacy attracted the enthusiasm of the Indians, but was massively rejected by the Spanish colonisers. Las Casas was forced to leave his diocese. From 1547 he worked in Europe, attempting to educate public opinion, and awaken the consciences of the authorities, the court, the counsellors, the ministers and the King.

This intense labour and tireless struggle to change prevailing attitudes and secure acceptance for a new model of colonisation, inspired by justice and solidarity, forms the background to Bishop Las Casas' famous debate with Canon Juan-Ginès Sepúlveda in Valladolid in 1550. Eager as ever to 'save' his country from the great collective 'sin' constituted by the plunder, oppression, enslavement and 'destruction of the Indies', in Seville in 1552 he published eight *Treatises*, apologetic and angry in style, but very well documented and with good doctrinal arguments. The first is the best known of his writings, the 'Short Account of the Destruction of the Indies' *(Brevísima Relación de la Destrucción de las Indias)* used by his opponents to discredit him, with the insinuation that he was denigrating Spain. In fact, the manuscript text of the book had been sent to the King in 1540, since the missionary bishop's instinct was to inform and influence leaders, and he appealed to public opinion only twelve years later, when he discovered that the sovereign had not found time to look at his complaints.

Unfortunately, almost down to our own time Las Casas' other writings remained unpublished, especially 'The Only Way of Bringing All Peoples to the True Religion', which summarises his underlying theological view of the Gospel, of evangelisation linked to the promotion of justice. The same applies to his two great 'Summas', the 'History of the Indies' and the 'Brief Apologetic History'. These three works, which Las Casas had in mind from the beginning of his life as a Dominican, offer us the true doctrinal message and the true image of the person of Las Casas, and explain his recognition by modern scholars as a true doctor of the Church at the dawn of the New World.

SOCIAL JUSTICE IN LAS CASAS' VISION, ACTION AND STRUGGLE

What I call the conversion of Las Casas was a complete change in the life of a man who considered himself, and was considered by others to be, a good Christian, a good priest, but discovered that the only true religion consists in combining the sense of God and the sense of justice. Recognising God as Father totally changed the life of this 'practising Catholic', leading him to universal love, to respect for the dignity of every human being, and to a quest for full rights for all in relations between individuals and in the construction and functioning of society.

This is the message of social justice, inspired by the practice and main thrust of the prophets' teaching. It constitutes the very stuff of Las Casas' life, and forms the guiding thread of his doctrine. In it lies his originality. He lived justice day by day. Through successes and failures in action, by means of study, linked to work and struggle, in dialogue with competent people, through constant analysis of situations and contexts, he continually advanced in his vision and practice of justice. More than the precious collection of teachings he left us in his writings, still not fully or accessibly assimilated, more important is the lesson he gave us in his journey by stages, in the consistency of his life as it gradually matured, allowing him to see more and more clearly and implement more fully the demands of social justice.

He saw justice as a primordial duty inherent in history. He did not think of it as a bundle of universal principles and norms for which he had to find means of application. He understood justice as a specific reality, from his first experience, which he describes as the origin of his conversion, the basic characteristic of the first community of Dominicans in America, seeing the demands of 'right' in the first 'social fact' of colonisation, the plunder and enslavement of the Indians. This original insight became a growing source of light and energy for him. In the half century he lived after his Pentecost in 1514 in Cuba, justice constantly expanded and developed into a series of concentric circles, becoming wider and more universal.

The universality of this understanding and this transforming energy derived from justice comes from his initial recognition of the human nature of the Indians: 'Are they not human beings?' This radical, crucial question he heard from the Dominican friars was one he took forward and used as a touchstone in all the problems and situations he encountered. Where human beings are present in society, there too must be justice, and be supreme.

From his youth, Las Casas had had a passion for law,

understood as the regulating presence of justice, the primordial virtue and value of society. For him, law was first and foremost 'natural law', the first demand and first norms that spring from a consideration of the inviolable dignity inherent in every human being. But he also valued positive law, and devoted himself to the study of the codes, the legislation, the prescriptions and juridical forms that governed the country, calling for their proper and effective application or demanding their amplification or correction, when the law was wrong or inadequate.

Accordingly, Montesinos' question, 'By what right?' was understood and proclaimed by Las Casas first as condemning a gap in the law, intolerable arbitrary behaviour underlying the conquest of America and the enforced subjugation of its population. The series of laws that followed from 1512 onwards were criticised by Las Casas insofar as they did not respect the Indians' human rights and did not give rise to a new positive law as the practical and effective implementation of this natural law.

It is fascinating to follow the growing energy that marks the sense, doctrine and practice of justice in Las Casas' career and writings. He continually advanced towards an ever clearer perception of the universality of rights, of better formulations and an increasingly sensitive feel for their applicability and the conditions needed to make them viable.

The most eye-catching side of his activity and his polemical writings – the only ones published in his lifetime – is the condemnation of the injustices and violence perpetrated by the Spanish conquistadors. Many did not see the central thrust of the thought and action of this man, whose concern was constructive in his efforts to design and implement exercises in social justice. Las Casas was always rooted in reality. He criticised all those who talked about America and its problems without direct knowledge, based on experience or information derived from contact with the things and inhabitants of the continent. Among the targets of his criticism were even the professors of Salamanca, including the one for whom Las Casas expressed greatest esteem, the 'eminent master', Fray Francisco de Vitoria. They became objects of the missionary's reservations when they talked about the things and people of America at a distance and in general terms.

Already, in the period between his conversion and his entry into the Dominican Order in 1522, Las Casas put at the service of a just and human colonial system all the qualities and administrative skill he had acquired in business. To persuade the authorities and win over partners for his ideas, he composed 'Memorials', real action plans, complete, consistent, detailed, proposing the formation of a network of communities of life and work, bringing together Indians and Spaniards. Not merely work, but health, government and the administration of justice – all were regulated in fine detail. He gave figures for the number of hospitals, doctors and nurses, schools and teachers, joiners and butchers. Outlay and income are calculated, wages and salaries are fixed justly and exactly, with the aim that the business would become prosperous, repay the capital invested and create wealth that would be distributed fairly among all the partners. Everything is well planned and even rigorously costed by this former businessman, now devoting himself with complete realism to a lucid and effective quest for justice and solidarity.

In other words, underlying Las Casas' apostolic and social action was a specific project combining the following main objectives:

• To establish fraternal contact between the peoples of America and Spain, on the basis of esteem and mutual respect;

• To create communities with the aim of recognising and practising equality of rights and valuing cultures for their differences;

• To combine evangelisation and the promotion of justice in a climate of freedom, so that people can accept or reject the faith offered to them.

This project, already present at the moment of his conversion, developed and guided the evolution of Las Casas' action plans and inspired his writings. In essence, the message of social justice, the idea of promoting full rights for all, was already present as early as the first Memorials of 1515, but the programme's working out in detail came in response to the problems and challenges of everyday life.

The following section attempts to highlight some of the essential points of this constant and sometimes difficult march towards social justice, which Las Casas always sought to insert into the interplay of interests and ambitions surrounding the colonial venture.

Obeying the criterion of urgency, Las Casas, as we saw, initially concentrated his interest on the Indians, and in 1515 received the office title of 'Procurator' or 'Defender of the Indians'. Since the native population of America was being oppressed and without protection, they became the first group for whose rights the missionary campaigned. At the same time, however, he also demonstrated that the welfare of the Spaniards was a constant concern. He wanted them to be protected by the law, but his primary aim was that they should practise the law. He praised the magistrates, judges and administrators who showed zeal for justice. In his letters and appeals to the King and the metropolitan authorities, he vigorously recommended those who were able and willing to collaborate in establishing an authentic and effective judicial system in the Colony.

It would thus be a mistake to present him as an unconditional defender of the Indians and an implacable foe of his fellow Spaniards. He vigorously denounced injustices in the person of the colonisers and in the colonial system in the light of the conviction he proclaimed that, without a real conversion that included the restitution of the property stolen and compensation for the damage done, the sin of injustice would lead both individuals and nations inevitably to perdition. This prophetic vision, reinforced by the Gospel, acquired an apocalyptic tone in Las Casas' preaching.

A similar, more serious mistake, has been made even by historians with regard to blacks. It is asserted that in order to preserve the Indians from slave labour, Las Casas supported African slavery. Today careful studies lead to the opposite conclusion, which is solid, if with some qualifications. At the beginning of his career Las Casas shared the prevalent view within Christendom that accepted African slavery on the (false) premise that the slaves were prisoners of war and were being shown mercy by having their lives spared and being reduced to servitude. Led by his love of truth and justice, Las Casas investigated and condemned African slavery as being 'as perverse as the enslavement of the Indians'. It is worth noting that his mature work includes a passionate and well-argued 'Short Report on the Destruction of Africa',[2] similar to his first book denouncing the 'destruction of the Indies'.

It will be clear that the universalisation of Las Casas' view of justice was not the result simply of an intellectual process, but of a journey within history, in dialogue with the challenges and conditions arising out of events. Another example illustrates his originality as compared with the attitude dominant in Christendom, closed to others and not allowing for differences. This significant example is Las Casas' attitude to women. In contrast to the machismo so blatant in his country, Las Casas showed himself particularly mindful of the rights of women. In his first schemes for communities combining Indians and Spaniards, he took trouble to specify that women should have good working conditions and that their work should be well paid. He insisted firmly and frequently that the injustices committed in the colonisation process were particularly serious when they affected families, caused unhappiness to women and destroyed the harmony of couples. It is also a pleasant surprise to find how much the bold and fearless campaigner revealed a sensitive and human dimension in his references to the indigenous queens, and lamenting the ill-treatment they received from the Spanish conquistadors.

A MODEL OF SOCIAL JUSTICE

In an attempt to summarise the results of current research and to encourage further exploration of the alternative colo-

2. This is the title of the work by Isacio Fernández Pérez, O.P., Salamanca, 1989. The same author has also written a book summarising the results of current research: *Bartolomé de Las Casas contra los negros?* (Madrid, 1991).

nial model put forward by the first Dominicans in America, the following sections highlight the radical originality and current relevance of the model of social justice that emerges from the work and doctrinal writings of Las Casas.

The primacy of rights over power

Las Casas never challenged the religious power (of the Pope) or the civil and political power (of the Spanish monarchy), which was cited as the basis for the legitimacy of the colonial venture. The missionary recognised the established powers. But he called on all those who held power to exercise their mission, which he described as: guaranteeing all rights, beginning with those of the Indians, as persons, as families, as ethnic groups and as peoples. He took for granted a legal system that guaranteed the rights of Spanish citizens. His central concern was to subordinate power to rights. The Pope, the monarch, all the authorities hold power only for the purpose of defending and promoting rights, and only retain power legitimately to the extent that they guarantee the exercise of rights. These are the main theses of the 'Treatises' published in Seville in 1552.

Hierarchy and priority in making rights effective

In practice, Las Casas recognised a hierarchy, above all one based on urgency, in his effort to make rights universal. He concentrated on guaranteeing and defending fundamental rights, because they are the basis of all the other: the right to life, the features that make life human, the right to health, freedom, possession and use of essential goods. These rights were to be guaranteed first to the poorest and weakest, who had no power to claim them for themselves. In the specific case of America, the urgent need was to begin by recognising and asserting that the Indians could be the subject of these rights, that they were the legitimate holders of the rights before the conquest and had to be reinstated in their rights with the appropriate restitution and reparation for the damage caused by the invasions, expropriations and acts of violence of which they had been, or were still, the objects.

People and communities are active subjects of rights,
which society has a duty to guarantee

Recognition of this fundamental principle, ignored in his time, led Las Casas to proclaim, at suitable moments, that the population should not just wait passively for rights to be given to them, but demand them and fight for them. It comes as a surprise to find this Dominican missionary going so far as to recognise the legitimacy of a sort of guerrilla warfare invented and practised in moderation by an indigenous leader, 'Prince Enriquillo'.

Political ethics: the priority of rights and freedom

Examination of Las Casas' doctrinal development shows that he reaches the stage of formulating a political ethics clearly stating the primacy of rights and freedom, the latter hailed as the supreme right. He proclaims that the source of the power exercised by kings and other authorities lies in the people, who confer legitimacy on governments by choice or tacit consent.

With perfect logic, Las Casas draws the conclusion that that is of supreme importance for America: its inhabitants have the right to pronounce, in a sort of referendum, whether to accept or not the presence of the Spanish colonisers in the New World.

Rights of persons and peoples – Restitution and reparation for
individual or collective injustices an absolute necessity

One of the most original features of Las Casas' theoretical and practical positions is his affirmation of the rights of both persons and peoples. When these rights are violated, he insists that the duty of restitution is both individual and collective. And he maintains that this duty remains in force throughout history: peoples are obliged to restore what they have taken from other peoples, and to make good the damaged caused. Las Casas is thinking specifically of the injustices perpetrate din the colonisation of America, but develops a new general doctrine, based on St Thomas's treatise on restitution, which he amplifies, extends and transforms, to take account of the new issues raised by the discoveries.

The community ideal: power-sharing, regional or federal

From the corpus of Las Casas' teachings on political ethics, a model of organisation emerges that could be called 'communitarian'. He accepts the divine authority of the Church and the divine origin of royal authority, a position rooted in the medieval tradition and even retaining some features of political Augustinianism. What is new in Las Casas' however, is his acceptance and support for the rights of small and medium-sized communities: he defends a degree of autonomy for regions and nations, which he says the supreme authorities have a duty to maintain and promote. The Empire, under the authority of the monarch, should therefore take on a confederate form that recognises the value of persons in their dignity, freedom and rights, while recognising and consolidating intermediate communities, *de facto* and as possessing their own degree of power. This politico-social edifice is crowned by the plenitude of spiritual power vested in the Pope, whose vocation is to recognise and confirm justice and universal solidarity, at all levels of social organisation, since 'grace does not suppress, but confirms and perfects nature'. Las Casas stresses the Thomist axiom, and gives it special force and a degree of urgency in the social sphere.

Conscience deserves absolute respect

A similar political ethics, essentially human and natural in content, but including a reference to the theology of the creation and incarnation, is upheld by Las Casas especially when he deals with 'the only way of attracting all peoples to the true religion'. This includes what was later described as 'freedom of conscience', which gives it a firmer and broader basis. In every human being, even one still regarded as an unbeliever, Las Casas recognises the capacity and the right freely to search for and embrace truth, and this personal and intellectual journey must be supported, while the decision to accept faith or not must be respected. On this point Las Casas is a precursor of Vatican II.

The rights of peoples to retain their cultures

Constantly and very competently, Las Casas devotes great

effort to observing the lives, customs, cultures and traditions of the Indians. He shows great respect for their way of life, and their models of family and community. Some of Las Casas' works, especially the 'Brief Apologetic History', are valuable evidence for cultural ethnology, and constitute an enthusiastic and soundly based defence of the right of the American peoples and all others to maintain their cultures and have them respected. This is one of the elements of Las Casas' ethical legacy with most relevance to our day.[3]

In conclusion I would stress how much the confirmation brought by centuries of colonisation and colonialism makes it more touching to reread today Las Casas' Testament, and the letter he left in draft form for the Pope, his fellow Dominican, St Pius V. Showing an awareness that his mission was 'to free the Indians of America', the octogenarian bishop of Chiapas puts forward a new model of a bishop, of communities, of the Church for the New World. Faith and evangelisation have to go hand in hand with social justice.

To his Dominican brothers of the priory of Our Lady of Atocha in Madrid, who came to bid him their last farewells, the old missionary, with his eyes on the crucifix and a lighted candle in his hand, confessed for the last time his only regret, not to have done all he could during his life for the Indians, and to defend their sacred rights. In this sentiment of generous and humble love, Fray Bartolomé de Las Casas closed his

3. These positions are summarised here from Las Casas' writings, read and analysed in chronological order of composition, bearing in mind the harmonious development of Las Casas' thought. The basic text, although the surviving copies are incomplete, is 'The Only Way of Attracting Peoples to the True Religion'. The 'History of the Indies' is a genuine moral and theological *Summa* developed within a historical framework. But the real treatise from which to study Las Casas' positions on the value and content of pre-Columbian cultures is the 'Short Apologetic History'. This monumental work contains a profound theology of the relationship between the Gospel and the Church and non-Christian cultures and religions. The conception and development of his ethical positions on social justice, on the absolute necessity of the restitution of stolen property and the obligation to make reparation for the damage done, is found in the eight Treatises published by Las Casas in Seville in 1552. In the last of these a political ethics gradually emerges that finds its finished theoretical formulation in one of his last writings, 'On Royal Power'. The Select Bibliography includes the Complete Works of Las Casas and a brief list of authors who are attempting to explore his message today.

eyes on this world on 18 June 1566.

Why not end these reflections on a confidential note? In the twilight of a life largely devoted to the study of the writings and person of Fray Bartolomé de Las Casas, I have come to a conclusion that I should like to share above all with my Dominican sisters and brothers. Looking at the great spiritual leaders, not excluding the holy Fathers and Doctors of the Church, and the Popes, I do not see, in all history, anyone who can compare with Las Casas for a life and mind totally devoted to social justice, to the study, defence and promotion of all rights for all. If there is any exaggeration in this expression of my conviction, put it down to the gratitude of a Latin American who feels indebted to this brave *sevillano* who chose to be a hundred per cent Latin American out of love.

SELECT BIBLIOGRAPHY

Complete Works of Bartolomé de Las Casas
I have used the critical edition of the original texts produced by the Instituto Bartolomé de Las Casas Foundation of the Dominicans of Andalucia, under the direction of Dr Paulino Castañeda Delgado for the fifth centenary of the discovery of America. There are fourteen volumes – vol. 11 has two parts – all published by Alianza Editorial, Madrid.

1 – *Vida y Obras, Introdução Geral.* 2 – *De Unico Vocationis Modo* (The Only Way of Attracting All Peoples to the True Religion). 3 – *Historia de las Índias* (T. 1). 4 – *Historia de las Índias (T.2),* 5 – *Historia de las Índias,* (T. III). 6 – *Apologética Historia Sumaria I.* 7 – *Apologética Historia Sumaria II.* 8 – *Apologética Historia Sumaria III.* 9 – *Apologia.* 10 – *Tratados de 1552* (these eight texts are the only writings published by Las Casas himself). 11.1 – *De Thesauris* (The Treasures of Peru). 11.2 – *Doce Dudas.* 12 – *De regia potestate,* 13 – *Cartas y Memoriales.* 14 – *Diario del primer y tercer viaje de Cristóbal Colón.*

Selected Writings about Las Casas
I. André-Vicente, O.P., *Fray Bartolomé de Las Casas y Los derechos del hombre,* Ediciones Cultura Hispanica del Centro Iberoamericano de Cooperación, Madrid, 1978.

Isacio Fernández-Pérez, *¿Bartolomé de Las Casas contra los negros?* Madrid, Editorial Mundo Negro, 1991.

Juan Friede and Benjamin Keen, *Bartolomé de Las Casas in History,* Northern Illinois University Press, Dekalb, 1971.

—— *Bartolomé de Las Casas, precursor del anticolonialismo,* México, 1974.

Gustavo Guti´rrez, *Dios o el oro en las Indias – Siglo XVI,* Instituto Bartolomé de Las Casas, Perú, 1990.

—— *En busca de los pobres de JesuCristo – El pensamiento de Bartolomé de Las Casas,* CEP Centro de Estudios y Publicaciones e Instituto Bartolomé de Las Casas - Rimac, Perú, 1992.

Lewis Hanke, *Bartolomé de Las Casas. Pensador político, historiador, antropólogo,* Sociedad Económica de Amigos del País, Havana, 1949.

Ángel Losada, *Fray Bartolomé de Las Casas a la luz de la moderna crítica histórica,* Tecnos, Madrid, 1970.

Marianne Mahn-Lot, *Barthélemy de Las Casas. L'Evangile et la Force,* Ed. Du Cerf, Paris, 1964.

—— *Bartolomé de Las Casas et le droit des indiens,* Payot, Paris, 1982.

—— *Bartolomé de Las Casas – une théologie pour le Nouveau Monde,* Desclée de Brouwer, Paris, 1991.

Carlos Josaphat Oliveira, *Contemplação e Libertação* – Tomás de Aquino, João da Cruz, Bartolomeu de Las Casas. Editora Ática, São Paulo, 1995. (There is a French edition of this book: *Contemplation et Libération – Thomas d'Aquin – Jean de la Croix – Barthélemy de Las Casas,* Editions Universitaires, Fribourg/ Editions du Cerf, Paris, 1993.)

—— *Las Casas – Todos os direitos para todos,* Edições Loyola, São Paulo, Brasil, 2000.

Helen-Rand Parish and Harold E. Weidman, *Las Casas en México, Historia y obra desconocidas.* Ed. Fondo Económico de Cultura do México, México, 1992.

Perez de J. Tudela, *Significado histórico de la vida y escritos del padre Las Casas.* Estudio crítico preliminar a Obras Escogidas del padre Las Casas: Historia de las Índias, I Madrid, BAE, t. 95, 1957 pp. I-CLXXXVIII.

7

Martin de Porres

Compassion in Full Bloom

BRIAN J. PIERCE, O.P.

HEALER AND FRIEND OF THE POOR

Martin de Porres died at the age of sixty after a long life held together by suffering and grace. One cannot help but wonder what his final years were like. Did he have the chance to look back on the complex, yet beautiful mosaic of his life and see all the different multi-coloured pieces fit into one harmonious whole? Was he able to see clearly and celebrate God's plan for himself and his people, even in the midst of the confusing times of conquest and colonization? One cannot look at the life of St Martin de Porres and not be moved by his graced capacity to transform suffering, his own and others,, into compassion. Speaking to the pilgrims gathered for Martin's canonization in 1962, Blessed Pope John XXIII said of the humble Martin, 'A springtime flower has opened in the Church.' Today we continue to be guided by this apostle of charity whose gift of compassion is a fragrant blossom waiting to bloom in each of us.

In 1594, aged twenty-two, Martin was admitted into the Dominican priory of Nuestra Señora del Rosario in Lima. It is a known fact that racism existed in the Church and in the religious orders of the time, and it is probably for this reason that Martin was received in the Order of Preachers as a *donato*, a kind of second class lay brother.[1] There is some controversy as

1. Guillermo Alvarez, O.P., has written on the topic of the racism in religious orders in Peru in the time of Saints Rosa de Lima and Martin de Porres: 'Rosa chose not to be a cloistered nun simply because the racial segregation in the monasteries was a sign counter to the gospel, a reason for scandal.' He bases his assertion on Rosa's correspondence with ecclesiastical authorities in Spain in an attempt to obtain permission for founding a monastery dedicated to St Catherine of Siena, 'where the sisters would be women of all social categories: Indians, Spanish, mestizas, Blacks and descendents of Moors.' Cited in Noé Zevallos, *Rosa de Lima, Compromiso y Contemplación*, 1988, Lima: CEP, pp. 2-3.

to whether Martin later professed vows as a full-fledged friar, or *hermano converso*, but what is of great value for the present discussion is that Martin seems to have reached early on a certain interior peace, a realism which allowed him to respond to the divine call to put his own experience of poverty and suffering at the service of others.

Stories abound which recount Martin's charitable visits to the African slave colony of Limatambo, on the outskirts of Lima. He would take bread and fruit and clothes to share among the hungry slaves, and spend time there healing their sick. His healing stories, those told by his Dominican brothers, as well as those remembered in the collective memory of the poor, are well documented and provide us with lively accounts of Martin's colourful ministry. He literally touched thousands, both rich and poor, through his compassionate presence.

What is curious is that Martin seems to have created a style of healing reminiscent of the long tradition of indigenous *curanderos* and African medicine healers. He even mixed a little spiritual magic into his healing rituals, seeking always a way of returning to the poor a sense of their own power as people of faith. Like Jesus, who used mud and saliva and other very earthy gestures for his healing encounters, Martin mixed his medicinal herbs with African and Incan spiritualism to create an outreach to the sick and marginalised of his time in a language that they could easily understand. His blending of spirituality and herbal medicine serves today as an affirmation to all who seek to reach out to the sick through the healing ministries of massage, hospice, natural and homoeopathic medicine, healing touch, Reiki, Twelve-Step groups and so many others. Martin's healing creativity encourages us to be bold in reclaiming a long tradition of popular wisdom often co-opted today by the powerful medical and pharmaceutical industries.

Brother Martin took advantage of his healing ministry to evangelize as well. He was freed from the duties of sacramental ministry to which the priests of his day occupied themselves, and this allowed him the opportunity to join with his beloved poor in their healing rituals and prayers, their processions and other popular devotions, where he mixed his grassroots medicine with stories from the gospels and the lives of the saints. The result was that he became the friend of the poor and an itinerant preacher-healer whose very life announced the Reign of God.

Popular religion and ritual continue today in Latin America to be one of the avenues where the poor experience their faith not as a passive following of institutional rules and rituals imported from afar, but as a truly liberating expression of their deepest faith. Popular religion awakens in the disenfranchised their own priestly vocation and call to respond actively as protagonists in the building of a new and more just world.[2] The Church as a pilgrim people of God accompanying the sick back to health, the enslaved to freedom, the dead to life finds a concrete expression in Martin de Porres. Martin is an icon in whom we see the face of Christ, which is simultaneously the face of our broken, yet redeemed humanity. For Martin, the Crucified Christ was God's I-am-with-you-always, and this great affirmation continues to be the guiding light for the crucified poor of Latin America and the world. No one has articulated this vision as well in our own times as slain Archbishop Oscar Romero who, like Martin, showed us what it means to be both pilgrim and prophet of God's compassion:

> With Christ, God has injected himself into history ... God's Reign is now inaugurated in human time ... Christ's birth attests that God is now marching with us in history, that we do not go alone, and that our aspiration for peace, for justice, for a reign of divine law, for something holy ... is already in the midst of us.[3]

FROM CONQUEST TO COMPASSION

Martin hardly knew his father growing up. He was raised almost solely by his Afro-Panamanian mother, Ana Velásquez. Juan de

2. See The Conclusions of the IV General Conference of the Latin American Episcopal Conference in Santo Domingo, October 1992, n. 97: 'The urgencies of the present moment in Latin America and the Caribbean cry out that all the laity be protagonists of the new evangelization, human promotion and of a Christian culture.'

3. Oscar Arnulfo Romero, *The Church Is All of You*, 1984, Minneapolis, Winston Press, 1984, p. 19. These words were spoken by Archbishop Romero in his Christmas Day homily in 1977.

Porres (or Porras, as some speculate) fathered Martin and his sister in a social and racial environment that treated the conquered Quechua and Aymara Indians and the imported African slaves as work horses. Peru was a Spanish colony built on the broken backs and held together by the blood, sweat and tears of the oppressed poor. Gold was god in colonial Peru, and everyone its servant.

Peru's social reality in 1569, the year Martin was born, was not all that different from many parts of our world today: a white dominant class which lorded it over a dominated majority of people of colour.[4] Martin's father, like so many of his time, was caught in a cycle of institutional violence, the violence of *la conquista*. No matter what he may or may not have felt for Ana Velásquez and their two children, he was a white Spanish gentleman and they were black. Martin was categorized, in the parlance of sixteenth century Peru, as a *mulato*, a child of Spanish and African parents. When Martin was nine or ten years old it seems his father did finally acknowledge some responsibility in raising his dark-skinned son, and took him for two years of schooling to Guayaquil, Ecuador. Was this his way of easing his own guilt – in a place comfortably far away from Lima's political status quo? Or did he truly attempt in those two years to heal the wounds left in Martin by his own parental neglect?

Today most Latin Americans are *mestizos*, people of mixed racial and cultural identity. Although this *mestizaje* is celebrated as a gift and source of cultural pride, as powerfully symbolized in the icon of the Virgin of Guadalupe, it is important to remember that the continent's *mestizaje* finds its roots in the concubinage and rape that were not uncommon in the colonial period. As a young boy Martin often would have been the object of jokes and discriminatory remarks, being called at times 'bastard' or '*perro mulato*' (mulatto dog). Racism, and its accom-

---

4. It is estimated that in the year of Martin's birth, 1579, there were about 4,000 African slaves in Lima. In 1614, Martin's thirty-fifth year, Lima had a population of a little more than 25,000 inhabitants. 10,386 of these were Africans and 744 mulattos – counting for almost half of the city's population. See, Zevallos, *Rosa de Lima*, pp. 32-27. For more information on the African heritage of Martin de Porres see Bruce Schultz, O.P., *Retrieving the African Roots of St Martin de Porres* (forthcoming).

panying machismo, linger on today in the peoples of Latin America, a toxic residue left in the wake of the conquest and its clash of cultures.

Peru's most important religious devotion, even to this day, centres on an image of Christ Crucified, known as the Lord of the Miracles. The dating of the image, which was originally painted on a wall in Lima and popular mostly among Lima's African descendents, is uncertain, but what is known is that it survived being destroyed in an earthquake in 1655, sixteen years after Martin's death. It was this miracle of divine protection that transformed the image of the Señor de los Milagros into a universally sacred symbol in the rapidly growing capital city.

Though we have no way of knowing for sure, we can at least imagine young Martin running to the Señor de los Milagros for consolation and guidance during his early years. We know that Martin learned early on, as he struggled with his own experience of neglect, abandonment and racial discrimination, to place his trust in God. He had a special devotion to the Crucified Christ, a devotion common in the Latin culture of his times. For the poor of Latin America, the image of the Crucified Christ is not a depressing or despairing image. Quite the contrary. For a people who know so deeply the crucifixion of daily oppression and the struggle for survival in a cultural and economic chess-game that leaves them sidelined as mere spectators, the blood running down the knees and back and face of the tortured Christ is a healing balm of incarnate hope. As with so many of his time and ours, Martin would have looked into the wounds of the Crucified Christ and heard from within the words, 'Be not afraid. I am with you.' Perhaps it was there, kneeling in silent veneration of the Señor de los Milagros, in the midst of Peru's social and racial upheaval, that Martin learned to recognize in the outstretched arms of Christ the all-embracing love of God. It was the experience of the divine embrace that allowed Martin to look within himself and discover the *imago Dei*, reflected in his own African soul and Latin heart. There, deep within his own inner sanctuary, he was able to contemplate the beautiful mosaic of God's handiwork.

Martin's awakening to the universality of God's love (see Galatians 3:28) serves as a signpost for the racial, ethnic and civil rights, struggles which have shaped our world in the past century. More than four centuries later we, too, have witnessed the devastation wrought in our world by hatred and violence. From Burundi to Kosovo, from East Timor to the clandestine graves of Guatemala, we cannot hide from the truth that our world today is still being crucified because of skin colour, cultural, ethnic and religious identity. In his own quiet way Martin de Porres prepared the way for the prophecy of another Martin, Martin Luther King, Jr, whose voice continues to echo across the globe in a clarion call for racial justice and true respect for human dignity and diversity. In 1963, one year after Martin de Porres was declared a saint and the patron of social justice, the other Martin spoke these words in front of the Lincoln Memorial in Washington, D.C.

> I have a dream that my four little children will one day live in a nation where they will not be judged by the colour of their skin, but by the content of their character ... With this faith we will be able to hew out of the mountain of despair a stone of hope. With this faith we shall be able to transform the jangling discords of our nation [world] into a beautiful symphony of harmony.[5]

Both Martins keep that dream alive before us today. Now it is our turn to live that dream into reality.

BIBLIOGRAPHY

Stanislas Fumet, *San Martín de Porres*, 1983, Buenos Aires, Carlos Lohlé.

Martin Luther King, Jr., 'I Have a Dream', *Ebony*, January 1986).

Antonio Mingote, with Emilio Lapayese and José María Sánchez-Silva, *Fray Escoba*, 1995, Palencia: MYR Ediciones.

Brian J. Pierce, 'San Martín de Porres: Apóstol del Amor Incondicional de Dios', awaiting publication in *Nuestra Iglesia*,

---

5. Taken from Martin Luther King Jr, speech 'I Have a Dream', 28 August 1963 in Washington, D.C. Cited from *Ebony* magazine, January 1986, p. 42.

2001, Managua: Editorial Lascasiana.

Oscar A. Romero, *The Church Is All of You: Thoughts of Archbishop Oscar Romero,* ed. James R. Brockman, SJ, 1984, Minneapolis: Winston Press.

Bruce B. Schultz, *Retrieving the African Roots of San Martín de Porras,* awaiting publication.

Noé Zevallos, Rosa de Lima, *Compromiso y Contemplación,* 1988, Lima: CEP.

8

Dominican Concern
for Social Justice in
Colonial and Post-colonial Africa

PHILIPPE DENIS, O.P.

The phrase 'justice and peace' is recent in the history of the Dominican Order in Africa, as it is in the rest of the world. The first inter-African promoter for justice and peace – Sidbe Sempore, a friar from West Africa – was appointed in 1980. Since then various initiatives were taken under the banner of justice and peace, particularly in South Africa. The concern for social justice is, of course, older. The institutionalisation of justice and peace only helped to increase the awareness of the brethren, while putting some financial resources at the disposal of those who wanted to promote specific social or cultural projects.

THE PORTUGUESE DOMINICANS UNDER THE *PADROADO* SYSTEM

Signs of a Dominican presence are attested in sub-Saharan Africa as early as the sixteenth century in present-day Congo and Angola and along the Indian Ocean, on the eastern side of the continent. In both areas, the friars belonged to the Portuguese province. In the seventeenth century, the Portuguese friars manned no less than twenty-five mission stations in South-East Africa. They played a significant, if controversial, role at the court of the *munhumutapa*. Frei Miguel de Presentação, the son of a local chief, became the first black Dominican in sub-Saharan Africa in the mid seventeenth century. He spent most of his life in India, where he taught theology and served as a prior.

Were there any manifestations of a concern for social justice in those early days? At first glance the answer seems to be No. Under the *padroado* system, which prevailed in the Portuguese empire until the early nineteenth century, the responsibility for the mission entirely lay in the king's hands. All missionaries, including the Dominican friars, were servants of the crown and preachers of the gospel at the same time. They were agents of the colonial enterprise. They had little understanding of the indigenous culture and always identified with the Portuguese army in its wars against the local African kings. They resorted to trade and owned slaves, although not as the same scale as the Jesuits who ran some of the biggest *prazos* of the Zambezi area.

In an age which values inculturation and economic development, these missionary methods may sound strange, if not shocking. Yet, when researching on the history of the Dominican friars in Southern Africa, I found that a least one friar – Miguel Range, the vicar general of the Dominican congregation of the Eastern Indies, under which fell the South-Eastern African mission – showed concern for social justice. In a report sent to the newly-founded Congregation for the Propagation of the Faith in September 1623, he expressed in unambiguous terms the opinion that the slave trade, because of its moral injustice, was one of the main obstacles to evangelization. The slave trade, he argued, could only provide arguments for the enemies of the faith, not to mention the English and the Dutch Protestants who tried to make conversions by promising the natives they would treat them better than the Portuguese. 'I know that these things are under the responsibility of the Catholic king,' Rangel wrote, 'but there is nobody who refers them to him. People only think of their own profit. They do not care about God, the church and the king. It is crucial that the holy church of God does not allow this situation. It is her duty to warn and instruct the faithful, and particularly those who play the main role in the conversion and salvation of the souls.'[1] Rangel did not mention specifically South East Africa in his discussion of slavery. But we know that the slave trade was widespread in the Munhumutapa empire as well as in Mozambique and that many priests, including Dominicans, were slave owners.

1. Miguel Rangel, *Memoriale de Rebus Fidei Catholici Indiae Orientalis*, quoted in Philippe Denis, *The Dominican Friars in Southern Africa. A Social History (1577-1990)*, (Leiden, Brill, 1998), p. 34.

The last Portuguese Dominican left Congo in the 1610s. In South-East Africa their presence continued interruptedly until 1834. We should also mention the French Dominicans' short-lived mission to Guinea in the late seventeenth century. The overall picture of the Dominican missionary endeavours in the early modern period is rather depressing. Hardly anything survived from the work of evangelisation accomplished in this period. Many friars were found guilty of moral misconduct and pastoral neglect. The documentation for the period, however, is fragmentary. There may have been other instances of genuine social concern, but they are not recorded in the sources.

THE AMBIGUITIES OF THE COLONIAL ENTERPRISE

By and large the friars were absent from Africa in the nineteenth century. The same cannot be said of the sisters, who came to South Africa and Rhodesia in great numbers. But this is another story. The most significant Dominican figure during this period is Bishop Raymond Griffith, an Irish friar who was chosen by the Congregation for the Propagation of the Faith to become the first bishop of the Cape vicariate in 1837. He died in 1862. He too was influenced by the prejudices of his times. He was a colonist at heart, politically conservative. Pseudo-scientific anthropological theories, which were nothing short of racism, dominated his thinking. With the then current pre-Darwinian literature he described the Khoikhoi as the connecting link between man and beast.

Later in his episcopal career, however, Griffith had the honesty and intelligence to acknowledge his errors of judgment. In a later entry of his diary, he expressed doubt about the theory of racial inequality.[2] His visit to the Xhosa chief Maqoma had a lasting impact on him. He was forced to admit that the chief's prayer was genuine, even if did not fit Christian categories. He then wrote about the need to establish non-racial schools in Stellenbosch, an area dominated by the Dutch settlers. It would be an abuse of language to describe Griffith as

2. J.B. Brain, ed., *The Cape Diary of Bishop Griffith for the Years 1837 to 1839* (Mariannhill: Mariannhill Press, 1988), p. 186. See Denis, *The Dominican friars*, p. 91-99.

a proponent of justice and peace. He never questioned the value of the colonial system. But at least he was open to challenge. This deserves to be recorded.

It had been Griffith's wish, at one point, to establish a Dominican community at the Cape. This project never materialised. Shortly after his death, a group of Irish Dominican sisters came to the Cape Colony, soon followed by a party of German sisters. The friars only arrived in Africa fifty years later. During the first half of the century, their presence was limited to two countries: Congo, and more specifically the Eastern Uele vicariate (later Niagara diocese), where the Belgian Dominicans established a mission in 1912, and South Africa, where the English and Dutch friars arrived in 1917 and 1932 respectively.

Like nearly all missionaries at the time, the Belgian Dominicans worked in close cooperation with the colonial government. With the help of the Dominicans sisters, they became involved in various social and cultural activities. They established, in particular, several vocational schools. None of these ministries, however, can be regarded as justice and peace work, to use today's categories. In 1964 thirteen friars and nine sisters, together with four Comboni fathers from Verona, Italy, were killed by a group of rebels in the diocese of Niangara.[3] The martyrdom of these Dominican and Comboni missionaries was the result of a troubled post-independence situation. It that sense it was an issue of justice and peace. This being said, all the victims were pastoral workers. They were not massacred because of a particular political or social stance.

The first English Dominicans were given parishes on the East Rand, in Natal, and in the Western Transvaal. In their correspondence with the English Provincial some of them distanced themselves from the 'colour bar' system. But they stopped short of criticising the government. A similar political neutrality characterised the first Dutch friars in the Orange Free State. In the late 1930s two English Dominicans, Finbar Synnott and Oliver Clark, developed a particular interest in the 'native question'. They pleaded for a more humane treatment of the

---

3. *Getuigen in Leven and Dood. Bisdom Niangara, Uele-Kongo 1964-1965.* Supplement to *Dominikaans Leven*, Gent, 1965.

black workers and expressed concern about the discriminatory practices at work in the Dominican parishes on the Rand. They reacted, however, as white liberals. Neither of them ever questioned the programme of racial domination which was gradually becoming entrenched in the Union of South Africa

CONFRONTING APARTHEID

The South African Dominicans eventually took a stand, individually and collectively, against the regime. What is striking, though, when one looks at the forty-year long history of their relationship to apartheid,[4] is how belated and ambiguous their 'conversion' to social justice was.

Their initial reaction to the National Party's electoral victory in May 1948 was in many ways short-sighted. Rather than looking at the impact of the announced programme of apartheid on South African society, they expressed concern for the restrictions that the government might impose on the immigration of missionaries from England or Holland. In the early 1950s several friars wrote on race relations, but they failed to condemn apartheid outright as if the new regime had to be given a chance. *Die Brug,* a magazine run by the Dutch Dominicans, maintained this position as late as 1967 – long after the Catholic bishops had declared apartheid 'intrinsically evil' in a widely publicised statement.

The first signs of a new attitude came in the mid 1960s in the wake of the foundation of the Christian Institute, the first Christian organisation in South African history to mobilise grassroots support against the government's racial policies. In 1964, while accepting that separate seminaries for blacks and whites were inevitable, Oswin Magrath, the rector of St Peter's Seminary, criticised the Church's complacency in racial matters and expressed sympathy for Africanism and nationalism. At St Nicholas' Priory, Stellenbosch, students and staff adopted a more militant mood under the influence of organisations like the National Catholic Federation of Students, the University Christian Movement and the Christian Institute. In 1968 they

4. On the South African Dominicans and apartheid, see Denis, *The Dominican Friars,* pp. 238-291.

assisted a group of coloured people forcibly removed from a nearby settlement. Around 1970 no fewer than four European-born friars were expelled from the country or barred from re-entry for having taken a stand against apartheid. The first of them, Rob van der Hart, was one of the eighteen members of the theological commission set up by the South African Council of Churches and the Christian Institute in 1968 to produce what would become the *Message to the Christian People of South Africa*. At St Peter's Seminary, Hammanskraal, race relations were openly debated, not without tensions among the Dominican lecturers who differed on how to respond to Black Conscious-ness-related student unrest. But all agreed to letting SASO, the student movement founded by Steve Biko, make use of St Peter's Conference Centre.

After the Soweto uprising in 1976 the majority of South African English-speaking Churches gradually developed a more critical attitude towards the apartheid government. Under the leadership of Albert Nolan who was elected provincial in 1976, the Dominicans constituted one of the more militant groups in the Catholic Church. In 1979 the vicariate's headquarters were transferred to Mayfair in a working class district of Johannes-burg. Nolan played in a significant role in the foundation and the development of the Institute for Contextual Theology, an ecumenical organisation which aimed to 'to do theology quite explicitly and consciously from within the context of real life in South Africa'.[5] He was one of the main writers of the *Kairos Document*, a theological manifesto calling for a more active commitment of the Church in the struggle against apartheid.

In one way or another almost all the friars were affected by the political crisis affecting the country, particularly after the declaration of the second state of emergency in 1986. Some of them were arrested and one had to go into hiding. The Domini-can headquarters and several other houses were raided by the security police.

---

5. Quoted in Larry Kaufman, *Contextual Theology in South Africa. An analysis of the Institute for Contextual Theology, 1981-1994*, unpublished PhD thesis, Pontificia Universitas Lateranensis, Rome, 1997, p. 15.

THE CHALLENGES OF POST-COLONIAL AFRICA

There are currently nine (male) Dominican entities in sub-Saharan Africa. All but two (South Africa and Congo) were established after the Second World War.[6] Compared to well established missionary congregations like the Spiritans, the White Fathers or the Oblates of Mary Immaculate, the Dominicans are late comers on the missionary scene. Yet they are evenly spread on the African continent. They contribute in many significant ways to the development of the local Church. This includes the field of justice and peace.

Four of the new foundations predated independence. The province of St Albert's in the United States established a mission in Lagos, Nigeria, in 1951. A group of friars from the province of Lyons arrived in Dakar, Senegal, in June 1955. They later expanded to Abidjan and Cotonou. Another group from the French (Paris) province started a community in the later months of 1955 in Douala, Cameroun. A team of Swiss Dominicans came to Bukavu, Congo, in August 1959. They were followed, in January 1960, by a group of Canadians friars, who established a community in nearby Butare, Rwanda. The Swiss Dominicans left Bukavu in 1966 to help their Canadian confreres to run the university of Butare.

During the pre-independence period it was probably in Dakar that the Dominicans showed the greatest concern for social justice and cultural development. Several friars were involved in Catholic Action movements. In 1957 a member of the Lyons-based *Economie et Humanisme* development institute, Victor Martin, arrived in Dakar to conduct a socio-religious survey of the city. In December of the same year, the founder of *Economie et Humanisme*, Louis-Joseph Lebret, delivered a paper on 'the conditions and requirements of a new civilisation' in the newly-established Dominican cultural centre. In 1960 Lebret handed over to Mamadou Dia, the President of the Council of Senegal, a triennial development plan drafted by *Economie et Humanisme*.[7]

6. On the Dominicans in Africa, see Philippe Denis, ed., *Histoire des dominicains en Afrique*, Paris, Cerf (forthcoming).

7. Gilles Soglo, 'Les dominicains en Afrique de l'Ouest (1954-1991', in Denis, ed., *Histoire des dominicains en Afrique*, chapter 7.

In 1963, the year of Kenya's independence, a group of American friars from the Eastern province arrived in Nairobi to run the national seminary for Kenya. Due to a disagreement with the bishops' conference, however, they left the country in 1969. They came back in 1985 and are currently involved in a variety of ministries in the country.

Several friars from Portugal came to Angola in 1982, resuming a century-old tradition of Dominican presence in Africa which had been interrupted in 1834. They established their first house in Waku-Kongo. Lastly we should mention the Dominicans from the Toulouse province in France who went to Reunion in the Indian Ocean in 1993 and are now in the process of opening a new house in Madagascar.

It is impossible to list all the justice and peace-related initiatives of the friars (not to mention the sisters) in post-colonial Africa. Three at least should be mentioned by name: the Songhai Project, an agrobiological development scheme in Porto Novo, Benin; Akagura, a street children organisation with a very innovative rurally-based training component, in Bujumbura and Makebuko, Burundi; and the Mosaiko Cultural Centre in Loanda, Angola, a training and research centre focussing on issues of social justice and development. Many friars are involved in less prominent but equally meaningful acts of solidarity: offering bursaries to needy children, helping a local community to resist corruption, rehabilitating alcoholics, educating women and assisting in the fight against HIV/AIDS, just to name a few.

Four countries where the Dominicans are present – Angola, Congo, Rwanda and Burundi – have been, and still are, involved in civil wars. For the friars concerned this constitutes a serious challenge, particularly when the issues causing conflict divide the Dominican communities themselves. Preaching, teaching and doing theology are crucially important in a context of war and ethnic division. It often requires courage. A new generation of African Dominicans is emerging. In matters of justice, peace and development, a daunting task is awaiting them.

9

Pro Foco Non Foro [1]

The Thomist Inheritance
and the Household Economy
of Father Vincent McNabb

HUGH WALTERS

Social justice, which treats the common good as a purpose of action, and brings all the virtues into our relationships with others, is not the only requirement of living in society, but some understanding of it is fundamental, both to liberal societies and to those of a more ancient stamp. Social justice incorporates the question of distribution of wealth, of how to deal with possessions, property, things.

The Church has recently uncovered the role of the laity in her understanding of the Christian life, and this aspect of social justice can perhaps be regarded as especially the province of lay people, who deal with the world of 'ordinary life': the life of production and reproduction, of work and family. It is not unreasonable to regard these aspects as central to modem life and indeed to Christian spirituality and philosophy. 'For instance, my sense of myself as a householder, father of a family, holding down a job, providing for my dependents; all this can be the basis of my sense of dignity.'[2] These call in different degrees and ways upon the ancient virtues of good sense or doing things well (*prudentia*), and art, or the skill of making things well (*recta ratio factibilium*).

How then might one conduct these aspects in the manner of a distinctively Christian calling? For the large number of middle class Catholics, this is the challenge of a vocation in the world,

1. '*Pro Foco Non Foro Agri Colendi*' was the Latin tag on Fr McNabb's headstone, arguing even in death that the hearth and not the market place was the reason to cultivate the fields.
2. C. Taylor, *Sources of the Self*, Cambridge University Press, 1989, p. 15

of the salvation of suburbia, of the holiness of married life and work.

The thought of Fr Vincent McNabb, the Guild of St Joseph and St Dominic, and Distributism should be included in this series because they are, quite simply, the most startling Catholic examples, in Britain this century, of the possibilities of ordinary life being thought about and lived in an extraordinary way.

Fr Vincent McNabb (1868–1943), who spent most of his preaching life urging the crowds of 'Babylondon' to return to the fields and the Catholic religion, was a champion of the household economy. A controversial figure, he lived as though he was still in the age of St Dominic, with a certain degree of exhibitionism, walking everywhere in his hobnail boots and homespun habit, keeping only the Scriptures and St Thomas next to his unslept-in bed in his room, which he swept with his hand. Eccentric he appeared to be, prophetic he may have been, but many people loved him, and at least revered and respected him; he was certainly a first-rate preacher.

Although ultimately it was his profession as a Dominican priest for which he should perhaps be remembered, he himself was animated equally by an amateur love of the land. In his collection of essays, *The Church and the Land* (1926), he begins by referring to the crisis in the fortunes of the Church – 'because the economic centre of gravity had become displaced by a subtle avarice which was endeavouring to serve God and Mammon.' This was the problem of the industrial town and led to what he called 'race suicide' by which he meant birth control, but which could equally well be extended in our day to more brutal methods of causing a declining population. In his view this was the consequence of the failure of industrialism and, as such, economics called forth the mystic – put simply, the industrial town was bad for the Catholic faith. He saw an apostolic duty to set forth the facts about this because he followed Pope Leo XIII in *Rerum Novarum* who declared: 'Every minister of holy religion must bring to the struggle the full energy of his mind and all his powers of endurance.' And the programme demanding this energy of mind and power of endurance was outlined in these simple words: 'The law should therefore favour ownership and its policy should be to induce as many as possible to become owners.' Thereafter, in language echoed by Latin American theologians, he talked of Exodus and exodus from Babylondon on Thames to the fields of England, a religious exodus to repopulate the deserted brown earth with the unemployed masses, to recreate Nazareth or Bethlehem where Christ learned a craft and lived in a family. 'Leave the garden cities and the flesh pots, not in order to scorn suburbia or to lead a simple life, but to worship God'.[3]

McNabb regarded the first few years of the community of the Third Order and the Guild of St Joseph and St Dominic at Ditchling Common as the closest thing to the embodiment of this ideal. The Guild was a fraternity of craftsmen and their families, begun in 1913. Starting as a non-religious exodus on a familial level by the Gills, it grew just before the war into the Guild, based on the life of the Dominican Third Order, and on self-sufficient principles, or, as Gill saw it, normal life before industrialism, in the Sussex countryside at Ditchling Common. Behind it lay the critique of industrial society of Distributism and the characters of G.K. Chesterton and Hilaire Belloc. The trio of personalities, Eric Gill, Fr Vincent McNabb and Hilary Pepler, created the spark that gave life to the experiment, a radical vision of land and hand work.

Hilary Pepler was a most remarkable man who turned his hand to many different occupations. Businessman, surveyor, one of the first social workers and organiser of meals for children in London County Council schools, author, printer, puppeteer, amateur actor and mime artist, Pepler moved to Ditchling in 1915 from the artistic and bohemian setting of Hammersmith where he had met Eric Gill and Edward Johnston the calligrapher, who both moved to Ditchling in 1907. Gill was perhaps looking for the basics in life and art, and found something of them in the country and Catholicism. In 1916 Pepler was taken by Gill to the Dominican priory of Hawkesyard

3. V. McNabb OP. *The Church and the Land* (London, 1926) Chapter 1, 'A Call to Contemplatives'.

in Staffordshire, a place where he hoped to discuss religion freely.

Gill had already met McNabb at the house of André Raffalovitch in Edinburgh, and struck up a fruitful exchange of views. McNabb baptised Pepler that same year and Pepler joined the Third Order soon afterwards, renaming his press St Dominic's Press. The Ditchling thing became a Catholic thing and in 1920 the two men, Gill and Pepler, who had moved to Ditchling Common, formed the Guild of St Joseph and St Dominic: a fraternity of craftsmen holding that 'the principle of individual human responsibility being a fundamental of Catholic doctrine, and this principle involving the principles of ownership, workmen should own their tools, their workshops and the product of their work.'[4]

The influence of these percolated down to E.F. Schumacher and Barbara Ward, who took the practical wisdom to a wider world; and there is a resonance and direct links with the *Catholic Worker* of Dorothy Day and Peter Maurin in the United States. Maurin borrowed much from McNabb with his thoughts on cult, culture and cultivation, his ideal of 'agronomic universities'. The looming ecological fears of the current generation strike a similar chord and the discussion of communitarian politics and the common good cannot ignore the understanding of virtue and excellence in making and doing that is the legacy of Thomism.

Distributism was and is controversial because it attracted some of the greatest Catholic minds of a generation in what many, both then and now, would regard as a futile exercise in 'poetry and preachment'[5] taking able Catholics away from parliamentary politics and ambition, scuppering more middle-of-the-road attempts to influence the Catholic population such as those of the Catholic Social Guild. It also attracted the contempt of those who turned to the Left in the 60s, partly because of its very real authoritarian (in some cases fascist) leanings, and its then unfashionable ultramontanist strain. It is

4. Brocard Sewell, *Like Black Swans*, p. 141
5. R. Neuhaus, *First Things* 52, April 1995 pp. 56–68

hard now to assess these criticisms. *Slant* is part of the Domini-can archives and not a lot else. State communism is of historical interest. It too is a failed experiment. (In 1990 the Supreme Soviet of the USSR as it then was, approved a law authorizing private ownership of the means of production, so abolishing the state's virtual monopoly.) The trades union movement is a muted voice, largely undermined by reasonable material stand-ards of living and the increasingly undifferentiated mass of consumers and producers that the nineteen-eighties produced.

The movement called communitarian-ism is perhaps the closest to anything resembling a challenge to the current ortho-doxy of liberal economics and polity, reinstating the notions of common good, subsidiarity and notions of the self embedded in communities and traditions. This is far closer to the views of Chesterton and company than their critics, and perhaps even more rhetorical and less specific in remedies than the Dis-tributists.

How are we to understand Distributism then? Since it can be regarded as applied Thomism this essay proposes to return *ad fontes*, to the thoughts of St Thomas on property which is where the Distributists claimed to find some of their inspiration, filtered through *Rerum Novarum*, and to place the movement in a broad historical context of thought about property.

When St Thomas analyses property in the *Commentary on the Sentences*, the *Summa Contra Gentiles*, his lectures on Aristotle and the *Summa Theologiae*, he is not talking of the early communal apostolic life of the early Church which could still be found in religious life. He is talking of ordinary ownership, and borrows his main line of thought from Aristotle's *Politics*.[6] The key texts in the *Summa Theologiae* are contained in q. 66 of the *Secunda-Secundae*, where he is discussing theft and robbery. Property is essentially about things (*res*), not, as later for Locke, ourselves, our life and our liberty as well as our possessions. Property involves ownership or control (*dominium*). This can be divided up into managing or taking care of them and distributing them (*potestas procurandi et dispensandi*) on the one hand, but also the

6. Aristotle *Politics* Bk II Ch 5, tr. A. Sinclair, Harmondsworth 1962, pp. 62–66.

use of things. Thomas does not in fact discuss quite how property is acquired – a lacuna leading to much diversion in later thought. The basic reason why this ownership is appropriate is argued from Genesis 1: the dominion given over the creation.

The main problem, though, is that of private property (*propriam possidere*): with what justification can someone come to appropriate for themselves what is common to all, or at least open to be appropriated by all? Thomas argues that private property is both permitted and necessary. The reasons for this are common sense ones, given human nature as it is: that everyone is more concerned to acquire their own things rather than what is common; common tasks will belong to everyone and no one; that it is simply more efficient and better organised to run one's own affairs, and finally that there is less to quarrel about. He claims that it is what is jointly owned that is the basis of the most frequent disputes. Here he was running up against the radical tradition of the Church Fathers, who by and large saw private property as the basis of disputes. To incorporate this tradition, Thomas in his next paragraph seems to take back what he said, in discussing the use of things as opposed to their management.[7] In this regard things are not held as private property but *ut communes* – as common, for the common good, the whole community. In need each should readily share with others. He quotes 1 Timothy, that the rich should give easily and communicate their wealth to others.

Private property for Thomas is an extension of the natural law, part of human law, made by agreement, a device of human reason. It has been claimed, not without some justification, that the history of natural law (particularly that to do with property) is 'an attempt to rearrange the elements of the puzzle left by Aquinas.'[8] The reason for this is the difficulty of reconciling the

7. See J. Finnis, *Aquinas*, Oxford University Press 1998, p. 190. I am thoroughly indebted to this fine book.
8. See I.Hont and M. Ignatieff, 'Needs and Justice in the *Wealth of Nations:* an Introductory Essay', in *Wealth and Virtue: The Shaping of the Political Economy in the Scottish Enlightenment* ed. Hont and Ignatieff, Cambridge University Press, 1983, p.27

very idea of private property (with its concomitant idea of developing the resources of the earth) with the ability of those in need to have prior claim to it. What in fact does private property amount to?

The limits of property rights clarify the rhetorical flourishes of those who wanted to abolish the distinction of mine and thine. Here Thomas relies on the discussion of almsgiving or charity (*eleemosyna*) to declare what became traditional teaching: some resources are essential for the survival of oneself and one's household; some are necessary to one's state of life and business affairs, or paying debts. These can be called absolute and relative necessity. Finally there are *superflua*, or luxuries. What should be done in justice with each of these elements of one's own belongings?

In times of extreme need, 'for anyone in that condition, all resources become common resources'.[9] There is no theft morally: people in this condition are simply taking from the common stock. They are entitled to do so. Likewise those who have what is necessary for one's state in life or *superflua* are under a duty in strict justice to help those whose need they are aware of Where there is dire need all around, the individual must judge what is best under the guidance of good sense. When there is no famine the rich ought by natural right to sustain the poor who do not have enough for a decent life out of their *superflua:* these are also held in common. Quite what is relatively necessary and what is superfluous is left up to individual judgement, a true judgement unswayed by consumerism, as we would say today. Yet, as Finnis says, for the distribution of *superflua* legislation is appropriate.[10]

Two very important points arise out of this discussion of property. Distributive justice, what is owed to the poor in strict justice, is a matter for every owner, every householder. It is not primarily a matter for the state, contrary to our modern assumptions. Ownership is a good thing, limiting the power of the state and giving the rich the opportunity to give of their abundance

9. J. Finnis, *op. cit.,* p.191
10. *ibid.* p.195

both in justice and in charity. The second point is that Thomas says quite clearly that a man cannot have more than enough without another having less than enough (II–II 118 a.1 ad 2). Finnis emphasises that even though economics is not a zero sum game, Thomas is still right to say this: 'For if we set aside the possible world in which everyone everywhere has enough to meet all their needs, *superflua* truly belong to others; anyone who keeps them is depriving, and indeed stealing from those to whom they should by one means or another have been made available.'[11] The thoughts of St Thomas are taken up with clarity by McNabb who wrote: 'Study not merely to give God his due by worship but to give man his due by justice. What is superfluous to your poor estate distribute. This is distributive charity; a virtue so sacred that crimes against it are the forerunners of inevitable doom'.[12]

After St Thomas, the subsequent history of these ideas follows a fascinating path. In Cajetan, it seems, justice becomes discussed under a threefold scheme of legal, distributive and commutative justice, where distributive justice becomes equated with the state's duty to the individual citizen, surreptitiously taking away the responsibilities of distributive justice from the ordinary household owner.[13] In Grotius an historical picture of the two 'competences' of Thomas was drawn: common ownership was only a short point in a simple and innocent life; private property came into existence as needs became more complex and property became a full and perfect right after a compact or agreement. In times of necessity this reverted to the original common ownership.[14] Property, he claimed, in a major redefinition of language, should only be applied to this sort of exclusive dominion over things. For Grotius also these property rights were expletive or perfect, capable of being guarded by legal justice, by law. Distributive justice was about compassion, generosity and foresight in matters of government.

11. *ibid.* p.196
12. McNabb OP., *op. cit.*, p.5
13. See Finnis, op. cit. p.217, note a, with references to Finnis, 1980.
14. Hont and Ignatieff, op. cit. p.28–29

The distinctive feature of Grotian jurisprudence lay in so reducing the scope of distributive justice that the right of theft in necessity or the right to buy grain at a fair price were theorized as exceptions rather than as rules as they had been in Thomist jurisprudence.[15]

The notion of right lay with the owners. This goes hand in hand with a shift to the language of rights rather than what is due in a relationship between people in regard to some thing: a shift towards the beneficiaries of relationship of justice. Legal justice was simply and rather confusingly general or social justice in Aristotle and Aquinas; by the time of Grotius the law had became equated with legal justice and came to underline property rights or exclusive dominion. All else was imperfect rights, as in Grotius, of the poor, or imperfect obligations of the rich as in Pufendorf.

What this later tradition signally failed to endorse was the demands of distributive justice either by the householder (Cajetan's followers), or by the law of the state (Grotius), or even the obligations in strict justice to care for the poor: in Pufendorf this was an imperfect obligation. By the time of David Hume justice has become associated almost entirely with the defence of property: 'It is on the three laws of the stability of possession, its transference by consent, and the performance of promises "that the peace and security of human society entirely depend."'[16] Justice is nothing other than rights to protect these, established by human convention. In Locke's thought the labour of the industrious and rational could be protected by laws of property.

The stage is thus set for the revolution described by Adam Smith. Smith is the harbinger of the commercial, market society with its division of labour and industrial capitalism. It has been claimed that the desire to reconcile the time-honoured paradox of the right to private property and the needs of the poor, occupies centre stage in the *Wealth of Nations*. Smith's answer to

15. ibid. p. 29
16. A.J.Ayer, *Hume*, Oxford University Press 1980

this, though, is through the market system: if scarcity could be overcome through the division of labour, it would not be necessary to choose between the claims of property and the needs of the poor. For Smith, justice, strictly speaking, was the enforcement of property rights: and in a market society nothing beyond this. Distribution of wealth, an imperfect obligation, a charitable action, could not be enforced at law.[17] In fact government and law were to protect the property owners who could raise productivity such that no one, not even the propertyless, would go hungry. This is what liberty was: the unhindered enjoyment of property rights that were productive.

This legitimation of accumulation under the rule of law, of an absolutizing of property rights, of the division of labour, clearly accompanied the growth of market capitalism. In theory the wage labourer would be better off than an African king; the practice produced Marxist socialism and a belated response from the Catholic Church under Leo XIII who saw with horror the factory system that destroyed the propertyless wage labourer and his family. It was out of this that Distributism was born.

Given this history since Thomas, it could be argued that Distributism and Ditchling were a real attempt to redress imbalances that had occurred in the understanding of distributive justice. First of all, distributive justice had come to be seen to refer to the role of the state, not the householder. Then any notion of distributive justice had reverted to private charity or benevolence in the face of a market society which emphasised the right to own productive wealth, and the belief in a market society that all would have enough. There was no need for redistribution in theory.

The Socialist answer was to restore the power of distribution to the state. The answer of Distributism was to transfer it back to the household (and, moreover, a productive household). Distributism did not have much place for the market belief that scarcity and consequently the problems of justice could be

17. Hont and Ignatieff, op. cit. pp. 24-5

solved by economic plenitude. This was a fantasy for St Thomas; it is a fantasy, full stop.[18] This perhaps is the major lesson to be learnt from the cries of the ecologists: that the earth itself cannot sustain the inroads of our way of life for much longer: the real world and real wealth is finite. There is not enough for everyone's greed.

The Distributist answer to industrialism as they termed the division of labour in a market society run on factories, had several strands. The most important principle however was termed 'The Restoration of Liberty by the Distribution of Property'. In this way they attacked monopoly or ownership in the hands of a few, and put forward individual ownership of any appropriate means of existence, including ownership of the means of production, credit and land. The most entertaining introduction, giving something of the style of the movement was that by Chesterton:

> [A] man felt happier, more dignified, and more like the image of God, when the hat he is wearing is his own hat; and not only his own hat, but his house, the ground he trod on and various other things. There might be people who preferred to have their hats leased out to them every week, or wear their neighbour's hats in rotation to express the idea of comradeship, or possibly to crowd under one very large hat to represent an even larger cosmic conception; but most of them felt that something was added to the dignity of men when they put on their own hats.[19]

At Ditchling each family led its own life, but the workshops, ideas and sense of worship drew them together. In describing the first days of the Guild of St Joseph and St Dominic on Ditchling Common Fiona MacCarthy writes:

> The seriousness of endeavour mixed with high spirited excitement at the novelty of things, almost a sense of daring,

18. See e.g. Hugh Wallers OP. 'The Monastic Ethic and the Spirit of Greenery' *New Blackfriars* March 1992 p. 177-187

19. J.P. Corrin, G.K. *Chesterton and Hilaire Belloc. The Battle against Modernity,* Ohio University Press, 1981 p. 107

comes over very strongly in the minutes of the early Tertiary meetings. It was a self consciously arduous programme. This saying of the office in public, systematically, by Tertiaries was in fact unusual. It has no equivalent in the history of the Dominicans in England. No one ever before, as far as one can see, lived a lay tertiary life with the commitment of Gill and Pepler's community at Ditchling.[20]

It is appropriate to look at the heart of the Ditchling community in this intense public recitation of the office, because from the perspective of suburbia it seems even more remarkable that a group of families should gather at such regular, positively monkish, times for prayer in common. Such recognition of worship as part of justice – justice towards God – betrays a distinctly Thomist inheritance.

Various nuances were added by the different characters who became associated with the ideal. McNabb looked upon Ditchling with the love he never gave a woman. He declared in his unpublished notes that 'we do not wish to go back to what is primitive but to what is primary.'[21] He was always concerned to put first things first. He felt the modem world had made an end out of what should only be the means. In this he shares the Church's mistrust of the pursuit of wealth for its own sake, a mistrust which goes back to St Thomas and beyond: economics is instrumental in the pursuit of the basic goods.

For McNabb these basic goods were a full family life lived by the hearth, close to the land, in praise of God. His understanding of the necessities of life involved poverty of work and thrift: wants must be measured by one's state in life. Poverty of work is the 'effective will to produce as much as possible of real wealth. By poverty of thrift is meant the effective will to consume as little as possible of real wealth ... If our hands provide more than is necessary for ourselves we must give to those who need it. These are not my ideas – they are the ideas of Christ.'[22] In the city was the shadow world of tokens, not things, money, not the

20. F. MacCarthy, *Eric Gill*, Faber and Faber 1989, p.
21. V. McNabb, O.P., Unpublished Notes in Dominican Archives. Edinburgh.
22. V. McNabb O.P. *Meditations on St John*, Aquin Press 1962. p. 40.

basic necessities, and 'the token nothings can excite an unsat-
isfied indefinite desire; which can at least fill the time if not the
heart of man'.[23] In the country the *superflua* of life were much
less evident; and *superflua* should be disregarded in the self-
sufficient voluntary poverty of the household which recycled its
envelopes (McNabb) or made its own custard from eggs (Gill).
Bethlehem and Nazareth, not Jerusalem; the hearth and home,
not the market with its machines; the land not the city.

Again, the roots of these thoughts can be found in Thomas:
'If the ultimate end were abundance of wealth, the economist
would be king'.[24] And this conception of the economics of the
household is far from irrational: 'Even if, unlike Aquinas, one
envisages economics as an understanding of capital formation,
production and consumption on a scale as wide as the political
community, if not of regional and world wide markets, Aquinas'
household-oriented conception of the basic human purpose of
economic activity can reasonably be sustained'.[25]

It is unclear quite exactly what has been lost when production moved beyond the household; whether it is a case of exile
and thoughts of return, whether there is always 'written in the
soul of suburban man, a home where he might discover his true
self.' Living in the suburbs of Manchester, a place which
McNabb did not want to make sanitary but impossible, I understand his sentiment but I rather think, with Dermot Quinn, that
the task is not to raze the suburbs but to raise them up.[26]
Although this too is poetry and preaching ...

McNabb eventually found Ditchling to be inadequately land-
based and this, along with his worries about the eroticism of
Gill's art, led to his disassociation from the place, in spite of
Pepler's best efforts. In the beginning, and in theory, however,
things were different. Gill's thought about work emphasised
the artful nature of work and the responsibility of the workman
to own the means of production, to become responsible as a

23. V. McNabb, O.P., *Nazareth or Social Chaos*, London, 1933, p. 20.
24. See Finnis, op. cit. p. 244 for this translation from the *de Regno*.
25. ibid.
26. D. Quinn, *The Chesterton Review* XXII Nos I and 2 February and May 1996
p. 34

maker. 'We are responsible persons, responsible for what we do and what we make. To what end is this doing and making? The greatest happiness of the greatest number, says the politician. my own greatest happiness and enjoyment says the individual ... 'that he may have something to give to him that suffers need' says the apostle; to share them without hesitation adds the Pope.'[27] Echoes of Thomas again – only this time arguing for a certain kind of economic freedom to make effective the Gospel of justice: the distributive charity, sacred virtue of McNabb, the good sense of the householder.

Gill believed that control of one's own work was an essential element of freedom for human dignity, and the recovery of the ancient pre-industrial alliance of beauty and usefulness in making things focused his talents as a stone mason, allowing him to strike the pose of the honest artisan. Indeed, both McNabb and Gill saw themselves as free workmen: In a preface to one of Gill's essays, McNabb showed his agreement with Gill: 'When a man is made a priest his hands are consecrated as the hands of an ergates – a workman (Mt 9:8) ... No craft in the world is at heart so free and so opposed to servile conditions as is the craft of the priest.' And Gill's even more startling clarion call to freedom in *Art Nonsense* declared: 'That State is a State of Slavery in which a man does what he likes to do in his spare time and in his working time that which is required of him. This State can only exist when what a man likes to do is to please Himself That State is a state of Freedom in which a man does what he likes to do in his working time and in his spare time that which is required of him. This State can only exist when what a man likes to do is to please God.'

The Thomist inheritance can be discerned in these ideas. For example, St Thomas had an understanding of servitude or serfdom. This involved the notion that it is a matter of human institution, not part of the natural law but a consequence of the Fall; however it is the service which is bought and sold: married life, being part of the natural law, still takes precedence, as do

27. E. Gill. 'Private Property', in *Essays*, London 1947. p. 34

other basic rights.[28] In Gill's view the factory worker was little
better than the *servus* of Thomas's day; indeed in some ways
worse off, because the mind of the worker has been corrupted
by the worship of money. 'The irresponsibility of the workman
is the first and simplest way in which to see our evil condition.
It is the first because the exercise of work is the formal reason
of individual appropriation.'[29]

In saying this Gill borrowed directly from Jacques Maritain's
Art and Scholasticism, the essential handbook for the Ditchling
community, originally translated as *The Philosophy of Art* by Fr
John O'Connor. Four hundred copies were published by St
Dominic's Press. In this book Maritain develops a Thomist
theory of making or art from the elements in St Thomas. There
is a property in making, thinks Maritain, because

> The work of art has been pondered before being made, has
> been kneaded and prepared, formed, brooded over, and
> matured in a mind before emerging into matter. And there
> it will always retain the colour and savour of the spirit. Its
> formal element, what constitutes it of its kind and makes it
> what it is, is its being controlled and directed by the mind..
> Artistic work therefore is specifically human work as opposed
> to the work of the beast or the machine; and for this reason
> human production is in its normal state an artisan's produc-
> tion, and therefore necessitates a strict individual appropria-
> tion. For the artist as such can share nothing in common; in
> the line of moral aspirations there must be a communal use
> of goods, whereas in the line of production the same goods
> must be objects of particular ownership. Between the two
> horns of this antinomy St. Thomas places the social prob-
> lem.[30]

This is Maritain's reading of the burden of the 'puzzle left by
Aquinas'. In Gill it becomes simply the right to ownership being

28. Finnis, op. cit. p. 184.
29. From *A Holy Tradition of Working,* an anthology of Gill's writings much to
be recommended, edited by B. Keeble, Golgonooza Press, Ipswich 1983, p. 124.
30. J. Maritain, *Art and Scholasticism*, London, 1930 p. 150.

a necessity, because 'only when there is full control of the means of production can there be proper and suitable manipulation ... unless I own the stone and my tools I cannot properly exercise my skill and intelligence as a stone carver. It is this necessity of manipulation which gives the right of property in the means of production'.[31] In other words, things are likely to be better made if they are made by workers who own their own means of production. Gill, in his vigorous way, sums up the difference between the realm of use and ownership by saying that in the realm of doing the sharing of use is primary, and in the realm of making the ownership is primary. He realises, though, as does McNabb, that ultimately the worker must submit to the demands of the common good; it is the giving not the making that is important, the exercise of charity, the practice of poverty: to give up, to go without, to praise God: art must give way to good sense in the realm of morality.

Gill writes, again and again, that the artist should be an honest workman 'making fitting furniture for a civilisation directed heavenwards.'[32] Holiness was beautiful, a holiness of imaginative making, forming products of knowledge and love, products of the mind of the artist and made by the hand, products which strike the whole man, body and soul. Thus even ordinary things can have the quality not only of use or serviceableness but of being pleasing to the eye and the mind. For the workman, 'Beauty comes to his work unasked when he works in a spirit of plain justice; when he considers simply the use of what he is making and the service of his fellows'.[33] Beauty is the reward of making well, with understanding and affection – it is difficult, thinks Gill, for factory made goods to exhibit charity, tenderness or sweetness, but they can still be pleasing to a degree in so far as they function well. Do they glorify God? Are they produced by responsible workmen? These questions remain. Ultimately, thinks Gill, the factory system rests on a separation of matter from spirit; industrialism tends towards

31. *A Holy Tradition*, p. 126.
32. ibid. p. 137.
33. ibid. p. 80.

death, the disintegration of the human personality in the pursuit of pleasure, leisure and an escape from the drudgery of routine in emotional thrills of high art or material comfort: 'no idea more noble or even more human than to have a good time'.[34]

What is striking about the whole Ditchling thing, whether browsing through the Dominican archives, or Fiona McCarthy's *Eric Gill*, or the writings of Vincent McNabb, is the quality of things that exert a pull on the imagination and senses. The description of Compline by candlelight in the kitchen at Hopkins Crank; the sharp conversations; the inherent logic at work in practice, from the New College Chapel war memorial, to the Stations at Westminster Cathedral:

> The body characterizes everything it touches. What it makes it traces over with the marks of its pulses and breathings, its excitements, hesitations, flaws and mistakes. On its good work it leaves the marks of skill, care and love persisting through hesitations, flaws and mistakes. And to those of us who love and honour the life of the body in this world, these marks are precious things, necessities of life.[35]

In this way the skill of the artist (worker, maker) and the good sense of the defender of the household meet. The claims of good sense or morality upon art, or making, find their focus in the question of the ownership and use of property, a windy crossroads through which the currents of tradition and the currents of the age continue to pass.

Ditchling was a community of a sort, of craftsmen held together to some extent by the force of the personalities but also by the Guild and the Third Order way of life. The life at Ditchling could not be sustained for long in its most fruitful phase. Gill's departure was something neither he nor the others really recovered from. Pepler tried to persevere with the self-suffi-

34. ibid. p. 138..

35. W. Berry, *What Are People For,* San Francisco, 1990 p. 194. See also A. Cunningham in *The Chesterton Review,* February and May, 1996, Special Issue on 'Fr. Vincent McNabb'.

ciency. However, McNabb's Luddite agrarianism, his antipathy to machines, his insistence on the land, was far from moderate: ultimately it was perhaps destructive of what was a focus for a group of talented craftsmen. Moreover, unlike the *Catholic Worker*, which is still going strong, there was no obvious outlet to the poor, no obvious way to practise the generosity McNabb himself practised in London.

In his elegiac way. Conrad Pepler, Dominican priest and son of Hilary Pepler, summed it up by saying that 'such community life necessarily sets itself up against the whole tendencies of the industrial society around it. So the effort to live out the ideal produces a very self-conscious set of men and women, and a highly developed self-consciousness necessarily breeds individualism if not eccentricities which militates against the nature of community life.'[36]

Yes, it was somehow puritanical; yes, Gill went seriously astray in his private life; yes, it was all amateur husbandry; yes, it was to a large extent poetry and preaching.[37] Yet, it might be asked,

36. Quoted in the stimulating essay on Conrad Pepler by Aidan Nichols, O.P., in *Dominican Gallery*, Gracewing, 1997, p. 361.

37. It continued in some form however until the 1980s. There were other figures who deserve more recognition than it has been possible to describe here, notably David Jones, Philip Hagreen and Valentine Kilbride. It is not prudish to say that Gill's obsession with sex was unfortunate – it is, at the least, unfortunate in any individual, or indeed culture. Art and Prudence: this distinction between making and doing finds its instantiation in the distinction between the work and the morality of the artist. In Gill's case one feels that perhaps he justified too much of his behaviour through this distinction, but it is there in Maritain in abundance, who states: 'Art in no wise tends to make the artist good in his specifically human conduct; ... as the artist is first a man and then an artist, it is easy to see what conflicts will rage in his heart between Art and Prudence, his character as Maker and his character as Man.' (Maritain, op. cit., pp. 14-15) He quotes Oscar Wilde: 'The fact of a man being a poisoner is nothing against his prose.' (ibid. p. 152) Only the saints can perhaps live well fully; but it is possible to see in Gill the difficulties of combining Art and Prudence, of not sacrificing his immortal substance to the devouring idol in his soul; and indeed to see how McNabb the Prudent man and Gill the Artist may have come into conflict (as did Pepler and Gill). Maritain makes it clear that Art aims a Beauty and in that way is independent of and metaphysically superior to Prudence: because it is more speculative and, following Aristotle, speculation is better than the moral life. 'It is difficult therefore for the Prudent Man and the Artist to understand one another. The Contemplative and the Artist on the other hand, both perfected by an intellectual habit binding them to the transcendental order, are in a position to sympathise.' (ibid., p. 85) Perhaps Gill could value McNabb the Contemplative

without Ditchling would Conrad Pepler have been the sort of character he was, running Spode House with a certain charm and manner? Would the contribution of the English Dominicans to Catholic life have made the same impact? Would Chesterton and Belloc have written with such verve about so much without this somewhat eccentric social theory of Distributism? Somehow I doubt it. And it is not wild or destructive. The household as a focus of distributive justice became progressively more obscured after Thomas had put forward his view that there were basically three sections of moral philosophy, relating to the individual (*monos*), the household (*domus*), the state (*perfecta communitas*), and expanded to include a locality or *vicus* in which to practise a trade.[38] The Distributists attempted to recover the centrality of the household in a very vivid way. This is still a task, for politicians, economists and anyone else who lives in suburbia. I shall let their memory trouble my thoughts.

---

and see his grandeur; likewise the Contemplative in McNabb could value Gill the Artist; but when Gill's art began to reflect his disturbed life, McNabb the Prudent Man could no longer find himself in sympathy. Perhaps this is to make the men too much the conveyors of metaphyseal ideas; but there is no doubt that they *were* animated by such things, part of a living tradition.

38. See Finnis op. cit., p.. 52, notes 1-6.

10

Stop War, Please

Dominicans and the Christian Peace Movement in England

VALERIE FLESSATI

'Enablers' was how Brian Wicker[1] described the Dominicans who provided a forum – whether at Spode House or in the pages of *New Blackfriars* – where radical Christian debate could flourish. 'Companions' is the word I would add to describe the role of Dominicans as they have accompanied Christian peace activists in the second half of the twentieth century. On that journey Dominicans have helped fellow pilgrims with their theological map-reading, and literally walked the same road, to Vézelay, Canterbury, Porton Down and Greenham Common.

PAX began in 1936 with the aim of 'resistance to modern warfare on grounds of traditional morality and principle'. Its founders had come to the conclusion that modern methods of warfare, with air attacks on civilians, violated the conditions for a 'just war' and that Catholics had the right, and even the duty, to refuse participation in future wars. This immediately set PAX on a path to confrontation with the hierarchy, whose attitude was conveyed in a letter from the Diocese of Westminster:

> The 'conscientious objector' has an erroneous conscience…
> He is entitled to respect and sympathy such as would be given
> to any misguided person … But error remains error … and
> no Catholic organisation may make it one of their purposes
> to support an attitude of conscientious objection which is at
> variance with Catholic teaching.[2]

As a result PAX could only continue its work by calling itself a society 'of Catholics and others' rather than a Catholic society.

1. See pp. 00-000, *infra.*
2. Letter from Valentine Elwes, Archbishop Hinsley's Private Secretary, to Hon. Secretary of PAX, 12 December 1936. PAX archives, London.

Loneliness was a common experience for Catholic conscientious objectors (COs) of the 1930s and 1940s. They often formed their convictions in isolation and thought they were the only Catholics who held them. Franz Jägerstätter in Berlin felt his burden of self-doubt lifted when he heard that the Pallotine, Fr Reinisch, had refused military service and suffered the death penalty before him. Gordon Zahn in the USA thought he was the only Catholic CO until he discovered the *Catholic Worker* and its civilian service camps. In England conscientious objectors were fortunate to discover Dominicans. Those who joined PAX often mentioned the German Dominican, Franziskus Stratmann, whose book *The Church and War* (1928) had reassured them that their attitude to war was morally valid. Gerald Vann had, from the outset, offered his support to PAX.[3] He wrote articles and pamphlets and addressed meetings. In 1937, no doubt having observed the problems encountered by PAX, he created the Union of Prayer for Peace as an orthodox Catholic association involving a promise to pray daily for peace which was taken up round the world, particularly in the schools run by Dominican sisters.

Gerald Vann's *Morality and War* (1939) became a bible for young men preparing for military tribunals. Manchester university student, John Heathcote, was one of them. With Vann's guidance and that provided by a *Catholic Herald* article[4] in which Victor White set out the limits to moral participation in the war, Heathcote was among the first to argue his case entirely on 'just war' principles – and to win noncombatant status. The absence of Catholic clergy appearing as witnesses at tribunals was noted by one judge in Leeds.[5] Through PAX Catholic COs found the few priests, including Vann, who would give evidence on their behalf. A PAX leaflet offering to put enquirers in touch with priests who could advise them was criticised by the Westminster diocesan censor:

It may well be that the 'priests' referred to are Dominicans, though to my knowledge they have not openly sponsored the

3. Letter from Gerald Vann to E.I. Watkin, 23 September 1936.
4. *Catholic Herald*, 12 May 1939.
5. *Yorkshire Evening News*, 13 June 1941.

movement under this name... I have recently had to refuse a nihil obstat to a book on war by Fr Vann OP which is vastly more moderate than Pax. The Provincial was annoyed since it had passed two Dominican censors ...[6]

In this difficult climate Dominicans helped COs to see their protest as a positive, and not just a negative contribution to society. In *Blackfriars* Vann wrote that in wartime society needed dissidents as well as conformists. The dissidents' way of serving their country was precisely not to participate: to create a new future by maintaining clear judgement, free of hatred, with the objective of a just peace always in view.[7] Conrad Pepler reflected further on 'The Part of a Pacifist' by suggesting that their task was to resist actively, concentrating on the positive work of charity which would heal the spiritual wounds of war. Theirs was a job of sowing rather than ploughing.[8]

In their thinking about social reform many PAX members were influenced by Distributism. Its most prominent advocate among them was Eric Gill, chairman of PAX in the last year of his life. They saw the roots of war in materialism and the profiteering of industrial capitalism. Pius XII was frequently quoted:

> In this age of mechanisation the human person becomes merely a more perfect tool in industrial production and ... a perfected tool for mechanised warfare.[9]

With Gill they believed that the solution lay in ordinary men and women embracing the things that made for peace, including poverty, and in creating 'a cell of good living in the chaos of our world'. A practical incentive was the need of COs to find alternative work on the land and many joined farming communities like the one established by Catholic families near the

6. Note from Canon E.J. Mahoney to Cardinal Hinsley, 20 July 1939. Westminster Diocesan Archives.

7. Gerald Vann, 'Patriotism and the Life of the State', *Blackfriars*, vol. XXI, no. 238, January 1940, pp. 16-32.

8. Conrad Pepler, 'The Part of a Pacifist', *Blackfriars*, vol. XXV no. 296, November 1944, pp. 401-405.

9. Pius XII, Address to the International Congress of Catholic Women's Leagues, April 1939.

Dominicans at Laxton.

Others felt that PAX was being diverted by an unrealistic search for a rural utopia. Its eccentric approach to modern life, contempt for industry and the state, and stormy relationship with the hierarchy, prevented PAX from attracting Catholics who might otherwise be sympathetic to its aims. What was needed was a respectable Catholic peace organisation backed by the Church. Gerald Vann was briefly involved, in 1944, with a new 'Society of the Peace of Christ', short-lived because it was no more successful than PAX in gaining episcopal support.[10]

However, in the last winter of the war a teacher in France called Marthe Dortel-Claudot started a prayer group which was soon endorsed by the Archbishop of Toulouse as the 'Pax Christi crusade of prayer for Germany' (later for 'all nations'). In 1946 Dortel-Claudot wrote to Cardinal Griffin. Pax Christi and the Benedictines were preparing a peace pilgrimage to Vézelay. Who might bring a cross from England? The Dominicans responded, and a band of thirty, mostly ex-servicemen, set out from St Dominic's Priory, London, in June 1946, on a gruelling three-week walk. The pilgrims prayed at wayside war memorials, shared the rations of local people, and their youthful chaplains, Simon Blake and Columba Ryan, sometimes preached six sermons a day.[11]

Two years after the Vézelay march some of its veterans organised a peace pilgrimage to Walsingham. But post-war peace activity was at a low ebb since people had returned to their studies and their jobs. A handful of committed PAX members kept the flame of peace concern alight in a Cold War Church. They kept in touch with friends abroad: Fr Stratmann, back in Germany, the *Catholic Worker* in the US, Pax Christi in France. They diligently wrote to the Catholic press in every debate about the hydrogen bomb, the need to deter communism, and the Pope's opinions on both.

In 1954 a new partnership began with the Dominicans when Spode House was renovated as a conference centre and the war-

10. Correspondence between Vann and Bishop Parker of Northampton, January-February 1944. Westminster Diocesan Archives.

11. *Pilgrim Cross: an Illustrated Account of the Vézelay Peace Pilgrimage 1946,* Oxford, *ca* 1946, Blackfriars Publications.

den, Conrad Pepler, arranged a weekend on 'Christian Peace and the Pacifist'. The PAX annual conference at Spode became a training ground for the formation of a new generation of Catholic peace activists. The agenda was now dominated by the nuclear issue and once again Dominicans furnished speakers (Laurence Bright, Columba Ryan, Henry St John, Anthony Ross among them) and tools for theological analysis. In 1956, at the invitation of the National Peace Council, Illtud Evans (a founder of PAX) took the part of moderator in a medieval disputation which was broadcast by BBC Radio. Ian Hislop and Laurence Bright debated the morality of nuclear war, concluding that atom and hydrogen bombs were immoral because they were uncontrollably destructive and indiscriminate in their effects. After the broadcast Brocard Sewell, the Carmelite, challenged Cardinal Griffin to declare whether these conclusions were heretical. If they were not, it meant that it had been publicly admitted that Catholics might indeed hold such opinions as those advocated by PAX. Sewell was rebuked for this 'impudent' letter.[12]

The wave of public concern about nuclear weapons which produced the Campaign for Nuclear Disarmament (CND) brought fresh support from Catholics and, in 1960, the new Catholic Nuclear Disarmament Group took its banner (in papal colours) to Aldermaston. Someone noticed that among the religious organisations the Catholics modestly brought up the rear, 'possibly with a subconscious sense of caution as an acknowledgement that Rome has not yet spoken'.[13]

Even Dominicans were rather cautious. When PAX drew up a list of sponsors Henry St John would only allow his name to be included if Archbishop Roberts also agreed.[14] Safety in numbers. Illtud Evans declined because the Provincial thought 'one OP is probably enough... A pity if an impression were given that Peace were a Dominican monopoly – or peculiarity!' He explained that:

12. Brocard Sewell, 'The Habit of a Lifetime', unpublished autobiography, *ca* 1980.

13. PAX Bulletin, no. 83, May 1960,

14. Letter from Henry St John to Charles Thompson, 25 April 1959.

our primary work at this juncture must be informal, helping individuals or groups, as at Spode, to formulate their views and inform their consciences ... Granted the extremely difficult situation vis à vis the Bishops, it is very important that nothing should be done unnecessarily to aggravate that situation.[15]

Various episodes illustrated the problem. In 1961 Laurence Bright was to conduct a day's retreat for Catholic peace activists. Hardly had they assembled at the Sion Convent in London when a telegram arrived from Archbishop's House forbidding any discussion of peace and war! Official opposition added a frisson of risk and excitement for young participants such as Angela and Adrian Cunningham who met at this retreat.

More serious pressure was brought to bear on Archbishop Roberts who was delated to Rome for associating with PAX. At Spode he had discussed the contents of his letter to Cardinal Tardini, Vatican Secretary of State, expressing his hope that the forthcoming Vatican Council would give priority to the morality of war and the rights of conscience. The PAX conference wrote to Rome supporting his proposals, with copies to Jesuit and Dominican leaders. Dissatisfied with the non-committal reply from the Master-General, Henry St John (who had chaired the conference) wrote personally, indicating his own concern and adding that he had refused permission to some Dominicans to lend support to anti-nuclear organisations which made a condition of membership the belief that nuclear weapons had rendered any future war immoral. Even if that was their personal belief, as it was his, this went beyond the official position of the English hierarchy and of the Vatican. He had advised them that what they could do was to offer guidance to individuals in the formation of their consciences.[16]

Spode stimulated the international community of those lobbying – with eventual success – for a declaration about nuclear weapons and conscientious objection from the Vatican Council. Speakers in these years included Eileen Egan, who had

15. Illtud Evans to Charles Thompson, 15 November 1960.
16. Henry St John to Charles Thompson, 13 December 1959.

started an American branch of PAX, Dorothy Day, and, from India, Bede Griffiths. There was a memorable weekend with Fr Pie Régamey, a French Dominican whose work on nonviolence brought Gandhian ideas to a Christian audience. *In Nonviolence and the Christian Conscience* (1966) Régamey suggested that Christians should start preparing themselves for 'possible acts of disobedience' in relation to war. In 1962 he was campaigning for a statute for conscientious objectors in France. At Spode his lecture was translated by Simon Blake who was himself becoming more involved in a new Christian grouping within CND.

Christian CND was a pioneer in purposeful ecumenism, organising religious services during CND's Easter events. Simon Blake strode at the head of a pilgrimage from Southwark to Canterbury in 1965. He gathered clergy support for protests against the Vietnam war, and, in the late-1960s, took the lead in a series of vigils at Porton Down which helped to put British development of chemical and biological weapons under scrutiny. On one of these marches Blake revealed his recipe for blisterless feet: he had learned on the Vézelay expedition to put a lump of lard into each boot, thus fusing foot, sock and boot into one friction-free machine.

By 1970 PAX was collaborating in all its projects with the small Pax Christi group which had become established in England: a monthly Mass for Peace, retreats and study days, and promotion of Pope Paul's 'Peace Sunday'. The two bodies merged in 1971, the older PAX members gracefully and willingly handing over responsibility to the more energetic and younger Pax Christi people. In 1974, at the invitation of the Prior, Peter Edgar, Pax Christi moved into the former parish club next to St Dominic's Priory in London. The luxurious (for the peace movement) premises enabled Pax Christi to expand its activities and host diverse events. Blackfriars Hall gave birth to the Campaign against the Arms Trade and became a factory for 25,000 placards when CND needed extra space because its 1981 demonstration looked like being a big one. After Simon Blake's sadly premature death, Pax Christi's main support within the priory came from Alan Cheales, and outside it from some prominent graffiti on the church wall: 'Stop War Please'.

This was unfortunately removed later, although the footpath it graced is now called 'Alan Cheales Way'.

With the deployment of Cruise missiles and the commissioning of Trident submarines, public concern about nuclear weapons mounted once again in the 1980s. Dominicans continued their by now traditional companionship to the Christian peace movements. This was especially true of Oxford, from where Roger Ruston, in particular, played a crucial part in the theological debate over the Church and the bomb. A member of the Bishops' Commission for International Justice and Peace, his pamphlet *Nuclear Deterrence: Right or Wrong?* (1981) applied 'just war' criteria to modern nuclear deterrence and brought up to date the arguments of Walter Stein's influential study *Nuclear Weapons and Christian Conscience* published twenty years earlier. The Peace Preaching course, created in the 1980s, deepened the scriptural and theological foundations of those involved in 'justice and peace'.

From Blackfriars in Oxford and elsewhere Dominicans lent their support to many initiatives: a liturgy at Greenham Common on the day in 1982 when 30,000 women surrounded the missile base; a monthly women's all-night vigil of prayers and psalms at Greenham's Blue Gate; regular recitation of the Rosary at Upper Heyford, and dialogue with chaplains and congregation at the base chapel there; tracking Cruise missile convoys and holding up white crosses in the darkness as they passed; delegations to Downing Street and a vigil during President Reagan's economic summit in London. 'God's people need bread not bombs' read the placards. Two decades after Fr Régamey proposed nonviolent 'acts of disobedience', a number of Dominicans felt called to civil disobedience as a radical gesture of opposition to policies of calculated mass murder which nuclear weapons represent. Defending his brethren in court, Timothy Radcliffe told the magistrate: 'Preventing genocide is a right and proper thing for a Christian priest to do'.[17]

On these occasions the presence of Dominican men and women, visible and photogenic in their habits, has been a sign of solidarity for the secular peace movement, a challenge to fellow Christians who would prefer to keep prayer and politics apart, and a surprise for the British public led to believe that peace campaigners were all communist traitors.

In the years since the Berlin Wall came down superpower confrontation has given way to more complex and fragmented international dynamics. All the more need, in the *Catholic Worker* phrase, for 'clarification of thought'. No satisfactory substitute has yet been found for the 'just war' framework which, after Christian peace activists gave it such exposure during the 1991 Gulf War, has become almost common coinage amongst politicians. For more than six decades Dominicans have helped the peace movements in England to develop Christian thinking on conscientious objection, nuclear deterrence, and nonviolence. Long may this companionship flourish in their joint effort to 'Stop War Please'.

11

Do the Baptised Have Rights?

The French Worker-Priest Crisis of 1953-4

FRANÇOIS LEPRIEUR *

'The members of the Holy Office use methods which, if they were in Great Britain, would soon land them in court. The Holy Office ruins reputations and destroys people's careers.' The English Jesuit, Archbishop Tommy Roberts, formerly Archbishop of Bombay, made these grave allegations in a full session of the Second Vatican Council. They are well illustrated by the way the French worker-priest crisis was dealt with between the summer of 1953 and the spring of 1954. Obviously I can only record such a richly complex period in summary form – almost telegraphically. But even such a résumé gives an eloquent demonstration of the way the hierarchical authority of that time functioned, particularly in regard to the human rights of the baptised.

WORKER-PRIESTS: ARE THEY REALLY PRIESTS?

The loss of the working class in the Catholic Church in France in the nineteenth century had for a long while made social issues prominent in French ecclesiastical thinking. The spiritual humanism with socialist leanings to be found, for example, in the influential periodical *Esprit* (founded by Emmanuel Mounier in 1932) was gradually accepted even by some members of the hierarchy. The publication in 1943 of the book by A. Godin and Y. Daniel, *La France, pays de mission?* – the question mark was included at the request of the ecclesiastical authorities – helped to spur concrete attempts to bridge the gap between the Church and the working class. By far the most outstanding among these was the decision by the bishops to permit some of the clergy to combine their priestly ministry with day-

* Translated from French by Colin Carr, O.P.

to-day sharing in the lives of manual labourers, in other words working beside them, joining their trade unions and living among them in working-class flats. So the worker-priest movement [1] was born.

After eight years there were about a hundred worker-priests in France, out of 40,000 clergy. More were preparing to join them. And elsewhere too: for instance, in the Walloon area of southern Belgium, a region with heavy industries, there were eight. These priests had established themselves in large urban centres – a third of them in the region of Paris. Twenty per cent were religious, including about ten Dominicans. Moved by a new spirit, they acknowledged that France had in fact become a 'missionary country'. Neither their background (rural or urban middle class) nor their clerical formation had exposed them to the world they were now encountering.

The life they led – so unusual for priests – had brought them close together. They were 'the Worker-Priests', a group somewhat apart, without a specific juridical structure (they related individually to their bishops or superiors); a group which had forged a strong, atypical identity, provoking mixed reactions. They had held several gatherings at regional and even national level.

From 1952 the hierarchy, under pressure from Rome, wanted to contain this unusual missionary 'experiment'. It set about things clumsily, in an authoritarian manner. The worker-priests sought help from some theologians – Féret, Bouéssé and, above all, Chenu – who all happened to be Dominicans. Chenu maintained that the time had come for 'the experiment to find doctrinal expression'; there was no need to rush; it *was* disturbing, but also full of promise.

These priests really did live in a world which the Church knew nothing about. Their work was hard and badly paid (food cost them 45% of their wages). The difficulty with housing was compounded by desperately poor sanitary conditions. They had furnished lodgings or small, insanitary apartments. They discovered another injustice in the lives of the workers – the

1. For the historical context of the crisis see *Quand Rome Condamne* (*Q.R.C.*), Terre humaine, Plon, Paris, 1989, 766 pp.

education of their children: compulsory schooling stopped at
fourteen. In short, they lived in poverty among poor people
who nonetheless were organized, unionized and militant.
(Strikes and social conflict were harsh and frequent in those
days.) By their solidarity through shared work and shared living
conditions they came to exercise a 'ministry of simple presence', as Chenu put it. But it was definitely an active presence.

Some people, however, thought it was not very pastoral.
Others, like the bosses who complained to the bishops or the
nunciature, thought it was unworthy for a priest. But how far do
you go in involvement, in the legitimate struggle for a better life,
with less oppression, less injustice in the distribution of the
fruits of production and of access to education? The majority of
these priests had opted to work in large enterprises with several
thousand workers – in steel, engineering, car manufacture and
pharmaceuticals, or else on the construction sites of the hydro-
electric barrages in the Alps which were being built then. Some
became dockers.

The most powerful union – and often the only one in the
large concentration of workers – was the C.G.T. The C.G.T. was
linked with the Communist Party, which was extremely influential in working class and intellectual circles. The Communists
would regularly poll 25% of the votes in French elections in
those days, and Communism was advancing powerfully on the
world stage. The Cold War was raging in Korea and in Indo-
China, where France was embroiled in an anachronistic colonial war. In the opinion of their opponents, these priests, with
their political and union involvement, were not complying with
the *motu proprio* promulgated by the Holy Office in July 1949, six
months after the fall of China to the Communists. It forbade all
Catholics from collaborating with Communists, even for specific limited purposes.

How far could you go in solidarity? To become active for
peace and join other 'progressive' Christians in responding to
the Stockholm Agreement – was that a case of simply being
manipulated by the Communists? In May 1952 two worker-
priests were beaten up by the Paris police during a pacifist
(some would say Communist) demonstration against General

Rigway, the new American boss of NATO. Public – and Christian – opinion began to have its doubts. Weren't these priests locked into a Manichaean view of society and the world? The tabloid press had made one or two attempts to lift the veil on the worker-priests 'secret' life, but they refused to give interviews and fled all publicity. Yet wouldn't the alternative be misrepresentation, betrayal and misunderstanding? Of course.

Some people expected these priests to play a conciliatory role in conflicts between management, white-collar workers and the unionized workers. Some admirers saw in them 'saints [who] go down into hell', to quote the ambiguous title of a famous novel by the Catholic author Gilbert Cesbron, *Saints vont en enfer,* which sold 300,000 copies. It was a generous *apologia,* but clumsy ('hell', note – the working classes were still seen as 'dangerous'). It was an *apologia* which demonstrated perfectly how difficult it was to speak adequately about the lives of these unconventional priests. The action in the novel took place *outside* the factory!

And others asked themselves questions. The voluntary poverty of these priests – poor among the poor – spoke with an undeniably evangelical accent; there was an obvious authenticity about it. And yet … were these men really fully-fledged priests? Priests who celebrated Mass daily, prayed, said their breviary? Could they find a place for all these things in their hassle-filled days? Other issues, too, fed a feeling of suspicion or disquiet among the lay people, the hierarchy and the clergy.

Whatever the answers, abolishing the worker-priests would not abolish the unacknowledged missionary problem which they were confronting. What was more, as their supporters said, they were beginning to win the confidence of those among whom they lived 'without looking for any come-back'. So? One thing was certain: the future of the worker-priests interested the Catholic Church as much as the French public at large.

THE VATICAN'S DIKTAT

During the summer of 1953 the French press carried a series of reports about measures aimed at blocking all new initiatives in the worker-priest project. They were the preliminaries to a much more serious decision which Marella, the papal nuncio in France, announced to the cardinals, bishops and religious superiors who had responsibility for any worker priests. The worker priests were to stop all union militancy and, worse still, stop working in factories. It was assumed that the religious, as the more docile element, would be the first to withdraw. Moreover, it had to appear that this decision, which was irrevocable, came from the French hierarchy, and everything had to be done with the utmost secrecy, out of view of the press.

In fact it was the cardinals themselves – Feltin of Paris, Liénart of Lille and Gerlier of Lyons – who prevented the Vatican strategy proceeding as intended. They felt that the decision was too abrupt and made without any awareness of the catastrophic effect that the suppression of the worker-priest movement would have on the working class. 'Rome must realise,' declared Cardinal Feltin, 'that after this the Church will be seen by the workers to be definitively allied with capitalism.' The credibility which these few men had gained for the Church would now be irremediably lost. This was why the prelates wanted an audience with the Pope, Pius XII. Meanwhile, the press got wind of what was afoot. Theologians like Congar, academics like Borne, journalists like Hourdin, took up the cause of these threatened men who had done nothing wrong. Everything hung on the French prelates' visit to Rome. The worker priests had their advocates and the press were alerted.

The prelates returned from Rome at the beginning of November. The former defenders of the worker priests, now completely at one with the Vatican, outlined a series of measures which added up to the fact that, while the mission directed to the world of the workers would be intensified, the future of the worker priests as such was in serious danger.

This ambiguity made for a very unstable situation. Some people wrote articles expressing hope. Cardinal Gerlier himself thought there was room for further negotiation. His confrere in Lille insisted there was no way that could happen: Rome had spoken, the Pontiff's decision was irrevocable. The hierarchy counted on the effects of the formation in religious life which the worker priests who were religious had been given.

The Jesuits withdrew at the end of December. By contrast the Dominicans – and they were the most important group – made no move. Yet, since the autumn, the pressures on Emmanuel Suarez, the Master of the Dominican Order, had been steadily growing. They came mainly from the Holy Office, of which he was a member by right. The demands for information on such-and-such a friar, the response to such a delation as, for example, that of Boisselot, Director of Éditions du Cerf, and the summoning of the theologian Féret, who appeared before a tribunal of the Holy Office, all point to this ever-increasing harassment. Meanwhile the worker priests wrote to their bishops, individually and collectively, to confront them with their pastoral responsibilities. After all, it was they who had sent them on this mission. How could they now justify their sudden change? The question was made all the more dramatic because, fundamentally, it remained unanswered.

THE FATEFUL DATE: 1 MARCH

Days passed; weeks passed. Finally, on 19 January 1954 the bishops who were involved published an official letter to the worker priests announcing that their work must stop on 1 March. Shortly afterwards news came of Suarez's 'raid' on France. The three French Dominican provincials were removed, the Director of Éditions du Cerf was dismissed, the three outstanding Dominican theologians – Chenu, Congar and Féret – were deprived of their teaching posts and had to leave Paris. Their very slightest contributions to debates were subject to episcopal authorisation, and even tiny articles written by them were subjected to the very strict censorship which had just been activated.

The French press reverberated with the event. Several of the major dailies devoted their editorials to it. François Mauriac made a lyrical plea on behalf of the 'sons of St Dominic'. Somewhat later *Le Monde* published a manifesto signed by dozens of intellectuals. There was a growing number of meetings and petitions. Supporters and opponents of the theologians underlined the link between those measures and the suppression of the worker priests. The French ambassador to the Holy See attempted to convince the Secretary of State and the Holy Office that this upsurge of public opinion did not come from the traditional opponents of the Church but expressed widely-held feelings, made all the stronger by the fact that the worker priests had not done anything wrong, and that the friars who had been purged were 'the glory of the country's Catholic intelligentsia'.

The message was no doubt received, but the Roman officials (the Pope was ill at the time) were more concerned with congratulating themselves on the obedience which the Dominicans had demonstrated in response to the harsh sanctions imposed on them. The hope was that their conduct would set an example to the worker priests who very soon would have to give up their work. At the end of February the worker priests gathered for the last time, out of earshot of the press (or so they hoped) at the Café de la Paix in Villejuif, part of Paris's 'Red' district. They each told the others what they personally had decided. More than half had decided to go on working, to remain in solidarity with their workmates. The gathering was intensely dramatic: they had all been presented with 'an impossible choice'.

If the story set the press alight, it was quite simply because the position of the worker priests was so unusual – in fact unprecedented: priest and worker, an unheard-of combination, a paradox which opponents found all the more objectionable because, given the laws of solidarity, it would entail regular dealings with Communist comrades. This was intolerable in those times of grave social conflicts, Cold War, the persecution of Christian churches behind the Iron Curtain, and the strength of the French Communist Party. The worker priests' project represented for Rome a 'diminution' of their priesthood.[2]

This understanding of their project was itself in need of a modicum of caution. Instead of the pre-emptive removal of these priests from 'the harmful atmosphere of the shop floor',[3]

---

2. This was a theme which the cardinals spoke of at great length during this period; see *Q.R.C.*, pp. 343-347, for example.
3. The expression is Cardinal Feltin's.

there should have been a more gradual approach. To be sure, there were those in the bosom of the Church – and not only the traditionalists – who protested that the worker priests were in the wrong place, doing the work of lay people. To be sure, in addition to the 'romantic' aspect of their situation, these priests were, all innocently, relativising the Tridentine theology of priesthood, elaborated in and for a Christian society, and challenging the life-style which incarnated it. But instead of the brutal axing of the project there should have been discussion. For now, the argument from authority was shutting the door on a very necessary, indeed vital, exercise in creative theology.

It is understandable that from now onwards the press and public opinion had questions to ask. Over and above the inexorable unfolding of the crisis, what shocked people were the methods used to resolve it; they made it apparent to everyone that the Roman Church was governed in a manner which was both 'totalitarian and paternalistic',[4] at the cost of great suffering for a good number of its members.

A TRAVESTY OF JUSTICE

In the repression suffered by all those who actively supported the theological reflection of the worker priests, Féret was the one subjected to the most searing encounter with authority. Having spent three weeks hanging around in Rome without knowing why he had been summoned there, he was questioned for nearly four hours by a tribunal of the Holy Office. As a good historian, he was not unaware of the inquisitorial misdeeds of the institution, but he had not until then experienced for himself the odiousness of the process of which he was the subject. Let the reader judge.[5]

The first shock: Féret very quickly discovered that for a long time he had been the subject of denunciations, some from his brethren but most from integrist theological circles which refused to address the kind of problems that he, as a responsible theologian, found confronting him, or from extremely reac-

4. Y.M. Congar, 'Chronique d'une petite purge', *Q.R.C.*, p.433. Throughout the crisis Congar kept a kind of journal.
5. You will find an account of this interview in *Q.R.C.*, pp. 410–412.

tionary political and social circles that were hostile to the Church's social teaching.

It is important to remember that the process against a theologian by the Holy Office began with denunciations which were anonymous, so unidentified delators, who had a guarantee that they would never be confronted by their victim, were able to make that victim an accused suspect. The Provincial of the Paris Province was protesting at that time to the Master of the Order (who, as a member of the Holy Office, was implicated) about the credence given to all the denunciations which were being heaped on several of his brethren. He added:

> I cannot help being shocked and scandalised that Rome is condemning and penalising religious without giving them a hearing. It seems to me to be a basic principle of natural justice, irrespective of the quantity or quality of the accusers, that anyone who is accused should be informed of the charges brought against him and have the opportunity to explain and defend himself. Otherwise there is nothing but a travesty of justice.[6]

In September 1953 Joseph Robert, a Dominican worker priest, had admitted, 'I feel troubled about the possible motives for a condemnation. We have been attacked and slandered. Our accusers have been believed and have remained anonymous ... To me it seems terrible that the Church, or rather certain authorities, accept this, and always do so. I have protested and I am grimly determined to go on protesting.'[7]

Next shock: the prosecutors were also the judges. Without knowing beforehand what is his dossier, the accused was delivered into the hands of his interrogators without knowing what to expect. As the questions were being asked he had to try and grasp what they are really all about – they are often long and complex – and at the same time formulate a response which the clerk would minute and require him to sign at the end of the interrogation.

The final straw was that the accused was alone before his

6. *Q.R.C.*, p. 413.
7. ibid.

judges. There was no sign of a counsel for the defence. The hearing ended with a threefold oath: to keep secret the trial itself, the names of the judges and the nature of the questions. Scandalized by this final demand, the defendant objected and replied: 'Inflict whatever penalties you want, exile me ... but you won't have my conscience.'[8]

In a normal court, after the cross-examination and the counsel's summing-up (of which there were none here) the judges would retire to consider the case and announce the sentence at least to the accused, if the court was held in camera. But in the present case the sentence was never published. So, equally, there was no right of appeal. Nevertheless, at the beginning of January 1954, the Pro-Prefect of the Holy Office sent two contradictory letters on the same day. The first was to Father Féret's superiors: no error had been found in his doctrine, so he could continue teaching at the Dominican pontifical faculty of Le Saulchoir. The second was for the Cardinal Archbishop of Paris, 'High Chancellor of the Catholic Faculty', saying the doctrine of this religious was not suspect, but his influence on the priests, clerical students and sisters was, on the other hand, 'inopportune'. So for the Rector, who, like the Cardinal, knew nothing of the first letter, there was nothing for it but to terminate the Dominican's employment.[9]

That whole world of delation, of suspicion, of secrecy, aimed at coercing consciences – those of the members of the Holy Office and of the 'suspects' – was the cause of enormous suffering, though those who were operating the machinery could not even see how unjust it was. The scandal was doubly grave when one considers that the institution claimed to embody the justice willed by Christ for his Church.[10]

8. On those last two points Féret simply promised to be discreet.

9. *Q.R.C.*, p. 427. Féret came back to this subject in a letter to Bishop Guerry, at whose request he wrote a long clarification in response to statements made by the Secretary of the Episcopate. The latter had just published in *La Documentation Catholique* of 12 June 1955 a 'letter on the Episcopate of France and certain current problems: a reply to various articles in the Press.' The writer made reference to 'measures taken against certain Dominican Fathers' when *Le Quinzaine* was condemned. Féret considered that the juxtaposition of the two events was shameful. See letter to Mgr. Guerry, June 1955, Archives de la Province de France.

10. *Q.R.C.*, pp. 414f.

A HIERARCHY UNITED BEHIND THE HOLY FATHER

The juridical arsenal (inherited from the Inquisition) deployed by the Holy Office was, however, just one part of the apparatus of government of the Roman Pontiff and the rest of the bishops; you can see the hortatory and repressive mentality of the hierarchy here, in the way they managed people and resolved the worker-priest crisis.

In 1953 the three cardinals had together come to Castelgandolfo (a move which annoyed Rome – Rome preferred audiences to be of single individuals). They had come to submit to the Sovereign Pontiff a 'directory' which they had been drafting since the previous spring. It would, they hoped, allow them to contain the worker-priest project without stopping the ground-breaking missionary apostolate which the worker priests were conducting. The Pope did not deny the disastrous effects of putting a stop to it, but that was what had to happen; he could no longer permit the experiment to go on, because he was convinced that it amounted to a 'diminution of priestly life'. Other ways had to be sought.[11] Of course it was a painful moment for everyone, but the Pope had spoken. There could be no beating about the bush.

The men who had to tell the worker priests for whom they were responsible what was the Pope's final decision were undoubtedly pained. Sometimes they did the job clumsily: this was the case with Cardinal Feltin when he met his worker priests in January 1954.[12] This embarrassed attitude was compounded by the glaring contradiction which they could not suppress; they were in effect saying: 'You have done an admirable job but in the interests of prudence you have got to disappear.' That was the substance of the communique of 19 January,[13] which put a stop

11. Canon Hollande's audience with Cardinal Feltin, 8 Novembre 1953. Cardinal Feltin referred to that meeting in January, when he addressed a group of worker priests.

12. See Henri Barreau, 'Prêtres-ouvriers, prêtres oubliés?', Golias n. 26, p. 72. Jean Desailly, Prêtre-Ouvrier, Mission de Paris 1946-1954, L'Harmattan, Paris 1997, p. 459.

13. 'The worker priests have done good work, but they had to be removed in order to protect them from the great dangers to which they were exposed.' Cardinal Feltin, Pastoral Letter on a current problem in our missionary apostolate, 27.2.1954. Documentation Catholique n. 1168, col. 263–270.

to the adventure. Was it duplicity on their part and on the part of the other bishops who participated in the decision – issuing admonitions about the painful crisis, calling for obedience from the worker priests, then from those who signed petitions and from the faithful in general? Not at all. Although they had firmly defended the mission to the workers, for three decisive reasons they rallied to the Roman decision.

Firstly, the hierarchy shared the Pope's suspicion that the worker-priest movement could lead to a watering-down of the priesthood. The last time they had expressed their fear had been in a letter to the Holy Office at the end of their first national meeting with worker-priest delegates, in June 1953. This is what Cardinal Liénart wrote to Cardinal Ottaviani on behalf of the Standing Commission of the Council of Cardinals and Archbishops of the Church in France:

> The exchanges of views have made clear just how much these priests have let themselves be taken over by the spirit of Marxism in their attitude and their actions. They have been led not only by their contact with the world of the workers but also by the tendency of articles by various theologians writing in *Jeunesse de l'Eglise* [a review much influenced by Maurice Montuclard, a Dominican who had recently been expelled from the Order] and *Le Quinzaine* [a 'progressive' Christian weekly to which Chenu was a prominent contributor]; the Bishops have, several times, had to draw the attention of their religious superiors to them. Because of this deviation which threatens to pervert the evangelizing enterprise so courageously undertaken by the worker-priests at the heart of the people, the Standing Commission has decided that a memorandum drawn up by Mgr Guerry should be sent to all the worker-priests setting out clearly the nature of the priestly mission which they have to fulfil and the errors which they must steer clear of.
>
> We hope that by setting forth firmly the pure doctrine of the Church, and by indicating clearly the path each one must follow and the reeds to be avoided, we will succeed in rescuing our worker-priests from the misleading influence of certain false spirits. And we will be sure to communicate to

your Eminence the results of these efforts as soon as we have obtained a more detailed report on this subject.[14]

Secondly, Rome had spoken. The determined approach of the three cardinals to Pius XII was unquestionably a measure of their concern to gauge exactly the Pope's will. They gave full authority to the dictum 'Rome has spoken.' The expression implies unwavering submission to the Pontiff's word, which enjoys unlimited power, obedience and reverence. From the abundant crop of episcopal texts coming from France at that time here are two quotations which convey the flavour of this unconditional devotion. The Archbishop of Bordeaux invited his clergy to be 'more and more imbued with papal thoughts and directives, because one always comes back to the realization that the Sovereign Pontiff has seen more clearly, deeper, further than anyone else, because he gazes from a higher peak.'[15] At the same time, the Archbishop's colleague at Angers spelled out to his diocesan priests that 'his Holiness Pius XII knows our problems, our difficulties and our anxieties better than anyone; nobody grasps them with more lucidity, from such a serenely exalted perspective. If we learn how to listen to him like obedient and devoted sons, he will guide us along the right path.'[16]

Thirdly, the hierarchy all shared the same idea of obedience

14. Letter of Cardinal Liénart to Cardinal Ottaviani, 29 June 1953. Archives of the diocese of Lille, dossier P.O., 1953. Unpublished text printed in 'Il était une foi ... les P.O'., *Prêtres ouvriers d'aujourd'hui et de demain*, Témoignage Chretien, Hors Série, 1994, p. 24. The members of the Standing Commission were to give their opinion of the memorandum to the worker-priests drafted by the Secretary, Mgr Guerry. Here, for instance, is the comment which Cardinal Liénart made; it illustrates the direction of his theological concerns. After giving his approval in general terms, he added: 'I just wonder whether, having agreed to discuss the position of the worker-priest in general, the document should not have stressed, in its conclusion, how impossible it is for the hierarchy to concur with an attitude which challenges the true mission of the Church and the correct idea of priesthood as these have been laid down by our Lord Jesus Christ.' (Letter of Cardinal Liénart to Mgr Guerry, 15 July 1953, Archives of the diocese of Lille, dossier P.O., 1953.)

15. Statement by Mgr. Richaud, 15.1.1954. Documentation Catholique n. 1166, col. 144–145.

16. Allocution of Mgr. Chapoulie, 7.2.1954. Documentation Catholique n. 1166, col. 144.

which claimed unconditional submission for the sake of greater unity – that of the bishops and that of the whole Church. As they said in their joint letter to the worker priests of 19 January 1954, 'You never go wrong if you obey.' Any suffering entailed – which is a communion in the Passion of Christ – must in their eyes be fruitful. Here again the writings of the bishops, which re-applied the Jesuit doctrine to the present circumstances, were frequent and unanimous.[17] So this view of the Holy Father, undergirded by an unprecedented personality cult, and its corollary of absolute obedience, excluded all debate, all right of dissent, any appeal to conscience. It was in this frame of mind that the French hierarchy set out to resolve the crisis. So all those who showed any form of opposition to this resolution had to be denounced, marginalised, even discredited.

REPRIMANDS AND REFLECTIONS

As we have seen, the first to feel the indignant suspicion of the bishops were the theologians. Bishop Ancel, who was very close to the worker priests, wrote to his fellow-bishops in July 1953: 'The worker priests have met some theologians who have constructed a novel theology to reassure them. Only an authentic document from the hierarchy will be able to oppose these pseudo-theological concoctions.'

Back from Rome in February 1954, the same bishop told Cardinal Gerlier that when he met Cardinal Valerio Valeri he confessed to 'preferring by far the Jesuit way of doing things to that of the Dominicans', and that in conversation with French priests he had mentioned Chenu by name. 'In fact,' he added, 'I believe that along with Desroches and Montuclard (two Dominicans who have left their Order) he is one of those mainly responsible not only for today's deviations but also for current acts of resistance.'[18]

Cardinal Saliège was indignant when he found a deep dis-

17. See chapter 6 of Q.R.C., entitled 'Soumission ou obéissance'.
18. Letter to Worker Priests, remarks of His Excellency Mgr. Ancel, 19 July 1953, Archives du diocése de Lille, dossier Prêtres-Ouvriers, 1953. Letter to Cardinal Gerlier, 20 february 1954, archives du diocèse de Lyon, dossier Ancel. On the serious disagreement between the majority of the French bishops and the Dominican theologians, see Q.R.C. pp. 212-230.

quiet among the worker priests at the end of 1953. He spoke out against those 'second-rate minds who have not done any higher studies and who grab our Mother, the Church, and shake her.'[19] Cardinal Liénart was just as virulent about Chenu when his article appeared in February 1954, 'Le sacerdoce des prêtres-ouvriers'. He saw it as rank insubordination. The very notion of 'worker priest' had been effaced by episcopal decree (had it not?) on 19 January, and here was this theologian calmly addressing a question which was no longer open to debate! The attitude was, he thought, doubly blameworthy because, in prolonging the discussion of the question with them and seeking to elucidate it, this theologian was feeding the disquiet of these priests who would soon have to 'submit'.[20]

Confronted with the genuine disquiet of Catholic intellectuals about the Church's mission, expressed in private or in the press during those months, the hierarchy could only see 'the resurgence of a thoroughly Gallican mentality', 'a breath of protestantism'.[21] If those same academics wanted to know on what basis the repressive measures were taken against the worker priests, which the Church authorities were now so anxious to see disappear, and against some Dominicans, they

19. Allocation of Cardinal Saliège to his clergy, 30.12.1953. Documentation Catholique n.1166, col. 144.

20. Letter of Cardinal Liénart to Chenu, 4 February 1954. Chenu had addressed this article in good faith to the cardinals who were directly involved in the crisis. Liénart wrote to him: 'Allow me to use this as an opportunity to tell you frankly what I think. I willingly acknowledge the freedom of a theologian to go deeply into a doctrine or to have a personal opinion on this or that matter. But he must not teach his followers a personal opinion as though it were a teaching of the Church when the Church has not yet pronounced on the question. And he is even less qualified to say how the Church should conduct its apostolate. The Pope and the Bishops are supposed to have become mere administrators; the higher authorities in the Church are deemed to be inadequately sensitive to certain delicate issues of the day. There is no lack of unauthorised experts who presume to take their place and direct the apostolate of clerics and laity. They do this through articles – often unsigned – in reviews, by circulating notes, through study groups and conferences. The result is a real confusion in people's minds, and, I would say, in the Church at large.'

21. 'Don't you sense a breath of free enquiry in the air, a whiff of protestantism, and, here and there, a loss of genuine Catholicism?' Mgr. Théas, 'La soumission au pape', Bulletin religieux de Tarbes et Lourdes, 14.1.1954, Documentation Catholique, n. 1168, col.288. 'Let us not listen to those who shout or complain

were invited to make an act of faith and not forget 'that, unfortunately, these questions are beyond the collective competence of the faithful.'[22]

The Catholic press was considered rebellious, and got a severe reprimand at the spring Assembly of Cardinals and Archbishops in March 1954. However, the Assembly could not touch the secular press; *Le Monde* and the review *Esprit* were immune from condemnation. The latter had published an article 'The Worker Priests and the Hopes of the Poor' by A. Béguin; its pertinence and lofty perspective had particularly irritated the ecclesiastics concerned. And there were others like A. Mandouze, J. M. Domenach and F. Perroux who joined strongly in the debate.[23]

The weakest link in the 'rebellious' press was *La Quinzaine*. It received explicit and sustained reprimands before being suppressed a year later. *L'Actualité Religieuse dans le Monde* officially lost its Dominican patronage. *La Vie Intellectuelle*, another Dominican review, was to disappear at the beginning of February 1957, thanks to the assiduity of the high-handed Dominican promoters of the 'restoration' which had started after the crisis of 1954.[24]

---

without thinking, "Rome doesn't understand; Rome doesn't know; the Pope is badly informed"; maybe what they really mean is: "Come on, let's just do what our conscience tells us and not burden ourselves with instructions from Rome." On this subject I will not hesitate to call what's happening a resurgence of a Gallican mentality which would quickly undo the links which unite French Catholics with the Supreme Head of Christianity.' Mgr Chapoulie, homily of 25.12.1953, Documentation Catholique, n. 1166, col. 143.

22   Letter of Cardinal Liénart to M. and Mde. Benoit. Universitaires grenoblois, 4.3.1954.

23   Q.R.C., 'Haro sur la Quinzaine', pp.152–155. The Assembly of Cardinals and Archbishops responded to the repeated lay initiatives to appeal to the Hierarchy by issuing a very violent communique in which each paragraph began: 'It is not true to say … ' Foreclosing any further discussion, they warned: 'No doubt some lay journalists are finding it difficult to understand the profound doctrinal, spiritual or religious reasons which lie behind these measures. Let them learn the true facts, or keep silent on this matter. The Hierarchy is speaking here of what is its own field: the priesthood. It is they, and not the journalists, who have the competence to define the conditions in which a priestly life is possible.' Congar commented at the time: 'These days I am painfully, agonisingly, aware of the great gulf existing between the Christian people and the processes of the hierarchy – especially Rome.'

24. *Q.R.C.* pp.438–452.

RESISTING IN A WORLD '*TOTALITAIRE ET PATERNALISTE*'

A considerable body of Christians, lay people and clerics, challenged the demands for submission which were spreading out from Rome, from the hierarchy, from everywhere. Or, rather, they joined in the resistance to this 'dictatorship by isolation' which, according to the French ambassador to the Holy See, was the hallmark of the final years of Pius XII's reign. Various intellectuals continued to point out what was at stake in this crisis, and the dangers which the Catholic Church faced as a result of the manner in which it was resolved. The editor of *Esprit* wrote in March 1954:

> The most dangerous aspect of all this is somewhere else: it is that in the very heart of the Church there will grow a hidden intimidation which interiorises censorship, makes it a habit of mind, thereby making barren the field of research, encouraging hypocrisy and double-thinking, and multiplying not true teachers but intellectual reptiles who will serve any power provided it silences their adversaries.[25]

But the worst affected, and irreparably so, were the worker priests; their very *raison d'être* had been undermined. Most of them chose to be dissidents. All refused to show that submission', that 'token of obedience', which Rome was so keen on. They had merely 'left their work'. Some of those who did 'leave their work' were to live with their remorse at having done what they were told. And others, hoping against hope, chose an 'active' obedience. So, for instance, the Dominican worker priest J. Screpel, with the backing of none other than Cardinal Liénart, worked with A. Depierre for the renewed acceptance of worker priests.

As for the theologians who had been disciplined, it was vital that their resistance was free of the anger they felt at first, or of bitterness. To achieve this freedom they drew on their profound knowledge of history. After all, had not Chenu's work *Le Saulchoir, une école de théologie* been put on the *Index* in 1942 especially because of the importance it had given to history in

25. J.M. Domenach, 'D'autant s'obscurcit la lumière', Journal à plusieurs voix, *Esprit*, mars 1954, p.406.

the theological task? They continued their work in exile. We could instance Congar's book *Le mystère du Temple*, written in Jerusalem, or *La théologie au XIIe siècle*, which Chenu wrote in Rouen. They had to be careful not to be defeated by a slow process of censorship which delayed their publications. They remained obdurately clearsighted both about the ecclesiological implications of the crisis [26] and about the mystique of obedience which prevailed at that time, even in the Dominican Order.

If the Dominicans who had been disciplined showed obedience, it was for prudential reasons. It was not a matter of plunging into a hopeless submission, but of clear-sighted recognition of what was at stake: the very Constitutions of their Order, which a good number of leading ecclesiastics in France and in Rome wanted to modify. So it was a question of preserving the one area of liberty which was canonically guaranteed! [27]

When the most acute phase of the crisis was over, Congar reflected on what Catholic life really was. The Church, he said, boils down to the Pope and his curia. Through the hierarchy they govern the masses of the faithful. Theological research is just about tolerated. In cases of disagreement there is no alternative to 'trustful and filial submission' – terms constantly used in the bishops' writings – other than disappearance. The dissident worker priests did not even have the option of 'reduction to the lay state'. Quite simply, they were excommunicated. In that scheme of things, everything hung on the arbitrary (even if benevolent) will of the omniscient Father, who expected in return the complete submission of his 'sons'. That

26. Cf Congar's 'La chronique de la petite purge', or the correspondence of Féret; e.g. Q.R.C., 'Centralisme et insensibilité apostolique', pp 419–427.

27. Y.M. Congar, 'Chronique de la petite purge', *Q.R.C.* pp.432f. 'Here we see the general ecclesiological basis of the Dominican episode. We are almost the only organised body of free thought in the Church ... We remain the only body which can, canonically, organise and act on its own accord: when a superior is elected and confirmed he is in charge ipso facto; our Chapter ordinations have force without the permission of the Holy See; we still have independent legislative power.' He deplores yet again the extent to which 'freedom of research and thought' is currently shackled, circumscribed by the Pope and the congregations 'sibi subjectae', which identify themselves with the Church. He goes on to note the correlation between the Order's juridical status, its independence in Church law and its independence of thought.

view of obedience could, Congar said, only lead to servility or revolt.

By contrast, the space inhabited by Dominicans was like a little island whose laws – potentially, and if Dominicans made responsible use of them – allowed independence of thought. So those Dominicans who had been disciplined retained a complete liberty of mind, heart and conscience. As an example of this attitude we could quote this robust and humourous observation of Chenu's, contained in a letter to one of his brethren written in the spring of 1954:

> There are times when, in the midst of darkness and stupidity, we come face to face with the harsh demands of obedience, in the Church more than anywhere else. But to do justice to those very demands, I refuse to accept a mystification, which makes of moral obedience an act of faith in Christ crucified, and reduces the theological virtue of faith to simple obedience to Church authority. This is a false exaltation of obedience, which entails its own inversion. Let's have no more complaints about the loss of a sense of obedience. As I said, my faith led me to obedience. But my obedience doesn't then escape from its own rational principles, and plunge me into a mournful mystery in which my victim soul uncomprehendingly accomplishes the redemption of the world.[28]

As for Féret, during the Second Vatican Council, at the request of Cardinal Frings, he drew up a detailed report of the procedures to which he had been subjected by a tribunal of the Holy Office. Thus he was able to contribute to the reform of that institution – a reform which the German prelate wished to set in motion.[29]

* * *

What I have written I see to be a brief incursion into a relatively recent episode in the history of the Catholic Church which

28. Letter from Chenu to one of his fellow-Dominicans: 'Pourquoi et comment j'ai obéi', in *Il est une Foi*, n.22-23, oct–nov 1989, pp.22–23.

29. This report was published in *Il est une Foi*, nn.22–23, oct–nov 1989, pp.13–20. B. Quelquejeu evaluated this reform of the Holy Office twenty years after its inception: cf 'Ralliement aux droits de l'homme, méconnaissance des "droits des chrétiens"', *Concilium* 221, 1989, pp. 129–143.

shows with harsh clarity the type of mind-set and the cultural handicaps which that venerable institution must overcome, if the human rights which it now promotes in civil society are to be respected within its own bosom.

FURTHER READING

In addition to my own book *Quand Rome condamne* (*Q.R.C.*), Terre humaine, Plon, 1989, consult ...

Arnal, O.L.: *Priest in Working-Class, the history of the Worker Priests 1943-1954*, New York, Paulist, 1989.

Perrot, D: *Les fondations de la mission de France*, Paris, Cerf, 1987.

Quelquejeu, B.: 'Ralliement aux droits de l'homme, méconnaissance des "droits des chrétiens"', *Concilium*, n. 221, 1989, pp. 129–143.

Vinatier, J.: *Les prêtres-ouvriers, le cardinal Liénart et Rome. Histoire d'une crise, 1944–1967*, Paris, éd. T. C. éditions ouvrières, 1985.

Watteleb, R.: *Strategies catholiques en monde ouvrier dans la France d'après-guerre*, Paris, éditions ouvrières, 1990.

Inédits du dossier des prêtres-ouvriers, *Il est une Foi*, n.22-23, oct-nov 1989.

12

Slant, Marxism and the English Dominicans

BRIAN WICKER

Dialogue between European Catholics and Marxists became significant in the 1960s[1] and the English Province of the Dominicans had a major hand in its promotion.

My personal memories of that episode focus upon three members of the province in particular: Conrad Pepler, Laurence Bright and Herbert McCabe. Each had a distinctive contribution to make to the dialogue. But all shared one particular gift. They were enablers. In other words, each of them helped to make things happen, by encouraging others more directly involved than themselves to have their say. Conrad Pepler's contribution was as the Warden of Spode House, the Dominican conference centre where much of the dialogue took place. He gave house room to the variegated groups who wanted to take part; and by standing back from the in-fighting he made the dialogue 'fizz'. Laurence Bright was the organiser at the centre of the network, and it was he who brought people into contact with each other at the beginning, and saw to it that what they said got into print, in various books as well as in the pages of *Slant*. In the later phases of the dialogue Herbert McCabe, as editor of *New Black-friars*, opened the pages of the periodical to the participants in such a way that they were able to conduct their dialogue at leisure and at suitable (sometimes excessive!) length in between the conference gatherings at Spode. He also

1. A precursor of the 1960s dialogue may be found in the book by J.M. Cameron entitled *Scrutiny of Marxism*, published in 1948 by the SCM Press in their 'Viewpoints' series. Professor Cameron, who later became the first Catholic holder since the middle ages of a chair in philosophy in a British university (Leeds) was a pre-war communist who had become a Catholic. His book was a dialogue in his own head between the two allegiances. It contains an extended discussion of Marxist ethics – a topic which was to become central to the later dialogue.

made lapidary observations of his own in editorial comments.

Conrad Pepler was a child of the Eric Gill / Ditchling circle. As such he was familiar with the early Catholic peace movement. The Catholic PAX society had been started on 8 May 1936 by a small group including a recent Catholic convert from Wales, J. Alban Evans, who had experienced difficulties over the concept of 'just war' in Catholic thought until he read a book by the German Dominican, Franziskus Stratmann (a leader of the anti-war movement in Germany) called *The Church and War*. By June of that year, Eric Gill himself had taken an interest in the new group – and he of course was a Dominican Tertiary, as was Conrad's father Hilary. So the Dominican influence on Catholic thinking about peace, and conscientious objection, was profound from the beginning.[2]

The link between PAX and the emerging 'Christian Marxist' dialogue of the 1960s was the campaign for unilateral nuclear disarmament (CND). Indeed, that dialogue, at least in Catholic circles, was a product of protest against 'the bomb', in at least two ways. Firstly, the campaign of the late 1950s brought British Catholics into working relationship with the political Left in a way that was quite different from the older association of Catholics with trade unionism through the Catholic Social Guild and the Catholic Workers' College. That older movement had been a product of papal teaching about the rights and responsibilities of labour. It had full ecclesiastical backing. But this new link with the Left meant opposing rather than following ecclesiastical guidelines. Of course, because of its work for conscientious objectors, PAX had long encountered opposition from bishops and priests. But soon the new Catholic anti-nuclear campaign found itself in deeper trouble, for not only did it involve opposition to prevailing ecclesiastical assumptions: it actually involved campaigning alongside atheistic Marxists (and of course others, such as Quakers). Secondly, Catholic objections to the bomb were not just emotional or political: they were deeply philosophical. Indeed some of us – certainly myself – found that thinking hard and long about the ethical problems of nuclear deterrence, and what it entailed by way of future

2. Not surprisingly, J. Alban Evans eventually became Fr Illtyd Evans, O.P.

actions and conditional intentions, became a key point of entry into real – as distinct from scholastic text-book – moral philosophy. Indeed I think it could be fairly said that the modern contribution to the revival of the classic tradition of Catholic moral reflection owed much to the need to work out exactly why nuclear deterrence was the wicked policy which the banner-waving campaigners in their bones knew it to be.

Conrad Pepler became host to the Spode House annual group meetings from which the dialogue with Marxism emerged. (These included not only the PAX group meetings but also the Spode philosophical enquiry group, the Spode literature and history groups etc., several of whose regulars became close observers or even participants in the dialogue with Marxism.) Out of this mixture of interests was born in 1960-61 the December Group. This had as its object 'to discuss social problems from a Catholic point of view independent of any official organisation'. Laurence Bright and Neil Middleton (managing director of publishers Sheed and Ward) were the moving spirits behind this effort to shift Catholic social thinking in a leftwards direction.[3] Herbert McCabe soon joined in. Various Dominican novices from the adjacent house of studies attended the discussions, and speakers included Dominican luminaries such as Cornelius Ernst, Fergus Kerr, Geoffrey Preston, Charles Boxer. Peter Benenson, the Catholic lawyer who founded Amnesty, was an early contributor.

Following the early meetings of the December Group came the publication in 1964 of the first issue of *Slant*. This was the product of Laurence Bright's energetic 'networking'. He had brought together in Cambridge, where he was living at Blackfriars, a number of Catholic graduates and undergraduates who were not only already involved in various left-leaning causes, but who were profoundly alienated by the atmosphere and practices of the University Catholic chaplaincy under its long-serving but reactionary chaplain, Mgr Alfred Gilbey. (Gilbey actually forbade women to attend his main Sunday Mass!) The

3. See Adrian Cunningham, 'The December Group: Terry Eagleton and the New Left Church', in *The Year's Work in Critical and Cultural Theory* (Blackwell, Oxford, 1991). Vol. 1, pp. 210–215.

Dominicans, of course, were not under the Gilbey thumb and could organise things independently, in the spirit of the December Group. Leo Pyle, Terry Eagleton, Adrian and Angela Cunningham and several others met with Laurence Bright and conceived the idea of a 'new left' Catholic magazine. Neil Middleton was prepared to help finance it so that it could be printed properly. Fergus Kerr prevented it from being called 'Bias' after noticing another publication of that name in Heffer's bookshop. Anthony Downing, who had the distinction of simultaneously being secretary of Cambridge CND and of the Cambridge Conservatives, served as editor of the first issues. Raymond Williams wished it well in an 'Introductory Note'.

Slant did not begin as a vehicle for Christian-Marxist dialogue. Its context was the hope and excitement engendered in the Christian sphere by the Second Vatican Council, and by the emergence of the secular 'New Left' among British intellectuals. But it was also shaped by the fact that most of those most closely involved in it were specialists in literary studies. Hence *Slant*'s early insistence on the connection between cultural values and social institutions, and its debt to cultural studies as advocated by early gurus, notably Richard Hoggart (*The Uses of Literacy*) and Raymond Williams (*Culture and Society*) – both best sellers. In *Slant*'s first issue I tried to show the theological implications of this new movement, hitherto ignored by Catholic thinkers. But underlying *Slant*'s arguments about culture and the idea of community lay two key assumptions – the Catholic Church, in its resurrected post-conciliar body, and Marxism as a revolutionary political movement would both remain major actors on the world stage. For some *Slant* contributors, given the struggle between Marxism and capitalism, the Catholic Church would eventually have to decide which side to back. There was no third way. But others saw the Church as constituting precisely the third alternative: a way through an otherwise unavoidable impasse. In the course of this struggle for the soul of the future certain battles within the Church would have to be won: against Church support for nuclear weapons, against the ban on contraception,[4] against the histori-

---

4. *Humanae Vitae* did not appear until 1968.

cal association of Catholicism with the political right. It was *Slant*'s job to push Catholics in the direction necessary for winning those battles.

It was not until its sixth number (Winter 1965) that *Slant* began seriously to confront Marxism as such, by discussing several recently published books and periodicals devoted to various aspects of Marxist theory. Then in the February/March 1966 issue Adrian Cunningham began a long study of 'The Continuity of Marx' which was concluded in August/September of that year. In between the two halves of this piece Terry Eagleton published one of the more notorious of *Slant*'s essays, on 'Politics and Benediction'. The central thesis of this interesting article is that 'in benediction the bread becomes dislocated from the practical, communal activity within which alone it has intelligibility, and is reified into an isolated commodity'. The argument then explains the implications for the worshipping community of this dislocation: 'the bread in its new condition takes on a mystifying eternal power, an abstract and unhistorical status, which increases its power over the group'.[5]

This article was representative of *Slant* in several ways. It pokes fun at a familiar bit of popular Catholicism, and does so in a provocatively outrageous manner. It employs Marxist concepts (reification, commodity-fetishism etc.) to do so, but is also rooted in some recent thinking about the sacraments (e.g., Herbert McCabe's *The New Creation*). It makes any reader who understands it, think about the subject. It displays impressive learning. It is highly theoretical. And it is unquestionably clever. All of these traits continued to feature in *Slant*'s subsequent work. Yet the discussion of Marxism was never more than a subordinate part of its concern, and labelling it a 'Marxist' journal was always a mistake. Confronting what it took to be the inadequacies of the Church was always the more important task.

Christian/Marxist dialogue was better developed on the continent of Europe, where Christians had to live cheek-by-jowl with socialists, than in Britain. Various *Slant* participants took part in meetings with Communists in Bonn and elsewhere during the 1960s: among them Giles Hibbert, O.P., who was

5. See *Slant* 9 (June/July 1966) pp. 16–17

more inward with Marxist thinking than most of his confrères. But none of them was involved in the depth of dialogue which became common in France, Italy, Spain and Germany.[6] And it seems startling now to notice that the work of Teilhard de Chardin became a focus of intense common interest to both sides. For most British Dominicans this in itself would have condemned any dialogue based on it to futility.[7]

Meanwhile *Slant* itself got more serious about Marxism from October/November 1966 onwards. In that number Neil Middleton asked: are 'we' serious? – because if we are then we have to understand that 'the Marxist revolution throughout the world must be repeated here'; i.e. in Britain. But so far, he suggests, *Slant* 'has touched only lightly upon the matter', and many of its articles 'have been, in effect, letting off steam'. But in the next issue Adrian and Angela Cunningham begged to differ. '*Slant*'s main function is not the formulation of its own political programme, but the shifting of the focus of Catholic thinking ... What needs clarification is not the political but the theological side of our position'.[8]

This divergence of view led eventually to a deeper rift, with some of the participants deciding that the Church was a lost cause. But Giles Hibbert tried, in the fourteenth issue, to show why the challenge implicit in this difference was not inevitable, in an article entitled 'Is This Christianity?' which became chapter one of his book *Man, Culture and Christianity*.[9] But for the time being, much of the interest shifted to more immediate (and probably more consensual) questions. Articles began to appear on problems in Ceylon, Algeria, China, Zambia, Pales-

6. For some details, see Roger Garaudy, *From Anathema to Dialogue* (London, Collins, 1967) pp. 28–30. *Slant* published two substantial articles by George Vass, S.J .,on Christian/Marxist dialogue in Europe in Nos. 18 (December 1967/January 1968) pp. 3–10 and 19 (February/March 1968) pp. 25–30.

7. See Laurence Bright, O.P., 'Teilhard: a Suitable Case for Dialogue?' in *Slant* 24 (March 1969) pp. 13–16. It should also be mentioned that in Slant 12 Laurence Bright had contributed an article on 'Priests and the university', following up work done by a sister organisation, the 'Downside Symposium' under the leadership of John Coulson of Bristol university.

8. See *Slant* 11 (October/November 1966) p. 25 and Slant 12 (December 1966/January 1967) p. 24.

9. *Man, Culture and Christianity* (London, Sheed and Ward, 1967)

tine, Vietnam, Latin America, South Africa. (Malcolm Magee, a Scottish Dominican working in South Africa, contributed on the last-named.) At the same time, *Slant*'s criticism of conventional Church life became even more pointed in two articles by Charles Boxer, O.P. on the parish and the Church as a community in the world, based on his experience as a 'locum' priest serving an army base belonging the British Army of the Rhine in 1965.[10] In the next issue he contributed an enthusiastic essay on G. Egner's book on contraception (a favourite *Slant* topic).[11]

Original dialogue between Marxism and Christianity in the columns of *Slant* itself began with No. 19 (January/February 1968) with a lengthy exchange between Martin Shaw and Martin Redfern, which was continued in No. 21 (June/July 1968). This exchange was the prelude to another which was published in *New Blackfriars* in the 1970s (see below). Meanwhile, Terry Eagleton had become editor in charge, and in No. 25 he expressed the hope that '*Slant* will carry a good deal more theology ... and less on parochial developments in the Philippines': a caustic reference to the Third World emphasis of several previous numbers. In No. 26 (July 1969) he published 'God the Future', by Herbert McCabe, and 'God the Past' by Timothy MacDermott, O.P., with a further comment by himself on 'The God debate'. No. 27 continued the theological theme by proposing a revolutionary role for the priesthood (Herbert McCabe on 'Priesthood and Revolution' and Terry Eagleton on 'Priesthood and Leninism') while Alban Weston, O.P. discussed the laity in the light of *Lumen Gentium*. In No. 29 I myself tried to clarify the question of how to spell out the concept of revolution, which I said is 'the problem that *Slant* needs to address itself to now'.[12] Unfortunately, soon after this the Sheed and Ward money ran out, so *Slant* 30 (March 1970) was the last issue. Furthermore, the core group of contributors was now dispersed to universities far apart from each other. In any case, I think they felt they had done as much as was possible within the

10. *Slant* 13 (February/March 1967) and Slant 14 (April/May 1967).
11. *Birth Regulation and Catholic Belief* (London, Sheed and Ward, 1967).
12. *Slant* 29 (January 1970) p. 7. A useful account of *Slant* and its achievement, by Alan Wall, was published in *New Blackfriars*, Vol. 66, No. 666 (November 1975) pp. 506–516 under the title '*Slant* and the Language of Revolution'.

Slant format. So the magazine came to an end, with articles by Adrian Cunningham and Terry Eagleton looking ahead to '*Slant* strategy' for the future, while on its final page was printed a useful *Slant* chronology, listing notable 'landmarks' on the journey from 1956 to 1969.

As the above summary shows, the Dominican contribution to *Slant*'s experiments with left-wingery was of key importance. But the Order's contribution did not end with the demise of *Slant* itself. For one thing, Laurence Bright had enabled a number of relevant books to see the light of day.[13] And a good deal of further discussion went on in the pages of *New Blackfriars* in the 1970s, under the editorship of Herbert McCabe (who had been restored to the post in October 1970, following a period of banishment after an incautious remark about Charles Davis's departure from the priesthood). He gave generous space to a good many *Slant* writers. I do not have space here to mention them all. But I will mention one example of an extended – perhaps over-extended – debate that took place on the question of Marxism and morality.[14] Some of the contributions (as indeed much else in the *Slant* venture) owed a great deal to Herbert McCabe's own work in the theology of the sacraments and later in moral theology.[15] The debate began with a thesis propounded by Denys Turner (then of University College, Dublin) that 'Morality is Marxism'. The thesis was that while Marx and

13. Terry Eagleton's final editorial in No. 30 mentions five, but there were several others which bore Laurence's trademark, as the *Slant* chronology indicates.

14. This debate in *New Blackfriars* lasted from February 1973 to April 1978. The items included were as follows: Denys Turner, 'Morality is Marxism' (February 1973 and March 1973) and 'Can a Christian be a Marxist?' (June 1975); Brian Wicker, 'Marxists and Christians: Questions for Denys Turner' (October 1975); Terry Eagleton, 'Marxists and Christians: Answers for Brian Wicker', also October 1975; Brian Wicker, 'Sincerity, Authenticity and God' (May 1976); Francis Barker, 'The Morality of Knowledge and the Disappearance of God' (September 1976); Terry Eagleton, 'Marx, Freud and Morality' (January 1977); Brian Wicker, 'Marxist Science and Christian Theology' (February 1977); Denys Turner, 'Marxism, Christianity and Morality: Replies to Francis Barker and Brian Wicker' (April 1977); Francis Barker, 'Science and Ideology' (October 1977); Dick Lobel, 'Giving Away Power', (January 1978); Denys Turner, 'The "Subject" and the "Self": A Note on Barker's Cartesianism' (March 1978); Brian Wicker, '"God" and Ideology' (April 1978).

15. Especially *Law, Love and Language* (London, Sheed and Ward, 1968).

Marxists tend to suppose that the scientific study of society (i.e. Marxism) supersedes moral theory, this is just a muddle about the concept of morality. The muddle arises from the collapse of the 'classical' concept of morality under the pressure of Enlightenment ideas. The debate thenceforth centred on the claim of Marxists to be the scientists of society. I raised the question how Marxism could accommodate the concept of absolutely illicit acts like torturing people, and Terry Eagleton tried to answer it. Francis Barker, an Althusserian Marxist, then entered the fray to defend the thesis that Marxism is the true science of society: i.e. that its findings, unlike those of theologians, yield genuine knowledge. Theology on the other hand is based upon mere tautologies which cannot yield real knowledge of how things are in the world. The debate from that moment onwards focused on the question whether theology could be genuine knowledge.

Re-reading that debate today is a curious experience. The contributions were very scholarly and sophisticated: but also strangely sterile. They had little to do with what human beings ought or ought not to do. The whole enterprise was extraordinarily abstract. Meanwhile, in the real world outside, people in Britain and America were getting ready to usher in the era of Reagan and Thatcher. Undisciplined squads of capitalist avarice were mobilising under nuclear umbrellas. CND was on the verge of its second period of greatness. And on the distant horizon, under the weight of its enormities and its impoverishments, the USSR was getting ready to disintegrate.

Slant accepted too easily, albeit understandably, that 'Communism is a fact. It is viable, stable, succeeding. It has come to stay'.[16] Despite the fact that all the *Slant* writers were resolutely anti-Stalinist, they did not realise how deeply the existence of states built allegedly on Marxist principles undergirded their theoretical loyalties to Marx and to the Marxist concept of revolution. In the end, it may be said, the old original PAX inspiration of principled non-violence and opposition to nuclear weapons outlasted the Marxist preoccupation with build-

16. See John Lewis, in *Dialogue of Christianity and Marxism* (London, Lawrence and Wishart 1968) p. 5.

ing a new Jerusalem. For while Marxist theory may have almost vanished, the battles *Slant* was first mobilised to fight have not yet been won. Morality has outlived Marxism. Christianity may be down, but unlike Marxism, it is not yet out.

13

Asia-Pacific

The Value of Networking

JIM NUTTALL, O.P.

THE COMING OF THE DOMINICANS

The histories of the growth of the Dominican Family in different parts of Asia – often initiated by the friars, soon to be complemented by sisters' congregations, frequently with active laity and the establishment of monasteries of nuns – intertwine with one another and with the missionary movements of the Church.

Throughout the fourteenth and fifteenth centuries Dominican friars and members of other religious orders were working together in Persia and India, and gathering information about China and other Asian countries.

In the sixteenth and seventeenth centuries friars from Portugal moved on from India to Sri Lanka, Indonesia, Timor and Cambodia. They established the Dominican Congregation of 'Santa Cruz of the East Indies' to coordinate and promote their missionary work. During the same time friars from provinces in Spain and Mexico established the Province of the Holy Rosary, first based in Manila, to enter and establish missions in China. After succeeding in this endeavour, they travelled to Japan, Taiwan, Hong Kong and Korea.

In ensuing years friars from France went to Turkey, Iraq and Vietnam; from Ireland to Iran, Australia and India; from Canada to Japan, joined later there by friars from Poland; from Germany to China and Taiwan; from the USA to China and to that part of India which is now Pakistan, where they joined the friars of the Roman Province, who had preceded them by some twenty-five years.

To know those histories and to know the men and women who made them would mean opening and lovingly reading the annals of those groups, and of all the congregations I have not mentioned.

In place after place, Dominicans were living in the complex and highly developed cultures of Asia and the Pacific, interacting with people throughout these societies. As Christianity developed in different countries, Dominicans were active in education, health care, religious dialogue and, sometimes, in the politics and labour movements there. In cities and in remote areas, friars and sisters served the poor and vast indigenous populations tirelessly, and defended them from the grosser attacks on their human rights. It is mostly from the poor and labouring peoples of Asia that the nucleus and the growth of the Church in Asia has come.

Throughout the years, Dominicans suffered persecutions along with their brother and sister Christians. During the Second World War many were interned in camps throughout the war zones, and later, during the Communist government's take-over in China, priests, sisters and lay people were interned. Many of them died; many came out in extremely weak condition.

All these stories contributed to the traditions of the region.

BUILDING UP A NETWORK

In Taipei in April 1974 the newly formed Federation of Asian Bishops' Conferences set out what they saw to be the ways of proclaiming the Gospel today in Asia. They said the first task should be the building-up of the local Church; the second, dialogue with the great religious traditions; the third, what the Federation called 'dialogue with life', in other words with the poor, deprived and oppressed, because the multitudes of Asia were in this condition. This last task was to bring into the Asian situation the affirmation made by the Synod of Bishops of 1971, in its document *Justice in the World*:

> Action in behalf of justice and participation in the transformation of the world fully appear to us as a constitutive dimension of the Gospel, that is, of the mission of the church for the redemption of the human race and its liberation from every oppressive situation.

This clarion call had gone out throughout the whole Catholic world and was being assimilated and translated into meaningful legislation by many religious orders and congregations. With the election of Fr Vincent de Couesnongle as Master of the Dominican Order at Naples in 1974, the terms 'justice' and 'peace' began to appear in writings in the Order as referring specifically to the need for the Order to promote in a practical way, both worldwide and in local provinces, organisations furthering the human rights of peoples. In 1975 the Master appointed his Assistant Fr Bernard Olivier as the Order's first General Promoter for Justice and Peace.

Attacks on human rights were becoming more frequent and more institutionally organized – that was the major motivation for action. In addition, Dominicans had got an added motivation for action: the imprisonment and torture – leading to one death – of members of the Order in Brazil over a period of four years by the military regime there. It only ended with their release in December 1973. In 1971 Fr Vincent, as assistant to the Master General, had travelled with Fr Fernandez to Brazil, had visited the friars imprisoned there, and had experienced the anguish of those times.

The General Chapter of Quezon City in 1977 commissioned the Master of the Order to appoint promoters for Justice and Peace at the regional levels – in other words, coordinators. The first Promoter for Justice and Peace for the Asia-Pacific Region was Fr Bob Mutlow of the Australian Province.

Bob entered the job with a natural willingness and a trust in God. He saw his role primarily as helping to put some organisation into the Justice and Peace ministries of the Dominicans in this vast region. In addition to the Dominicans of the countries of his own area – Australia, Aotearia New Zealand, the Solomon Islands, Indonesia and Timor – he set out to meet Dominicans in Japan, Korea, the Philippines, Taiwan, Hong Kong, and the Indian Subcontinent (India, Pakistan and Sri Lanka), with hopes of reaching the more difficult places, like Vietnam, Indonesia and East Timor, in the future. Iraq, Iran and the other countries of the Middle East joined the Asia-Pacific Region by the time of the Goa Conference of 1995.

He came as a friend, preaching the compassion of Luke's

Gospel and urging friars, sisters, nuns and laity to appoint Promoters for Justice and Peace and give them job descriptions to coordinate the efforts of the local Dominican Family to collaborate at all levels in their countries with people of good will, so as to strengthen, protect and increase the human rights of all. The work for Justice and Peace unites us with people of every religion and philosophy, with all people who hold the dignity of the human person as basic.

To a far-flung Dominican Family, by August 1984 very much an Asian family, Bob issued an invitation for the first Dominican Conference on Justice and Peace in the Asia-Pacific Region. It was held at the Maryknoll House in Stanley, Hong Kong. This Conference, following closely on the Order's General Chapter at Rome, took up the theme of the Preferential Option for the Poor. Men and women came from Australia, Aotearoa New Zealand, the Philippines, Japan, Taiwan, India, Pakistan and Hong Kong.

As became typical for these meetings, there was enthusiastic sharing, good input and serious planning. We were visited one evening by Christine Tse of the Asian Center for the Progress of Peoples in Hong Kong, to introduce us to the 'Hotline Asia' service for responding by letter-writing to emergency situations of abuse of human rights in Asia. It was this kind of networking that we were planning ourselves.

In the final statement of the Conference, the participants resolved to bring home to their communities the basic message of the Conference: that questions of justice and peace had a central place in everyone's life and in our lives collectively. Justice was to be given priority in the studies and experiences of our formation programmes. Members of the Conference returned to homes in different parts of Asia Pacific to look at ministries in the light of the increased awareness of the call to work for justice and to build a living structure of networking within the Dominican Family.

One important piece of the networking is the region's newsletter, *Mission and Justice*, which Bob had started, publishing it from Australia. To it we all could contribute articles of interest concerning justice issues. After Bob, Fr Luke Rawlings took over, and now he and Sister Patricia Woodbury edit it. This service of the Australian province reaches people in every corner of the region.

It took a while to get used to this ministry of promotion of justice and peace, and there were skeptics who were critical of the efforts being made to reorganise us in these directions. However, horrific events going on in the world and in our own back yards were conscientising all to the increased dangers to human rights and the need to seek solutions.

Already the 1984 Conference in Hong Kong had recommended that promoters be appointed for all provinces, vicariates and congregations, and that the regional promotion be given to a team of a man and woman. This recommendation was adopted, and ever since 1988 a friar and a sister have worked as co-promoters for the region, the first team being from Pakistan, then from India, and now from New Zealand.

The second and third regional conferences, in 1988 and 1991, were especially devoted to the rights of women and children. The fourth regional conference, held in Goa in 1995, was the first in which the laity joined the religious as participants, and the first which included participants from the Solomon Islands and Indonesia. At the fifth, held in 1998 in Sydney, participants for the first time came from Iraq, Vietnam and Papua New Guinea.

It was at this conference that we first divided our large region into four sub-regions with a coordinator (known as 'the liaison person') for each. This, we hope, will assist collaboration among Dominicans in countries near one another. The regional co-promoters for Justice and Peace attend at the regional conferences of Dominican superiors and give reports.

Certain broad conclusions were reached at the conferences. For example, it was felt that there was a need for research towards developing a more adequate spirituality of justice and to greater animation in the local Church. It was also clear that there had to be greater collaboration with other people, outside the Order, engaged with justice issues. Also, there had to be more collaboration among Justice and Peace promoters. In a number of countries and on the regional level, collaboration in formation has brought the dimension of justice clearly into our formation programmes.

Furthermore, our contemplative nuns in the region give the strong support of their prayer to the work of the Dominican Family in this apostolate, and a nun in Korea who for some time corresponded with a man on death's row who had been unjustly condemned, was instrumental in bringing about the involvement in the affair of the Church in Korea and of our regional network, leading eventually to the man's acquittal and release.

The excellent leadership of our last two Masters of the Order, Fr Damian Byrne and Fr Timothy Radcliffe, and also of Edward van Merrienboer, Simon Roche, Jean-Jacques Pérennès, Pablo Romo and Kevin Toomey, have helped us to be more united and effective, 'acting in behalf of justice and participating in the transformation of the world', as the bishops in the 1974 Synod had put it.

The presence of Philippe LeBlanc at the Franciscan International/Dominican seat on the United Nations High Commission for Human Rights together with our responsive generalate at Santa Sabina have made a great difference to us in Pakistan, when we have needed assistance in responding to injustices in our country – for example, discriminatory laws mandating the death penalty for blasphemy and violent attacks on minority peoples by extremists.

The growth of Dominican Family awareness, within countries as well as on the regional level, has been the greatest blessing which has come to us in the Asia-Pacific region. The factors which have led to this are many, not the least of these being the networking and collaborating there has been in this area of Justice and Peace. However, it is also truly a gift from the Spirit, and is the heart of our preaching and witnessing.

ISSUES TO WRESTLE WITH

Here there is only space to focus on the contributions which Dominicans in the Asia-Pacific region have made to groping with outstandingly difficult issues: refugees and guest-workers; rights of women and children; indigenous people; economic and cultural slavery.

Refugees and Guest-workers

A great number of the world's refugees – something in the region of eight million of them – live in Asia Pacific. As violence and warring escalate in Afghanistan, Tibet, China, Sri Lanka, West Timor and the Moluccan Islands, the numbers increase.

The Maryknoll Sisters of East Timor, who were forced to leave in the wake of the violence inflicted by pro-Jakarta militias, followed the refugees to Darwin in Australia, but returned when the peace-keepers were able to clear the way. Again, the situation is extremely tense there.

In Japan, in Matsuyama and in Tokyo, Dominican Sisters of Maryknoll and the Roman Province care for guest-workers from the Philippines and for refugees from North Korea. They provide shelter, counselling and religious services, particularly for the women who are most vulnerable to abuse and violence. In Matsuyama the friars of the Holy Rosary Province work closely with the sisters.

Dominicans work with the Vietnamese in Hong Kong and the Philippines. Fr Joean Houlman ran schools for the Vietnamese in the huge camps of Aranyaprathet and Phanat Nikhom in Thailand, as well as helping to reunite members of families and secure for them visas to Australia, Aotearoa New Zealand the West.

Rights of Women and Children

Throughout the region Dominican Sisters and laity minister with women and children in a variety of situations. Along with their pastoral outreach through schools, health care, parish apostolates, inter-religious dialogue, evangelization and special ministries, Dominican women unite with women's rights organizations to work for legislation and social change which will gain for women their rightful recognition as equal citizens.

Apostolates with women lead to a ministry to the whole family and the recognition of the rights of the child. In many places Sisters run training programmes which enable poor women to increase their earning power, thus benefiting the whole family. Whereas in most parts of the world Domincans minister to people of every stratum of society, in Asia we are most often found among the poor and marginalised, and the

Sisters are the ones who take up residence in the poorest of neighbourhoods to serve and be with the people.

Health education, community development, and the running small schools in which children who are caught in the trap of child labour can also get an education, are ways in which Dominicans are able to bring liberation to children.

The San Juan Chapter of Dominican Laity in Metro Manila administrates the St Martin de Porres Charity Hospital. Here patients who could not afford treatment anywhere else are fully taken care of.

Indigenous People

In Asia, indigenous tribal people form a significant part of the population. They depend on their traditional ways of living and supporting their families. Economically challenged, many tribes are behind in education, health care and economic development.

Many of their leaders realize that their people must accept change, but, at the same time, they do not want to lose their identity. In Aotearoa New Zealand, Northern Iraq, parts of India and Taiwan, the indigenous cultures are strong, and they struggle for the recognition of their political rights, rights in ownership of land, and, in places, their own sovereignty.

Our Solomon Islander friars and sisters, as they evangelize their people, bring to the Order the riches of their culture and spirituality. At the other end of the region, sisters and laity minister among the Kurdish populations.

The Conference on 'Evangelization among the Indigenous Peoples of Asia', held at Hua Hin in 1995, stated:

We acknowledge that over the centuries God has been speaking to indigenous peoples through their cultures. Thus we seek a new evangelization at the heart of these cultures, a profound encounter between the core values of indigenous peoples and biblical faith.

Such an encounter can only takes place where deep trust and honest friendship is established.

Economic and Cultural Slavery

The continued presence of many forms of human slavery in Asia-Pacific mocks our best efforts at striving for human rights. Child prostitution, bonded labour, drug dependency, AIDS and poverty are some of the forms of this slavery. The Dominican Family Justice and Peace Committee in Taiwan has estimated that 100,000 women under the age of eighteen are trapped in a life of prostitution. In the Committee's own words: 'Sold, swindled or lured into the sex trade, they are virtual slaves of pimps that string them out on drugs and keep them locked indoors, where they must service up to forty male customers a day.'

In India and Pakistan farm labourers can be kept at bare subsistence wages, and build up large debts to the landowners. This makes the whole family the landowner's slaves. They must do his will at work, and submit to his abusive behaviour. In the Sindh Province in Pakistan these poor workers are often locked into jail-like compounds at night.

Although these situations could be discussed in different categories of Justice and Peace issues, they are especially related by the interplay of economic and cultural factors that bind people so strongly in slavery that it is extremely difficult to break the hold. Even where legislation is in place forbidding these practices, they continue to exist because of the power invested in the upper classes in these countries. The landowner in Pakistan who keeps his workers on starvation wages and even keeps them physically bound to his land thinks he is God's agent and is doing a noble thing to provide that much for them.

Individual efforts to combat slavery of these kinds, though they are often heroic and keep hope alive in human hearts, nevertheless only begin to scratch the surface. Only people of good will, of all beliefs, working together at all levels of society, can hope to bring about change of this kind.

THE DOMINICAN CHARISM

Focusing on particular issues, on particular problem areas, it is easy to overlook what has been done by some individuals. There are particular Dominicans and congregations that have undoubtedly contributed greatly to the growth of awareness of Justice and Peace issues in the region by their commitment to the poor.

Fr Pedro Salgado, of the Province of the Philippines, is a prominent writer on economic and political issues. The late Fr Michael Shirres was apostle of the Maori people and writer on theology in context. Sister Naseem George was Chairperson of the Justice and Peace Commission of the Major Superiors' Leadership Conference of Pakistan 1993-9. Sister Mary Britt ministered for many years with refugees in Australia. Fr Prakash Lohale of India and Sister Reetha Mechery brought about great advances in our networking. Sister Mary Anna Baird of Aotearoa New Zealand worked for women's rights. Many of the congregations of Dominican Sisters in Asia are committed to the rights of the poor and marginalised, and the Dominican Families of Iraq, Vietnam and East Timor keep hope alive in people in exceptionally difficult situations.

Asia Pacific is a region undoubtedly full of problems of intimidating magnitude, but I dare to believe that in this region the Dominican charism is particularly effective and adaptable. Perhaps because of our Dominican Family's structures, extending beyond the world of active religious life into the laity and into contemplative union with God, we seem to be able to join with many people and groups in the struggle, whether it is in preaching and writing, or group organizing, or at the grass roots level in pastoral ministries in remote areas. Throughout this enormous region Dominicans seem to be known for their full-hearted involvement in the ministries which challenge the powers of oppression.

14

Teaching by Recent General Chapters and Masters

VIKTOR HOFSTETTER, O.P.

This chapter presents statements from Acts of General Chapters on the commitment of the Order of Preachers to Justice and peace. My hope is that the selection I've made reflects the enormous richness of the work and study on justice and peace in the Order over the last few decades. Since general chapters occur every three years,[1] their Acts not only gather the thinking of those attending, but also reflect the activities of various groups and members in the time between chapters.

We will look at chapters held over the last thirty years. This is because the document *Justice in the World*, issued by the Synod of Bishops in 1971, set a new context for work in this area. It declared a principle which situated social justice within the mission of the Church, of evangelization and preaching:

> Action on behalf of justice and participation in the transformation of the world fully appear to us as a constitutive dimension of the preaching of the gospel, or, in other words, of the Church's mission for the redemption of human race and its liberation from every oppressive situation. (n. 6).

The Apostolic Exhortation *Evangelii Nuntiandi* of Pope Paul VI (1977) is the other major reference for reflection on mission, evangelization, preaching and justice and peace in the Order. Here is the relevant key passage:

> There are close links between evangelization and human advancement, that is development and liberation. There is a

1. The first Chapter in a sequence is an elective chapter (choosing a Master of the Order) and consists of priors provincial and representatives (diffinitors) from the provinces – one diffinitor or more depending on the size of the province. Three years later, the General Chapter consists of diffinitors only, and three years after that there is a chapter of provincials. To complete the cycle and start another, there then follows, after three years, another elective chapter.

connection in the anthropological order because the human being who is to be evangelized is not an abstract being but a person subject to social and economic factors. There is also a connection in the theological sphere because the plan of creation cannot be isolated from the plan of redemption which extends to the very practical question of eradicating injustice and establishing justice. There is, finally, a connection in the evangelical order, that is the order of charity: for how can the new law be proclaimed unless it promotes a true practical advancement of human beings in a spirit of justice and peace? This is what we intended to assert [at the Synod of 1974] when we pointed out that in the work of evangelization, we cannot and must not disregard the immense importance of those questions which are so much at issue today: questions concerning justice, liberation, progress and world peace. If we disregard these we are likewise disregarding the teaching of the Gospel about the love of our neighbour who is suffering and in want. (n. 31).

JUSTICE – A PRIORITY

The General Chapter of Quezon City (1977) proposed Justice in the World as a priority to the whole Order. Thus it took up the challenges presented in the synodal and papal document. But the previous chapter (Madonna dell'Arco, 1974) had already addressed some of these issues. This was the chapter which elected Vincent de Couesnongle as Master, and it was inspired by the spirit of renewal stemming from Vatican II. Its *Letter on Contemporary Problems* was in the form of a pastoral exhortation because the chapter-members believed that the Order as a whole and in each community must search for solutions to these questions and challenges.

I. – Preaching the Gospel in Today's World
1. What world?
The world in which we live is just emerging and a new awareness of humanity is taking shape (cfr. human rights, developing countries of the Third World ...). It is a world profoundly affected by continuous and rapid change, by instability, by the questioning of old values and certainties .

At the same time it challenges us to give reasons for our hope.

It is a world torn apart by wars, by rivalries – between rich and poor, between races, social classes, ideologies, economic interests, and even more so between young and old, men and women. It is a world deeply marked by injustice, where large parts of humanity suffer under the weight of society being organized in the interest of a few and by the idolatry of money; a world where hunger still exists, where even values of Christian civilisation serve as a pretext to justify oppression...

This is our world; we are influenced by it and we live in solidarity with it. In sharing these concerns and hopes, aware of the signs of times and believing in the action of the Spirit, we must welcome the life-giving Word of God, and together must read and share the gospel of salvation.

We cannot really understand the needs of our world, and thus be mediators of salvation, unless we share today's human condition ...

2. Which mission?

The charism of preaching, recognized by the Church in St Dominic, is the foundation of the mission of the Order of Preachers. Because of our Dominican vocation, we have to be prophets of a new world, proclaimed in Christ, to a world that is still seeking itself, emerging in suffering and pain, but also in hope, though this is still uncertain.

St Dominic himself, the *vir apostolicus*, received his call at a time of deep turmoil, when a new type of society was emerging. The pope greeted the first friars as 'new prophets'.

We are carriers of this spirit, this mission we inherited for our modern world. We meditate, in humility but also trusting in the divine promise, on the passage from Isaiah that the liturgy applied to St Dominic: 'My Spirit is upon you and the words I have put into your mouth will not leave your mouth, nor the mouth of those of your race, nor the mouth of those of your race of your race, for ever and ever, says the Lord'. (Is 59:21 – old office of Saint Dominic).

3. Which Gospel?

(a) The Good News we are sent to preach is the salvation

in Jesus Christ, that is the total liberation of humanity: liberation from sin, liberation from the blind forces of destiny, of taboos, of legalism, of lies and of death; in short, liberation from all that alienates the human being: 'he has anointed me to bring good news to the poor. He has sent me to proclaim release to the captives and recovery of sight to the blind, to let the oppressed go free … ' (Lk 4:18). This liberation is the work of a God who acts in history and who, through the Covenant, has come to proclaim and install … a new world: the kingdom of God.

(b) This Gospel, the Good News of liberation, we must announce in its integrity, enlightened and with the courage to comprehend and proclaim all its dimensions and all its challenges. Because the Word of God continuously challenges humanity, it challenges us today in particular ways: to be witnesses of an eschatological reality already present, and thus to build a new world where love is recognized as the supreme value, the new law. We are still far from it …

The proclamation of the gospel invites us to a new critical awareness, discerning and denouncing all dimensions of sin. Thus the gospel has a 'political dimension' since it not only calls for individual conversion … , but for the transformation of structures of injustice, and of relationships between persons and peoples.

Our world is particularly challenged by the fundamental affirmation in the gospel of the inalienable dignity of every person, men, women, children: each one is created in God's own image, loved by God, saved at the price of Christ's blood and promised his glory …

II. – In what spirit do we live?

We only can be faithful to our charism by living in a certain spirit, under certain conditions.

1. We believe that a major concern for us must be to witness to the gospel in an open dialogue and in fraternal encounters with all peoples, cultures, especially those beyond the Christian context … Our charism must lead us to the frontiers.

2. As Christians, but especially as preachers, we must build

a Church for the world of today ... The Church needs to regain its evangelical face. It is important to know what kind of Church we want ... A Church which is powerful, rich, strong and linked to the powers of this world? Or a servant-Church, poor, weak and disarmed in the eyes of the world? Do we really want a Church where the action of the Spirit and the charisms sown among the people of God are not at risk of being crushed by the all too human rigidity of its institutions? We believe it is time to choose ... We must know where our solidarity lies ...

3. We can only be prophets of the kingdom if we preach by our life as much as our words.

– living in solidarity with the poor;

– listening to the poor, giving them a voice, lending them our voice;

– liberating ourselves from the powers of money, revising our life-style;

– fighting for justice and accepting that we must suffer for it ... (*Letter on Contemporary Problems*)

The General Chapter of Quezon City (1977) dedicated a large part of its deliberations to 'Our Apostolic Mission in Today's World'. In declaring the Order to be *in statu missionis*, that is, sent to all peoples especially the poor (LCO[2] 98), it expressed the conviction that God will bring about his salvation in the human history and in this world. The Chapter proposed four priorities, of which the third is Justice in the World. Here are the major passages:

The Mission of the Preacher and Justice in the World

1. We live in a world where many human beings are victims of injustice – injustices which are not inevitable but are intrinsic to social structures based on the pursuit of egoistic interests and power.

2. In today's world there is a new awareness of injustice: we must share it and make it our own. Moreover, for many

---

2. LCO – *Liber Constitutionum et Ordinationum*: The Book of Constitutions and Ordinations of the Order of Preachers. Constitutions may be changed only by the decision of three successive General Chapters, meeting at intervals of three years.

people the credibility of the Churches is linked directly to their attitude towards entrenched injustices. The credibility of those who are professed to preach the gospel is especially affected by this.

3. Justice is a constitutive element of the preaching of the gospel. There is no respect for the image of God in every human being when one tolerates fundamental rights being denied to many. And there is no charity without a will of justice for all (see declaration by Synod of 1971).

We wish to present some pressing recommendations to the whole Order.

4. If we want to be faithful to the charism of the Order ..., we must take care to preach the gospel in all its dimensions, especially in its implications for justice in the human community (see LCO 132, I).

After the example of the incarnate Word, we must show special concern for the lowly, the poor, the oppressed, the isolated, the frustrated; it is with them that we need to establish our fundamental solidarity in the spirit of the gospel (see LCO 109).

5. We ask that in the whole Order the major conclusions of the document *Justice in the World*, 1971, ... be examined, especially those applying more directly to us:

(a) that we examine our ways of behaving towards others in the Order as well as those around us, our use of goods, our lifestyle in relation to those among whom we live;

(b) that all the brethren be granted 'suitable freedom of expression and thought. This includes the right of everyone to be heard in a spirit of dialogue, preserving a legitimate diversity within the Church'.

6. In our own countries and on the international level we must work for a more just society. We have to be aware that, more than we realise, all we say and do has a political implication. Whether intended or not, our evangelical word will almost always have an impact on the political level. Even our silence.

Regarding politics of all kinds, we need a critical awareness inspired by the gospel. And we must remember that denouncing the structures of injustice and defending the rights of the poor, like defending religious freedom, are part of our prophetic mission. Dedicated to the truth, we must accept that sometimes we are accused falsely: 'Blessed are you when you suffer every kind of calumny for my sake ... ' (Mt 5:11).

7. The Order has to fulfil a specific task in theology. Today its contribution, in collaboration with specialists in other areas, should be to study the following problems:

(a) the relationship between the kingdom of God and temporal society, between the kingdom and social justice;

(b) how to integrate theological reflection and analysis of structures of injustice ... and reflect on the means of transforming the world in view of the kingdom of God;

(c) how to integrate research and promotion of a new economic world order;

(d) the advancement of women in the Church and in society (*Acta* n. 19).

JUSTICE AND PREACHING

The General Chapter of Walberberg (1980) re-emphasised the declarations of previous chapters, recalling also those of the Missionary Congress (1973) and the relevant Church documents. In looking at the four priorities[3] in the light of the Dominican tradition it showed how the commitment to justice and peace affects our preaching today:

1. Prophetic preaching

We are in the best tradition of our Order when our preaching is prophetic (LCO I, 5). Preaching that is purely theoretical and abstract captures neither the spirit of St Dominic nor the hearts of the people. Prophetic preaching is no mere sharing of knowledge but joyous proclamation of the living, life-giving Word of God. We must announce the full gospel message ... Therefore a serious discernment of

3. The General Chapter of Quezon City (1977) set out four priorities for the Order. These were: the Order's theological heritage; justice in the world; evangelising a dechristianised culture and secularised Christianity; and integrating the media into preaching the word of God..

the signs of the times in the light of principles and sustained by our prayer, is needed. In the past our preaching has been effective when the Order knew how to discern the signs of the times in troubled periods of history.

In order to discern the signs of the times we need to hear the cry of the poor, of the oppressed, the excluded, the sick, and those who suffer persecution because of race or religion or because of their commitment to justice. God speaks to us through their complaints as well as through the silence of those living in apathy, solitude and desperation.

2. Preaching and poverty

In the life of St Dominic and in the Order, preaching and poverty are intimately related. Poverty is not only an act of renunciation. It is also a witness, a means that serves the credibility of our preaching, a sign of authenticity and honesty. This is urgently needed today more than ever.

We live in a world where the division between rich and poor is growing. This is true for rich and poor nations as well as for individuals and groups ... There is an increasing awareness of national and international structures creating dependency and poverty. If, in this kind of world, we appear to be more aligned with the rich than with the poor, our preaching is not credible. How can we free the rich from the domination of money and other material goods if we do not live simply and soberly (LCO 31, 1)? And how can we hope that the poor accept our preaching seriously if we are not close to their way of life (LCO 31, 2)? It is very important that in the Order poverty be and is seen to be a specific sign of our preaching ...

3. Preaching and compassion

After the example of Dominic our preaching must be based on compassion – a deep compassion for all those who suffer because of the selfishness and the injustice of others. Compassion alone can give us the goodness and the capacity to recognize the signs of the times. Compassion alone can lead us to the humility that prepares us to listen and to speak, to welcome and to offer, to submit to and to use influence, to be evangelized and to evangelize.

This kind of compassion and humility comes only from a deep union with the God of Jesus Christ. We are united with God when we imitate the compassion of Christ and his humble service. Compassion and humility are the source of a true understanding of the signs of the times, and that itself is nourished by prayer and contemplation. We contemplate God who reveals himself in Scripture and manifests his will through the signs of the times. This is the spiritual foundation of our preaching.

4. Preaching and theological reflection

Our preaching has always been based on a profound and scientific study of theology. The deep crisis of the modern world, the scandal of poverty and increasing levels of injustice, the clash between different cultures, contacts with dechristianized people – all are for us a source of challenge. Our practice of theological reflection must prepare us to penetrate in depth the meaning of all these situations in the mystery of divine providence. Contemplation and theological reflection do not make us competent to find adequate means to transmit the gospel today. But they are true means to ensure that our preaching be really doctrinal and not only an abstract and intellectual presentation.

Social justice – the third priority

The Good News of Jesus Christ cannot be proclaimed in today's world unless we proclaim, at the same time, the inalienable dignity of every person, called to be sons or daughters of God. Neither will the Good News be proclaimed without our denouncing the injustices that our society imposes … on the poor. Thus our preaching can bring hope to the poor and be a true call to the powerful …

Here are some principles for action:

(a) promote the study of social justice in theology and spirituality;

(b) research and publish informations on serious injustices;

(c) promote formation in social analysis so as to discover the causes and the development of unjust structures in society;

(d) respect human rights, especially the rights of cultural and racial minorities, the rights of refugees and immigrants, the rights of religious freedom;

(e) alert people to the danger of the arms race;

(f) evaluate the credibility of Church institutions ... (*Acta*, n. 17).

THE OPTION FOR JUSTICE AND PEACE

The elective General Chapter held at Rome in 1983 invited the Order to a triple option – the option for the poor, the option for justice, and the option for peace. This gave the issues of peace and the option for the poor greater importance and also meant an opening towards the Third World – something that found expression in the chapter commissions dealing with the mission of the Order in Africa, in Asia and in Latin America respectively, and in the election of, first, Albert Nolan and then Damian Byrne as Master of the Order. Here are some of the chapter statements on justice and peace:

Some situations that challenge us:

– The misery, poverty and dependency in which a great part of society is found today constitutes a continuing violation of human dignity. This situation of injustice is truly a social sin to be denounced by us untiringly.

– Among the wealthier peoples, economic crisis follows upon an abundance of material things. A new kind of poor arise: the young, the old, immigrants, the unemployed, those who are found to be physically and socially handicapped, the marginalized, etc.

– Poverty of this kind is neither accidental nor by chance. Indeed, the mechanisms of modern society themselves work together to make the rich richer and the poor poorer ...

– In many nations, the ideology of 'national security' brings in unusual forms of militarism, where armies do not defend the supreme autonomy of their own nations but, rather, take action against their fellow-citizens through arbitrary detention, torture and all kinds of violations of the human person. The stronger foreign nations withdraw their aid and often use these military systems for their own advantage and privileges, even in the name of Christian culture, but not of Christian life, which leads to true liberty.

– A still more serious danger threatens humanity – the arms race, especially the nuclear arms race. Because of this, the nature of war is changed fundamentally: it does not offer an adequate solution to conflicts, even limited ones, but rather it has effects beyond anything that can be thought or imagined. Expenditure to prepare to wage war and to defend against war are the greatest scandal in the face of poverty and want in the world.

– All these things considered, the Christian faith cannot be lived and preached except in situations necessarily involving conflict and having political implications that must be discerned, judged and addressed in a responsible way (*Acta*, n. 234).

JUSTICE AND PEACE AND THE MISSION OF THE ORDER

Lines of thinking present in the previous chapters, especially n Rome, became the main focus of the General Chapter in Avila (1986). In defining the mission of the Order today as Mission on the Frontiers, it put issues of justice and peace into a broader context. It declared justice and peace to be one of the five frontiers for the mission of the Order, with 'The Challenge of the Marginalised' as another, and closely related, frontier. *The Letter on Contemporary Problems* of the 1974 Chapter had also spoken of mission on the frontiers. Here is the relevant text of the Avila Chapter:

The Mission of the Order has been and must continue to be a mission 'on the frontiers'. This follows from the affirmation of the missionary and evangelizing character of the Church by Vatican II and by post-conciliar documents like *Evangelii Nuntiandi*... , and makes the original project of Dominic very contemporary. It is the responsibility of the whole Dominican Family to put into practice the specific mission of the Order in the contemporary world ... In line with the previous chapters, this Chapter puts forward five frontiers as the major challenges for the Order and its mission today.

1. The frontier between life and death: the challenges of justice and peace in the world

The most urgent and the most dramatic problems facing humanity today are of historical character. They are linked to systems, structures, social, economic and political practices that put a great number of human beings at the margin between life and death.

The most urgent questions for contemporary humanity are those of justice and peace. Along with these problems there are many situations where human beings are pushed to the edge, even to death. Poverty, injustice, violence, war and death flagrantly contradict the Christian ideal of life for all.

Without a commitment to justice and peace it is not possible to experience and live out the kingdom of God; it is not possible to have genuine evangelization. This commitment to justice and peace – analysis, reflection, solidarity – authenticates Dominican mission ... The compassion of Dominic for the poor, for sinners, the afflicted, the sick ... urges the Dominican community to become actively present on the frontier of life and death in contemporary society. The examples of Bartolomé de Las Casas, Montesinos, Pedro de Cordoba in Latin America, of Domigos de Salazar in the Orient, and the work of Fr Lebret enlighten our mission.

2. The frontier between humanity and inhumanity: the great challenge of the marginalised

The structures of contemporary society place more and more people on the edge of a life that is inhuman, if not subhuman. There are various categories of marginalised: indigenous peoples who suffer material poverty as well as cultural, social and political marginalisation; victims of apartheid, immigrants, dissidents, certain workers, women, the young and the old ...

Without communion, reconciliation and solidarity ... it is not possible to experience and live the kingdom of God; it is not possible to have genuine evangelization. The marginalised are to be the privileged of the mission of the Order, and their situation is a challenge to our reflection, evangelisation and solidarity. Situations of inhumanity are a clear sign of the absence of the kingdom of God.

Compassion and mendicant itinerancy led Dominic to the marginalised people of the thirteenth century: the poor, heretics, pagans. Dominic saw the Dominican community as a 'fraternity' so as to be a preaching, a proclamation of the gospel, a challenge to the feudal structures of society, of the Church and of medieval monastic life. The mission of the Dominican community is to inaugurate and show forth a new model of human relationship. (*Acta*, n. 22)

JUSTICE AND PEACE – STUDY AND FORMATION

As previous Chapters had done, the General Chapter of Avila made specific recommendations for study and formation; to support its mission on the frontiers the Order needs focused programmes of study and of formation. In the General Chapter of Oakland (1989) the Commission on Studies took up the challenge to give Dominican studies a new vision.

The vision and hope of Dominic, the history of the Order, as well as the General Chapter of Avila, invite us to accept the challenge of a 'mission on the frontiers', to respond to the great challenges of our time, especially in seeking justice and peace in solidarity with the marginalised. 'We have as our special function the prophetic office by which the Gospel of Jesus Christ is proclaimed everywhere both by word and example, with due consideration for the conditions of persons, times, and places so that faith is awakened and more deeply penetrates all life so as to build up of the Body of Christ … ' (LCO 1 § IV).

In our fragmented and insecure society, threatened by war and poverty, this witness requires great courage and competence. Fear suffocates that 'open speech' (Acts 4:31, see *Gaudium et Spes*, 62; *Dignitatis Humanae*, 2) which characterized the preaching of the apostles. We have been at our most creative theologically when we have dared to let ourselves be interrogated by the problems that have burden people. Our tradition of profound dedication to study helps strengthen our faith and clarify our vision so that we may be effective preachers, freed by truth from illusory securities.

It was evident from the earliest days of the Order that there is an intimate connection between prophetic preaching and right thinking. St Dominic's mission to the Albigensians expressed a deep reverence for the God who creates all things and became flesh for our salvation. St Thomas carried forward this fundamental orientation through his study of Aristotelian philosophy, enabling him to give a proper intellectual foundation to the theology of the goodness of creation, and the consequent rejection of dualism. The insecurities of our age also tempt us to take refuge in false dualisms of mind and body, spirit and matter, religion and politics, dualisms that promise invulnerability. A proper philosophical foundation, with the help of the human sciences, is vital if we are to preach the good news of the incarnate God who dwells among us.

All around the world we can see to the rise of religious fundamentalism, within and outside Christianity, which offers the false security of a faith without ambiguity. It is only a rigorous study of the Scriptures that can enable us to invite men and women to share with us the unending journey into the mystery of the life of God in Christ …

Our study not only grows from our common life within the Order, but it is ordered towards disclosing how we are all one in Christ. Thus there is an intrinsic relationship between fruitful study and the search for a just and peaceful world in which women and men enjoy their full dignity as children of God. To speak truthfully is an act of justice. As the Dominican Promoters of Justice and Peace wrote: 'Our experience and reflections upon this political culture has opened our eyes to a world of lies. This atmosphere of lies seems to be limitless, even denying the civil humanity of women, ethnic and cultural groups. The misuse of words like "democracy" and "human rights" furthers this culture of lies. Hypocrisy and illusion become the norm of political behaviour' (*IDI*, November 1988).

In particular we may note that in contemporary civilisation, science and technology have created a neocolonialism greater than ever before – that between rich and poor countries and within specific countries. Those who do not have access to modern technology are out of the race right from the beginning. So science and technology have been used to reinforce materialism and generate intellectual poverty and radical injustice, globally and locally. We therefore encourage the provinces to encourage study by brothers gifted in such areas as law, economics, politics and peace studies, so that science may contribute to the building of a just world rather than its fragmentation and impoverishment. (*Acta*, n. 109)

JUSTICE AND PEACE IN CHANGING TIMES

The changes of recent decades, including the fall of communist regimes, have greatly influenced the Order's commitment to justice and peace. The deliberations of the 1992 elective General Chapter in Mexico, understandably, reflected these historical changes. While the Chapter coincided with the commemoration of 500 years since the landing of Christopher Columbus, great attention was also paid to the challenges of the mission of the Order in Africa and Asia. It is to that Chapter's Commission on Preaching that we look for reflection on justice and peace issues in this wider context:

1. Just as in the time of the European conquest of what was to be called Latin America and its inhabitants, Dominican preaching is faced with the challenge posed by the historical situation in which we live. In the present as in the past, millions of women and men suffer the lack of recognition of their dignity and value as human beings.

2. We certainly have witnessed enormous changes in recent years: in Europe and in the part of Asia formerly under Soviet domination, opportunities have arisen for democracy and freedom ... this freedom is seen as an important responsibility in a difficult context.

In fact, in many countries, in Europe as well as in Asia, Africa, and Latin America, democracy is more apparent than real, or else it is threatened by different forces or by the widespread indifference of the people in the face of the management of public affairs ...

3. Perverse economic systems, communist dictatorships, and regimes inspired by neo-liberalism prevent the majority of human beings and their families from satisfying their primary needs. Many women and men emigrate in search of casual labour in countries more developed than their own, with the risk of being excluded and becoming objects of hate, rooted in deep racism and xenophobia. Inequality of opportunities and of situations as well as the aggravated increase of misery will accentuate this general phenomenon of migration in future years. Internal disequilibrium within the rich countries will increase, particularly since unemployment is structural.

4. In many countries, if not in entire regions, development and wealth benefit a minority only and separate them to an even greater degree from the majority. Many forms of poverty are present everywhere in the world. These processes are heightened by current use of high technology, which contributes to the accumulation of power in the hands of a few.

5. It is true that, for the present, the threat of nuclear war is remote, but the risk of conflicts remains. The awakening of nationalities in certain countries clashes with the repression of the dominating powers and is translated in terms of violence whose destructive process no one seems able to control. Although nuclear disarmament treaties have been signed, the developed countries (and sometimes poor countries) go on creating still more sophisticated and powerful arms, in the conviction that they have the duty to intervene wherever in the world their interests appear to be threatened.

6. On the other hand, the irrational and unlimited exploitation of natural resources threatens the future of humanity. Earth, water, and air are riches that should not be exhausted by the people of today to the detriment of their descendants.

7. All these world problems affect, in one way or another, all the countries of the planet, more than ever interdependent with one another. They cause people to fear one another and to close in on themselves with their privileges. Comforting themselves with false securities, they neglect the require-

ments of justice. No one can consider himself or herself protected from various forms of injustice or violence.

8. On the other hand, we must recognize that there are still too many Christians who align themselves with the dominant values of the rich nations, who are insensitive to the cry of the impoverished, wounded and exploited person, and show little concern for the risk now facing the future of humankind. This is contrary to the priority choice in favour of the poor proclaimed by the Church in following the requirement of Jesus Christ who identified himself with the poorest in the great Parable of the Last Judgement (Mt 25:31-46).

9. Thus every threat to humans, to their life, dignity and liberty, constitutes a challenge for our preaching. The gospel word, today as always, proclaims Christ, the New Person, who calls all persons to rise up, to take their own destiny in hand as well as that of the communities to which they belong, with their particularity and originality.

10. In spite of all the failures and desperation around us, our preaching proclaims that God, the Totally Other, has taken flesh in Jesus, source of all justice and peace. Going beyond all forms of false securities, our preaching wants to bring hope to the world. (*Acta*, n. 66)

JUSTICE AND PEACE IN SEARCH OF A SPIRITUALITY

The quest for a spirituality for the commitment to justice and peace is found in many Chapter documents. Sometimes it is clearly stated, sometimes only alluded to. The passages quoted in this final section point to an even more important question: In what way is the Order's commitment to justice and peace linked to the contemplative dimension of its charism? We certainly find such a link in the example of St Dominic 'bearing the poor, the sinners, the downtrodden, and the afflicted in the inmost sanctuary of his compassion'.

In recent General Chapters the four priorities first elaborated at Quezon City have become central in any assessment of our fidelity to the mission of the Order. These priorities are invoked throughout this *relatio* ... Here I will merely are invoked throughout this *relatio* ... Here I will merely share some brief reflections on our commitment to justice and peace. I have been deeply inspired by my contact with so many brothers and sisters who live this commitment with joy and suffering. Often their work for a better world seems doomed to frustration when every country seems to be absorbed into the all-powerful Market and it becomes harder to dream of a transformed world order. We may feel tempted to despair, to fatalism. Do we do all that we can to support and encourage those members of the Order who have taken a brave stand? Do we show our appreciation that their commitment is a preaching of the gospel?

This commitment for justice finds a wide variety of expressions, as we work for the healing of those hurt by a world order that is often cruel, in quietly working with the poor in our neighbourhoods, in recognising their dignity and supporting their just claims ...

Crucial to our preparation for the Dominican life is that of formation in a Dominican spirituality. Felicíssimo Martinez Diez, O.P., wrote: 'Dominican spirituality should be above all a Christian spirituality, a spirituality of the following of Christ. Jesus is the only one to be followed ... What Dominic tried to do was to show with his word and example a specific way of following Jesus ... ' Following Christ always includes an invitation to walk with him to Jerusalem, not knowing what awaits, sometimes uncertain and afraid like the disciples, to share his passion and suffering. This is not a popular vision of the Christian life, but unless we share some such vision of our journey with Christ then we will not form brothers who can endure the crises on the road with joy and hope ...

During the meeting of CIDAL[4] in Santo Domingo this year, I was deeply moved to listen to the Promoters of Justice and Peace in Latin America sharing their experiences. It was evident that one cannot accompany a people suffering great poverty and injustice without a deep life of prayer, a spirituality that sustains one when God seems absent and when all one's efforts to bring about a better world seem frustrated.

4. Conference of Latin American Dominicans.

We cannot be preachers of hope unless we are sustained by a life of both community and personal prayer.

In so many parts of the Order I have found a desire for us to recover the contemplative dimension of our life. Unless this is sustained by our communities then, too often it withers and we lapse into activism. This aspiration for silence in the presence of God does not denote a *fuga mundi*, for it is our necessary sustenance to share the sufferings of the people of God. Too often when brothers, especially the young, ask for more space for prayer in their communities, they can be seen as lazy, escaping the demands of apostolic life. Nothing could be less true. (Timothy Radcliffe, O.P., Master of the Order, *Report to the Caleruega General Chapter*, 1995)

In his last letter to the Order, a letter addressed to the Dominican Nuns, Fr Timothy pursues this reflection on how our spirituality must be based on the contemplative dimension of our charism in order to sustain us in our commitment to justice and peace.

Compassion is part of your mission, sharing Dominic's gift 'of bearing sinners, the downtrodden, and the afflicted in the inmost sanctuary of his compassion' (LCM,[5] 35 § I,). Dominic's God is a God of mercy. Compassion means unlearning that hardness of heart which sits in judgement on other people, shedding the armour that holds others at bay, learning vulnerability to another's pain and confusion, hearing their cry for help. We learn this first of all in our communities. Do we dare to be touched by the suffering of the sister next door? Do we dare to take the risk of hearing her half-expressed requests for help? If not, then how can we embody Dominic's compassion for the world?

Compassion is more than feeling, but opening one's eyes to see Christ among us suffering still, as Las Casas saw the crucified Christ in the Indians of Hispaniola. It is an education of the heart and the eye, which makes us attentive to the Lord who is with us in the crushed and wounded. Compas-

5. LCM – *Liber Constitutionum Monialium*: The Book of Constitutions of the Nuns of the Order or Preachers

sion is thus truly contemplative, clear-sightedness. As Borg-
man, says, 'To be moved and shocked at what happens to
people and what this does to them is a way of perceiving
God's presence. Compassion is contemplation in the Dominican sense'. Contemplative compassion is learning to
look selflessly at others. As such it is deeply linked to the
hunger for a just world. The Order's commitment to justice
easily becomes ideological if it is not born of contemplative
compassion. 'A society that doesn't understand contemplation won't understand justice, because it will have forgotten
how to look selflessly at what is other. It will take refuge in
generalities, prejudices, self-serving clichés.' (Rowan Williams,
Open Judgement, London, 1994, p. 244). (Timothy Radcliffe,
O.P., *Letter to the Order: A Contemplative Life*, 29 April 2001)

Responding to the great changes in the early 1990s, the
Regional Promoters of Justice and Peace, with the General
Promoter, tried to formulate a spirituality for our commitment.
At their meeting in 1991, they presented the following reflec-
tions:

These new conditions have come about within a very short
period of time. The pace of life throughout the world has
quickened. This fast pace prevents reflection which could be
a source of liberation because, in a climate of contemplation,
people could perceive and create alternatives. Instead, this
rapid pace of life produces more fear within people.

Recognizing those forces in our world which work to unify
nations and peoples in fear, we, as followers of Jesus and
Dominic, are challenged to promote instead a unity based on
hope. We must keep hope alive. This hope is grounded in a
spirituality with the Paschal reality at its centre: life will
overcome death; love will triumph over hate.

The temptation to hand ourselves over to despair in the
face of current global realities must be countered by a spirituality which sustains us throughout the struggle for justice.
Rooted in the seeds of hope present in our world, such a
spirituality integrates several elements:
    – Relationship with others brings us to relationship with

God. In this communion which celebrates diversity there is no 'other' of whom we are to be afraid.

– Gospel-centred spirituality gives us the courage to respond to injustice, to recognize our own brokenness and to extend a healing hand to our sisters and brothers in need.

– Spirituality which sustains us is possible only in community. Communities which are a reference point for Gospel living become sources of hope for us and for others in our suffering world. Such communities serve to remind us that the Dominican Family, the Christian Family and the Family of God are in truth one family which transcends all boundaries.

– Truth informs our spirituality. To have real knowledge and direct experience of those who make up the Body of Christ crucified today strengthens us in the face of this world's lies and disinformation.

– Changes in today's systems and structures of death require that we undergo personal and communal conversion. We recognize that no person can experience authentic liberation unless all people are liberated from injustice, poverty and fear.

Such a spirituality will necessarily lead to action for justice and participation in the transformation of the world. As we look to the next three years we recommend that as an international Family we demonstrate in our life and mission how to be about hope and how to be prophetic in our commitment to justice and peace. In particular, our communication, formation and way of life should authenticate our commitment to the Gospel of Jesus.

'Justice is the pearl to be discovered in the oyster of mercy and compassion.' (St Catherine of Siena)

Epilogue

Looking Backwards, Forwards and Around

JOHN ORME MILLS, O.P.

The people writing these pages – all of them in one way or another concerned with social justice or peace issues – have looked at how one very old and in many ways unique Catholic religious order has responded to justice and peace issues in the course of 785 years: the 785 years from its foundation to the start of the Third Millennium. The authors have not set out to write a comprehensive history, but to focus in each essay on one individual or group of individuals, placing them in the context of the world they belonged to. Let us start this epilogue by asking ourselves whether we can see in the achievements of these Dominicans any kind of consistent pattern, any recognisable stance – in other words, a distinctively 'Dominican' way of reacting to what is going on in society.

This, though, is a question much easier to ask than to answer. Some of you think our choice of subjects has been too esoteric to make an assessment of this kind possible. Of the personalities we have written about, neither Eckhart,[1] Antoninus,[2] Vitoria,[3] Las Casas,[4] nor even McNabb[5] could be called 'typical' fourteenth, fifteenth, sixteenth or twentieth century Dominicans by any stretch of the imagination. Eckhart's contemporary, William Humbert, the Inquisitor who in 1310 sent the Beguine mystic

1. John Orme Mills, 'The Medieval Rhineland: Eckhart and Popular Theological Preaching', pp. 48-62, *supra*.
2. Richard Finn 'Recovering the Aposlolic Life: Antoninus of Florence', pp. 63-76, *supra*.
3. Roger Ruston, 'Francisco Vitoria: The Rights of Enemies and Strangers', pp. 77-95, *supra*.
4. Carlos Josaphat, 'Las Casas: Prophet of Full Rights for All', pp. 96-117, *supra*.
5. Hugh Walters, '*Pro Foco Non Foro* The Thomist Inheritance and the Household Economy of Father Vincenl McNabb' pp. 133-151, *supra*.

Marguerite Porete to the stake, was much more a 'typical' fourteenth-century Dominican than Eckhart, who shared some of his most original thoughts with a throng of Beguine women.

No one is likely to be surprised at the inclusion of an essay on Thomas Aquinas,[6] the Dominican who most profoundly shaped the Dominican way of seeing the world. In addition, although his name is not always mentioned, all of these essays – with possibly one exception – directly or indirectly reflect ideas of St Thomas. It is his influence, more than anybody's, which has given a special flavour to the Dominican contribution to Catholic thinking on justice and peace. In our opening essay Richard Finn placed in its world St Thomas's treatment of justice in the *Summa*.[7] In our fifth essay Roger Ruston not only pointed out how Vitoria's teaching on natural law, the law of nations, just war theory and non-combatant immunity has influenced modern thinking but he also said something about its roots in the *Summa*.[8] Hugh Walters, in our ninth essay, mentioned the influence on the Distributists of St Thomas's teaching on property.[9]

At the same time, though, we have to remember that for five centuries St Thomas's role in the Catholic Church has extended far beyond the Order. How satisfying it would be to be able to boast that the Church's first and most influential social encyclical, Pope Leo Xlll's *Rerum Novarum* of 1891, had got Dominican origins! The truth is that certainly St Thomas' thinking made a very important contribution to it, but – St Thomas excepted – the role of Dominicans in the events leading to the drafting of it was modest indeed, in spite of the fact that many of those events took place in Fribourg.[10] Thomism as it was commonly known in the Church, being for so long the basic ingredient of every course in every seminary, was only

6. Nicholas Sagovsky, pp. 31-47, *supra*.

7. Richard Finn, 'Early Voices for Justice', pp. 19-30, *supra*.

8. *supra*, pp. 77-95, especially pp. 89 ff.

9. *supra*, pp. 133-151, especially pp. 136-140.

10. Guy Bedouelle: 'De l'influence réelle de l'Union de Fribourg sur l'encyclique *Rerum Novarum*', in '*Rerum Novarum*': *Ecriture, Contenu et Réception d'une Encyclique* (Actes de colloque internacional organisé par l'Ecole Française de Rome et le Greco no 2 du CNRS. Rome 18-20 avril 1991), Ecole Française de Rome 1997.

identifiable with 'the spirit of the Order' here and there, now and then.

Many modern Dominicans working in justice and peace would say that quite as much as the thought of St Thomas it has been the anti-autocratic Constitutions of the Order, with all their checks and balances, and the Dominican way of life – partly monastic and scholarly and partly apostolic – which have over the centuries given a special flavour to Dominican work in justice and peace, and drawn Dominicans to this kind of work. But this is not easy to prove. If it is true, why have so many Dominicans in history, including some good and famous ones, had aims and values very different from the aims and values which have led other Dominicans to combat violence, oppression and want? We may say fairly confidently that there has been something distinctive about Dominican work of this kind, but this does not mean we can take it for granted that so long as there are Dominicans it is sure to go on flourishing. But then, if the teaching of General Chapters of the last thirty years [11] is to be our guide, there should be hope that the commitment will in no way diminish.

The time has come to take a brief glimpse at what Dominicans have been saying and doing in this area during the last few years. It is now twenty-two years since dedication to justice and peace was listed at the Quezon City General Chapter as one of the four priorities central in any assessment of our fidelity to the mission of the Order. There has been a lot of progress since then, but in 1995, at the Caleruega general chapter, the Master of the Order, Timothy Radcliffe, was raising the questions:

> Do we need more co-ordination so that in times of crisis, for example in Rwanda and Chiapas, we can offer immediate and effective support? Do we need to establish a full-time desk, which can support the Promoter of Justice and Peace in his demanding work, or establish new kinds of international networking within the Order?[11]

11. See 'Teaching by Recent General Chapters and Masters', *supra*, pp. 201-221.

12.. *International Dominican Information (I.D.I.)*, Santa Sabina, Rome, September 1995, p. 161.

The fact is, of course, that needs were changing, that the world was changing.

In December 1995 occurred the First Inter-African Dominican Meeting on Justice and Peace, to organise a network of communications for mutual support.[13] A couple of years later the North American Promoters for Justice and Peace were encouraging Provinces and Sisters' Congregations 'to overcome feelings of political disempowerment' through networking.'[14] At about the same time Antoine Lion of the Province of France was initiating the setting-up of an international Dominican network of brothers and sisters dedicated to the fight against AIDS.[15] To an increasing extent Dominicans were recognising that they could not wrestle with the problems of our time on their own, and the Internet was opening up new possibilities.

During this period Philippe LeBlanc was appointed as official representative of the Order at the UN, being attached to what is now called the Office of Franciscans International and Dominicans, which has status at the UN as a non-governmental organisation (NGO). This enabled him to speak at the UN Sub-Commission on Human Rights at Geneva about human rights violations in countries where Dominicans were actively involved, in other words about the outrages that had occurred in the Great Lakes Region of Africa, in Chiapas in Mexico, and in Shantinagar and Khanewal in Pakistan.[16] In August 1998, after two years of activity, the UN adopted a resolution on the human rights situation in Mexico.[17] The Order was beginning to make its voice heard in a new way.

Increasingly, though, Dominicans working in justice and peace have found themselves working closely with other groups – most frequently with other religious, but quite often with groups of different religions or none. Often now they are working more closely with non-Dominicans with whom they can

13. See *I.D.I.* February 1996, p. 26.
14. See *I.D.I.* September 1997, p. 167.
15. *I.D.I.* January 1998, pp. 12-13.
16. See *I.D.I.* September 1997, pp. 168-9.
17. Office of Franciscans International and Dominicans, Geneva. See *I.D.I.* pp. 189-190.

share their specialist interests (interest in the refugee problem, ratification of the Landmines Ban, women's rights in Islam, or whatever) than they are working with their brothers and sisters, most of whom do not know precisely what work they are doing and do not seem particularly to want to know. This trend is not limited, of course, to justice and peace activity, and it was discussed at length at the general chapter at Bologna in 1998, as it was seen as undermining community life.[18]

The developments just summarised have grown as the world-wide abuse of human rights has grown. Reading the three essays about important movements of the Cold-War period – Francois Leprieur's essay on the French worker-priest movement and its destruction,[19] Brian Wicker on lhc Marxist-Christian dialogue,[20] and Valerie Flessati on the Christian peace movement[21] – one is conscious that emphases have changed. The need for the Church to get across to the working class is more desperate than ever, and so is the need for conflicting ideologies to seek common ground and for war to stop, but now our attentions seem to be increasingly focused on a succession of rather different crises. In the words of the communique to the Order issued by the 1999 meeting of the Order's International Commission of Justice and Peace:

> We listened to stories of suffering, especially in Iraq, Kosovo, East Timor, Rwanda, Burundi, Chiapas and Colombia. Concerns were also raised about contemporary forms of slavery such as child and forced prostitution, forced migration, trafficking in human organs, and unjust labour practices.[22]

It is not, of course, that in the past there were no crises of this kind, no forms of slavery. For two decades Andre Lascaris of the Netherlands Province tried to bring Dutch experience to the

18. General Chapter of 1998, Bologna: Acts nn. 127-134 ('The Life of the Community as a Common Project').

19. 'Do the Baptized Have Rights? The French Worker-Priest Crisis', *supra*, pp. 162-181.

20. '*Slant*, Marxism and the English Dominicans', *supra*, pp. 182-191.

21. 'Stop War, Please: Dominicans and the Christian Peace Movement in England', *supra*, pp. 152-161.

22. *I.D.I.* September 1999, p. 161.

religious conflict in Northern Ireland, and during the same period Albert Nolan of the Southern African Vicariate was fighting apartheid. And these are only two of scores of such stories.

No, it would appear that what has changed is in us: it would appear that we are coming to see the abuse of basic human rights as a cancerous disease which, having been satisfactorily dealt with in one bit of the body-politic, crops up somewhere else. As the Human Rights Index 1999 reports in the London *Observer* 'Indeed, the past 12 months, if anything, have witnessed a worsening state of affairs for the victims of torturing governments, repressive regimes and murderous opposition groups.'[23] In this situation something important is being said by, for instance, the Sisters of St Catherine, who resolved to remain in Iraq though this might mean death in a NATO bombardment,[24] and by the American Maryknoll Sisters who fled from East Timor at the 1975 Indonesian invasion and then returned.[25]

Here, already, we are looking beyond the end-date of our series. For it is fairly obvious that one of the challenges which Dominicans of the coming age who are concerned with justice and peace issues will have to confront will be an increasing devaluing of the individual human being. Here is a trend which may not result in as much suffering as global warming will bring, but Dominicans are likely to see it as more immediately their concern, for fighting it is fighting a war of the spirit.

The past can inspire us, but it is over. How can we help to make people prepared for what most probably lies ahead? We could, for a start, take note of the answer which the International Commission for Justice and Peace offered in June, 1999, to the question: 'What can the Dominican Family do?' By that was meant what exactly could it do to help the Dominicans living and working in the middle of ugly political and social crises. The Commission did not think we should all jump on planes to these hot-spots, or even post off food parcels to them.

23. 24 October 1999, p. 26.

24. Report of the Journees Romaines Dominicaines 1995. *I.D.I.* November 1995, p. 223.

25. See *I.D.I.* April 1997, p. 85.

It thought we should

> Inform ourselves about what is truly at stake. Encourage economic and socio-political analysis of the root causes of conflict. Promote theological reflection on questions of war and peace, on hate, on reconciliation and healing. Organise fund-raising efforts. Promote inter-religious dialogue.[26]

That sounds sensible, even if not terribly exciting.

Many Catholic publishers are saying their customers no longer want to read about 'justice and peace'. Why? Presumably because they do not think it sounds 'terribly exciting'. Ironically, very few of the Dominicans we have written about in this series would have even understood the term 'justice and peace'. If they had been asked what they were doing, almost certainly they would have said that they believed they were bringing the gospel of Jesus Christ to bear on problems in the world around them. And are those of us who at the threshold of the Third Millennium say we are 'concerned about justice and peace issues' really doing anything very different?

---

26. *I.D.I.* September 1999, p. 162.